Gendering
Italian Fiction

Gendering Italian Fiction

Feminist Revisions of Italian History

Edited by
Maria Ornella Marotti
and Gabriella Brooke

Madison • Teaneck
Fairleigh Dickinson University Press
London: Associated University Presses

Associated University Presses
440 Forsgate Drive
Cranbury, NJ 08512

Associated University Presses
16 Barter Street
London WC1A 2AH, England

Associated University Presses
P.O. Box 338, Port Credit
Mississauga, Ontario
Canada L5G 4L8

The paper used in this publication meets the requirements of the American National Standard for Permanence of Paper for Printed Library Materials Z39.48-1984.

Library of Congress Cataloging-in-Publication Data

Gendering Italian fiction : feminist revisions of Italian history / edited by Maria Marotti and Gabriella Brooke.
   p.   cm.
Includes bibliographical references and index.
ISBN 0-8386-3771-X (alk. paper)
   1. Historical fiction, Italian—History and criticism. 2. Italian fiction—Women authors—History and criticism. 3. Women and literature—Italy. 4. Feminism and literature—Italy. I. Marotti,
PQ4181.H55G46 1999
853'.081099287—dc21   98-29649
                                       CIP

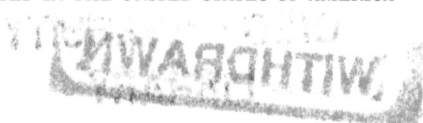

Maria Ornella Marotti
Per le mie amiche

🍎

Gabriella Brooke
To my husband

Contents

Preface

Gabriella Brooke

THE PRESENT VOLUME IS THE RESULT OF A COLLABORATION THAT both follows and deviates from the traditional path of academic alliances. The relationship between Maria Ornella Marotti and me was born out of mutual empathy and respect. Although our paths first crossed during the 1994 AMERICAN ASSOCIATION FOR ITALIAN STUDIES meeting in Madison, Wisconsin, it was only the following year that we became friends.

At the 1995 AAIS meeting in Tempe, Arizona, we both had organized sessions centered around historical fiction by women and were scheduled to read papers in each other's panels. Meeting over a cup of tea before our sessions, we soon realized that we shared both personal paths and unusual academic careers. A Ph.D. in English, Maria Ornella Marotti had started off as a Mark Twain scholar and had published a book on his posthumously published papers. Bound by family reasons to the Santa Barbara area, she had accepted a position as a lecturer in Italian at the University of California, Santa Barbara. By then, she had already edited two collections—one on American autobiography and another on Italian women writers. With an M.A. in counseling psychology, an M.A. in romance languages and an M.F.A. in creative writing, I too had unusual academic credentials. An assistant professor of Italian at Gonzaga University, I had spent the previous ten years researching and writing my first historical novel. In Tempe, we discovered that we shared a passionate interest in fiction by women and especially in historical fiction.

Our sessions at the AAIS conference were particularly stimulating and filled with insights. We realized that historical fiction written by women had acquired an important place in Italian literature even though little had still been written on the subject. After the sessions, we continued talking, and eventually, over yet another cup of tea, the idea of the collection was born. We decided to solicit papers from most of the people who had spoken at our sessions, and also at a 1994 Modern Language Association (MLA) session on the same subject—organized by Maria Ornella Marotti. The response was enthusiastic, and soon we had our collection together. Maria Ornella Marotti took care of the first critical editing of each article submitted to us. She also wrote the introduction. I did the second reading and contributed two essays. We made all decisions together, including selection of papers, format of the collection, and choice of publishers to contact. I wrote the application for and obtained a grant from the Gonzaga Research Council to help defray expenses, coordinated the final editing, and dealt with editors.

During a glorious week in August, at Priest Lake, Idaho, with both of us holed up to ready the manuscript for its first and—as it turned out—only trip to the publisher, we took long walks in bear-haunted forests, watched spectacular sunsets on the lake, ate an apple cake with too much baking soda in it (the filling was good though), and went over and over each article.

The result is this collection. We hope it will bridge a gap in Italian literature and stimulate more work in this important area. The reinterpretaion of history by Italian women writers deserves continued attention and research.

Acknowledgments

WE WOULD LIKE TO THANK THE FOLLOWING PUBLISHING HOUSES which granted us permission to reprint: Mondadori for permission to quote from *Un inganno dei sensi malizioso,* Einaudi for permission to quote from *Le strade di polvere,* Penn State University Press for permission to reprint Boscagli's article "Brushing Benjamin Against the Grain: Elsa Morante and the *Jetztzeit* of Marginal History" and Alfred A. Knopf, Inc. for permission to print quotations from *The Dust Roads of Monferrato.*

Our thanks go also to Mario Aste, editor of *Italian Culture* for permission to reprint parts of Brooke's article "Sicilian Philomele: Marianna Ucria and the Muted Women of her Time" and parts of Marotti's articles "Literary Historicism and Women's Tradition" and "Feminist Historians/Historical Fictions" and to Douglas S. Curry, editor of *RLA: Romance Languages Annual* for permission to reprint parts of C. Lazzaro-Weis "History, Fiction and the Female Autobiographical Voice". We wish to thank Daniela Cavallaro for permission to print parts of her interview with Dacia Maraini, Dacia Maraini for permission to print quotations from her *Isolina* and Francesca Sanvitale for permission to print quotations from *Il figlio dell'impero*

Our heartfelt thanks to Sr. Phyllis Taufen, Associate Professor of English at Gonzaga University, who helped us revise the manuscript in its early stages. Thanks also to the Gonzaga Research Council for its financial support of this project, to Linda Pierce and Connie Som at the Gonzaga Foley Library for their priceless help in locating difficult to find articles and bibliographical information. And special thanks to Sandy Hank, Julia Bjordahl and Marti Abrahamsom for help in solving many technical problems.

A final personal thank you from Gabriella Brooke to Dr. Pia Friedrich, Professor Emerita at the University of Washington, mentor and friend, for her warm support and advice.

Gendering
Italian Fiction

Introduction

Maria Ornella Marotti

IN *ON THE HISTORICAL NOVEL* (1984) A TRANSLATION OF *DEL ROMANZO storico*, 1850, Manzoni rejects the historical novel as a genre. Even though this is the genre in which he produced his masterpiece, *I Promessi Sposi* (1840) [*The Betrothed*], Manzoni rejects the historical novel because its mixture of history and invention proves to be of scant instructional value, and it also fails to conjure up a unified belief in readers' minds (Manzoni 1984, 63–66, 73). Manzoni predicts the impending death of this genre that strays away from the truth (78, 126). Although in the short run his predictions are accurate, when in the second half of the nineteenth century the historical novel fades away evolving into the realistic novel, in the long run, Manzoni's foresight is instead refuted by the twentieth-century flowering of historical novels, and in particular of women's historical fiction.

Much of Italian women's literary production consists of interpretations of women's positions in present and past history. Through fictional and nonfictional forms of narration, writers give voice to those who have been silenced, and create stories for those who were excluded from history. Furthermore, through deviations from male standards, women writers create historical narratives that challenge predominant interpretations of history. Women's historical texts, thus, raise questions about the relation between women and history and between history and literature.

In *The Content of the Form*, Hayden White defines as nonhistorical those groups who did not produce, preserve, and use a written historical record of their past (1987, 55). Even though White refers to entire cultures, and not a gender, I borrow his definition to describe the position of women in Western civilizations, and, in particular, within Italian culture. Even though Western women are partly and implicitly inscribed in the histories of their civilizations, they did not produce the narration of their specific history. A desire for reappropriation of their submerged history may account, therefore, for the proliferation of historical texts by women in modern and contemporary Italian literature.

Women writers writing in this genre enter a long established European and phallogocentric tradition. For this reason, while attempting to establish a typology of women's historical novels, one has to take into account Lukács' well-known work (1965) on the historical novel. In studying the early evolution of the historical novel, Lukács claims that two initial fictional models were established at the beginning of the nineteenth century: the novel based on the principles of the Enlightenment and the romantic novel (7–107).[1] These initial models planted the seeds of both the ideological and the structural features of the genre. While novels in the Enlightenment tradition interpret the past as a history of the people, and look at events as progressive steps toward the French Revolution (93), the romantic novel turns a nostalgic glance at the past as at a time of irretrievable harmony. While the Enlightenment novel places the common people at the center of the narration and uses history as a wider background of events ultimately shaped by the people (84–85), the romantic novel—mostly conservative in political outlook—uses main historical figures as literary protagonists, the only ones capable of rising above the chaos of historical events, which are often portrayed as acts of God or nature without any relation to the will of the people (91). Whereas the Enlightenment novel, steering away from main historical figures, refers to historical events in accurate historical terms, the romantic novel tends to reinterpret both historical events and their protagonists in a consciously subjective manner (90).

Just as women's history, despite its specificity, is still part of the history of humanity, women's fiction entertains relations of transcodification and influence with its male counterparts. However, for the specific purpose of furthering our understanding of women's historical fiction we need to revise the Lukacsian framework. In doing that, we can easily trace different streams. At one end of the spectrum, we have novels with historical protagonists in which authors offer, through fiction, a rereading of history, a reinterpretation of the psychological motivations of main historical, mostly female, figures. At the other end of the spectrum, there are novels in which the fictional protagonists are placed at the margins of history, excluded from the mainstream because of circumstances often linked to gender. The different groups of novels illustrate different aspects of feminine and feminist thought. By identifying with exceptional women, the first group of writers express the plight of the rare emancipated women of the past in a world ruled by men. The impact of exceptional women in the sphere of action and influence, where they have carved a place for themselves, is evidence of women's potential for greatness. The second group of writers affirm, on the contrary, women's difference in and extraneity to a world in need of radical change. It is clear, as we shall see, that most of Bellonci's fictional work pertains to the first category, while texts by Dacia Maraini, Maria Rosa Cutrufelli, and Elsa Morante belong to the latter category. Anna Banti and Marta Morazzoni seem, instead, to occupy an intermediate place between the two categories. In *Artemisia* (1947), Banti demonstrates the illustrious woman's isolation and marginalization. In her collection of historical stories, *La ragazza col turbante* (1986), Morazzoni places famous persons or works of art in the midst of a fictional world; although the protagonists are historically representative, she deals in her stories with unrepresented aspects of their lives.

Having observed similarities, it is even more interesting to our purpose to define deviations from the Lukacsian model. First of all, novels in which protagonists are major female historical figures do not express nostalgia for an irretrievable past, because there is no golden age in women's history. More importantly, it is impossible for women writers to identify a line of progressive steps moving from the past toward a present and future liberation. Women's history is made of discontinuities and of moments of hard-won temporary liberations, not of revolutions. The Lukacsian model thus partly fails to define women's historical novels exactly because the historical Marxist interpretation, which is its foundation, refers to a general history that does not include in its narration women's history.

Quite significantly, Lukács praises Manzoni's choice of protagonists among the working people rather than dynastic figures, and his accurate historical reconstructions, which the novelist separates in his narration from the fictional parts of *I promessi sposi* (Lukács 1965, 82). On the other hand, Manzoni rejects the historical novel because it violates historical truth. Despite their totally different ideological creeds, both Manzoni and Lukács thus express their beliefs in the existence of historical truth. This belief in the truth of history is indeed the foundation of general history as it is recorded and narrated in history books. However, it is exactly this truth that contemporary feminist fiction has come to question and deconstruct.

Lukács saw the historical novel as a reenactment of the historical process, with the fictive world creating a microcosmos of the world of history. Its characters were supposed to represent human general types. Women's historical fiction violates this assumption by giving an ex-centric and marginal status even to main historical figures—a characteristic that women's fiction shares with historiographic metafiction, as demonstrated by Linda Hutcheon (1988, 113–14).[2] Not only is this evident in works by postmodern historical writers Silvana La Spina and Laura Mancinelli, but also in other historical fictions with main historical figures as protagonists, such as Francesca Sanvitale's *Il figlio dell'impero*, Maria Belconci's *Rinascimento privato*, and Anna Banti's *Artemisia*.

In her recently published *Plotting the Past* (1996), Cristina Della Colletta defines as "critical historical novels" fictions that "imply a revisionist attitude with respect to the historical records" (15). By contrast,Vittorio Spinazzola uses the term "antihistorical" for novels that question the well-established conventions of the genre and refuse the idea of continuous historical progress (1984, 3–49). Whereas Della Colletta's definition coincides with the kind of analysis which has been the fulcrum of the present volume, Spinazzola's definition is unacceptable in this context because it does not take into account the recent evolution of historical studies and its impact on the historical novel.

In their effort to reread history, women novelists parallel, and sometimes forerun, tendencies that are evinced by various streams of feminist historiography. In ways that are similar to the approach taken by feminist historical research, some women's novels try to point to the presence of women in the making of the historical process. In so doing, they challenge historical knowledge, as it has been recorded, and its devaluing of women's agency. More importantly, historical fiction by women seeks to give value to ordinary women's lives and to assert, just as some streams of "herstory" do, that personal and subjective experiences indirectly impact public and political spheres (Scott 1988, 24, 27).[3] Finally, as feminist historiography challenges the universality of history that excludes women's particularity, women's fiction works in the same direction by creating narratives about women that encompass subjective experiences.

One must note, however, that Italian historical fiction by women is not solely focused upon women's stories. Just as feminist historians suggest that one needs to rewrite general history if we agree that women's presence has to be inscribed, novelists seek to revisit history through a different perspective. Male protagonists appear in these fictions by women, but they are reinterpreted and inserted within a feminine and/or feminist discourse, which destabilizes the culturally constructed categories of man and woman.

However, the historical novel does not deny historical facts. Events did actually occur in the past. But how can we know that past? What can we know of it? Historical knowledge is thus problematized. It can no longer present us with timeless universal values. The novel's skeptical revisiting of the past is paralleled by the evolution of official history as a discipline. In their effort to include in historical rewriting the marginal and ex-centric, the new historicist and feminist perspectives offer a reevaluation of both the method of historical research and the writing of official history. Most of the historical narratives during the early decades of our century were shaped by positivist concern to separate the literary and the historical—fiction and facts (Hutcheon 1988, 95). We have now come to understand that both official history and literature are discourses and that our knowledge of the past is a textualized one—that is one based on narratives that interact with each other (La Capra 1985, 128).[4] Not even personal events are accessible to us through pure memory, but rather through their remains (Veyne 1971, 309). Moreover, much literary theory and philosophy of official history recognize the similar conventions and formal techniques shared by the two separate fields of the novel and the historical narrative.

The development of the historical novel reverberates with questions about historical knowledge. In fact contemporary historical novels revisit the past with irony and skepticism (Eco 1993). Not only is this true of postmodern texts, but also of texts that cannot be fully ascribed to this contemporary trend. Isabella D'Este's carnivalesque performance in *Rinascimento privato* can be seen as an example of this contestation of official history, while the theme of travesty and the breaking down of gender boundaries in *La briganta* can also be seen as a destabilization of the gender categories upon which Western historical thought is predicated.

Italian historical fiction by women should be viewed as part of a general trend in historical writing—fictional and nonfictional. Strongly impacted by the Manzonian tradition, the historical novel has developed in Italy either with a powerful focus on private stories of the marginal and ex-centric or through a reinterpretation of uncommon and neglected facets of the lives of major historical figures. Riccardo Bacchelli's novels earlier and Sebastiano Vassalli's more recently are among the most notable examples of this kind of fiction, which is also connected to new tendencies in historiography toward the construction of a cultural history, as most notably evinced by Carlo Ginzburg's work.

Although women's historical novels are related to these tendencies, they do not lack their own specificity, which is demonstrated by a clear awareness of gender in the structuring of the private stories that they narrate. Even when their protagonists are male characters, gender plays an important role in women's novels, either through the focus on the most vulnerable facets of the characters' personalities, or through a parodic treatment that unmasks power games in the patriarchal recording and interpretation of the historical process. A recurrent feature of Italian women's historical novels is also the frequent use of personal forms of narration, either autobiographical, diaristic, or epistolary. While this narrative structure draws from the origin itself of women's fiction—that is, personal writing—it also demonstrates that the specificity of women's historical writing is based on the blurring of the boundary between private and public spheres because the public is always subtly and yet powerfully impacted by the private.

In her essay in the first section of this volume, Carol Lazzaro-Weis points out similarities and connections between women's autobiographical and historical writing. A similar motivation—the drive to revise the errors and omissions of past history—unites these two genres, which are hard to critically delimit and define. Autobiographism is both one of the motivations behind the authors' writings and a recurrent narrative form in women's historical novels. Lazzaro-Weis discusses the complex relationships between autobiography and history and between life and art in a large number of women's texts, including Grazia Deledda's *Cosima*, Anna Banti's *Artemisia*,

Dacia Maraini's *La lunga vita di Marianna Ucrìa*, and Maria Rosa Cutrufelli's *La briganta*. She points out that women of the generation preceding the current one protested the separation between life and art for women "through their use of literary memory." Contemporary women writers return instead to the historical novel not to "privilege a private, artistic yet isolated sphere," but rather to "rewrite woman's history from a personal and critical point of view."

In the essay, "Revising the Past: Feminist Historians/ Historical Fictions," I show similarities between feminist historiography in Italy as practiced by Gianna Pomata, Annarita Buttafuoco, Anna Rossi Doria among others, and some of the most notable female historical novelists of our century. I trace a progressive evolution of the genre and one major turning point that marks a shift in the focus of narration from a critical rereading of the history of the representative—the illustrious women of the past—to the re-creation of the history of the unrepresented—the silent and obscure masses and individual stories that went unrecorded by official history. While the former group of texts foreruns some of the tenets of feminist historicism, the latter group of novels seems to more closely coincide with these theories. A particularly illuminating example is Clara Sereni's *Il gioco dei regni*, in which fiction, memory-based history, and historical research are fused to map a women's genealogy.

Approaching the same text from a different perspective, Giovanna Miceli Jeffries reads it through de Certeau's theory of everyday practices "as sites of secondary productions of culture superimposed on the official cultural production." In "Unsigned History: Silent, Micro-'Technologies of Gender' in the Narratives of the Quotidian," she argues that "women's practices and productions of the everyday life are unrecognized pillars as well as gears moving history." New Historicism's organicistic approach to history can allow the rewriting of an inclusionary history. After a discussion of various streams of feminist thought, Miceli Jeffries examines female characters of caretakers in Sereni's and Di Lascia's novels as examples of women's roles as "tacit users and at times subverters of the dominant discourses and culture."

The other two sections of the volume mainly comprise studies dealing with single authors and, in some cases, single works. The section entitled "The Representative" includes essays examining novels that are for the most part centered around major historical and/or literary figures. In some cases these major figures are imaginary and/or verisimilar rather than based on the textualized recording of history. In "'Uno sguardo acuto dalla storia': Anna Banti's Historical Writings," Paola Carù discusses Banti's poetics of historical writing. The writer first refutes Manzoni's rejection of the historical novel, while she formulates her own autonomous definition of the historical novel as a "hypothetical interpretation of history." In Banti's novels, history is interpreted through female eyes, which look at reality from the off-center position of their double marginalization, caused both by their femaleness and their status as outstanding women. Her female characters, whether they are actual historical figures or invented and placed within a verisimilar historical background, are rebels who struggle to break the silence and invisibility to which they are confined. They often experience empowerment through female bonding. Banti thus takes on a pioneering role because she foreruns some aspects of the Italian feminist theory of "entrustment."[5]

Banti's contemporary Maria Bellonci constructs in *Rinascimento privato* a novel of "a possible maturation of the female self from within the margins of a masculine socio-symbolic order," as Gerda Reeb argues in "*Rinascimento privato:* A Historiographic Carnival." Even though the protagonist of the novel is Isabella d'Este—hardly a militant feminist figure—this character authorizes a confrontational female version of history through her carnivalesque performance of, and resistance to, the sociohistoric role assigned to her. The carnival thus becomes the ambiguous (non)site on which history can be readdressed and reappropriated. As Reeb argues, the subversive strategy endemic in the carnival is a crucial tool of a feminine appropriation of both history and the genre of the historical novel.

A thorough historical research and a desire to be faithful to the textualized knowledge of official history is a trait that is shared by both Bellonci and Francesca Sanvitale, the author of *Il figlio dell'impero*. However, as Davida Gavioli points out in her essay, the result of Sanvitale's painstaking research is a new kind of narrative form that defies definition. This novel is the result of "Sanvitale's profound self-consciousness about history seen not as an objective recording of the past but as a re-construction and conscious re-ordering of past events into a narrative." Gavioli argues that even though Sanvitale does not challenge the veracity of events, she creates a new historical text by the particular events she selects to narrate and by her choice of plot structure. She undermines the traditional notion of the objectivity of historical narration by reinscribing a historical figure who had been erased by official history.

A fictional reinscription of well known historical and literary figures is done also by Silvana La Spina in both her novels, *Quando Marte è in Capricorno* and *Un inganno dei sensi malizioso*, discussed by Gabriella Brooke. While in the former novel La Spina creates a fictional and yet verisimilar historical narration based on the friendship between Jacopo da Lentini and Pier delle Vigne, in the latter novel she uses parody, myth, and fairy-tale to shape a postmodern fantasy that deconstructs the patriarchal historical recording of events. Because of the unreliability of the narrator, the reader is reminded in this text that "History cannot be known as it was," as Brooke points out.

Another boldly experimental postmodern text is *I dodici abati di Challant* by Laura Mancinelli. Lauretta De Renzo analyzes the metahistorical use of history in this contemporary novel that subverts gender roles through fantasy. History is thus rewritten and reinterpreted because "it cannot be accepted as a cause/effect relation and a chronological sequence; the multitudes who are lost in its interstices create another possible history." The essay shows how images of food create the main structure of the subversive discourse of the novel.

The third section of the volume contains six essays that deal with novels centered around fictional, semifictional, and non-fictional characters cast against an historical background. The common thread among the essays is the lack of historical representation of characters who, even when they led lives that could be traced to existing documentation, were silenced, oppressed, and eventually erased from history.

In "Women Writing History: Female Novels of the Resistance," Bernadette Luciano discusses two Resistance novels: Renata Viganò's *L'Agnese va a morire* and Lalla Romano's *Tetto murato*. In their novels, Viganò and Romano attempt to correct the omission of women from the recorded history of a period in which women actively participated in Italy's civil war. With her main character, Viganò represents the thousands of disempowered Italian women who, prior to the Resistance, had little hope of playing a decisive role in history. However, Agnese dies outside of history, disappearing even from the final part of the novel. Romano provides, instead, an alternative vision of the Resistance and of history, as Luciano argues:

"Rather than starting from a political myth, Romano explores the possibility of human solidarity occasioned by rare historical moments."

In "Brushing Benjamin against the Grain: Elsa Morante and the *Jetztzeit* of Women's History," Maurizia Boscagli discusses Elsa Morante's materialistic historicism in terms of Walter Benjamin's concept of *Jetztzeit*—the simultaneous flow of official history and the separate history of the common people, victims of abusive power. In interpreting the unfolding of personal lives, both Morante and Benjamin resort, however, to a nonmaterialistic philosophy. While for Benjamin "the revolution is possible, and the oppressed will be redeemed in history," for the Italian writer "the past is 'completed' not through the revolution, but through the recourse to an eternal time, a cyclical time in which life and death unceasingly partake of each other and are no longer opposites."

In "Feminist Historiography and Dacia Maraini's *Isolina: Una donna tagliata a pezzi*," Rodica Diaconescu-Blumenfeld discusses Dacia Maraini's text in terms of new feminist historiography. The issues of the recovery of a lost life and of the subjectivity of the historical narrator—that is, "the deconstruction of the ideal of absolute objectivity" that "politicizes the subject/object relation"—are evident in this text that combines historical research with fiction. Maraini reconstructs a tragic act of violence against a woman by using "various forms of search and inscription that correspond to Isolina's obliteration." In so doing she inscribes the silencing and obliteration of women.

Gabriella Brooke's essay is centered on another work by Maraini, *La lunga vita di Marianna Ucrìa*. Brooke traces the mythical subtext of the novel to the myth of Philomela, the raped and mutilated Greek mythical heroine who succeeds in communicating through weaving an illustration of the abuse to which she had been subjected. Similarly, Maraini's heroine uses writing as a means of self-expression and self-definition, thus liberating herself from the patriarchal silencing to which she had been condemned. Through myth Maraini reinterprets a master story and deconstructs traditional historical discourse.

Traditional historical narrative is also challenged in another contemporary text, *La briganta* by Maria Rosa Cutrufelli, as Monica Rossi demonstrates in her essay. Rossi examines the theme of cross-dressing in this early terrorist novel based on the historical events of *brigantaggio* (banditry) in post-unification Italy. The protagonist, a noblewoman who joins the *briganti,* (brigands) thus renouncing her inherited social and gender roles, challenges women's absence from history, while trying to come to terms with her own passions and her role as a killer. In the interview by Cutrufelli that concludes the essay, the Sicilian author discusses both her method of historical research in preparation for the writing of the novel and some of the themes of her work. In her research she challenges the biased methods of male researchers who ignore women's presence both in historical events and in the actual findings in the archival texts. In her fiction, she explains, she uses transgressive and extreme behavior as a way of exploring women's hidden desires; she thus allows women's sexual desire and liberating actions to surface. In the last essay of the collection, Stefania Nedderman demonstrates the symbolic value of objects in Rosetta Loy's *Le strade di polvere.* Through their metamorphoses, objects epitomize the transformation and the aging of human beings, and especially of women who, while numerous in the text, are absent at the beginning and the end of the story. "The surface structure of the novel thus mimics history's treatment of women, contained inside the history of the male progeny," Nedderman argues.

Despite the authors' diversity of approaches, the volume achieves unity in its discussion of women's historical fiction by tracing both the evolution of and the recurrent themes in this area of Italian modern and contemporary fiction. Although novelists, unlike feminist historians, have not undertaken the task of a systematic rewriting of Italian history or, for that matter, of Italian women's history, their provocative reinterpretations of archival sources, bold formal experimentation, and the alternative and ex-centric perspectives from which they write invite a rereading of official history as we now know it. Departing from patriarchal texts, novelists protest women's and marginal groups' exclusion from official history, while they create a new narration of history based on a female symbolic order.

Notes

Parts of this introduction have appeared in my article, "Literary Historicism and Women's Tradition," published by *Italian Culture* 13 (1995). I wish to thank the editors of this journal for permission to reprint.

1. Lukács indicates that Stendhal's work should be ascribed to the enlightenment tradition whereas Victor Hugo's and Alfred De Vigny's historical novels fall within the category of the romantic novel. Alfred de Vigny's *Cinq Mars* should be considered the "manifesto" of romantic novels based on the most subjective and imaginative reconstructions of history.

2. Linda Hutcheon's work on the postmodern has proven particularly inspiring in the shaping of this volume. Even though only some of the novels here examined fall entirely within the category of the postmodern, her observations on the relation between historical narratives and contemporary novels are particularly useful and illuminating.

3. To this purpose, Scott points out that "the private sphere is a public creation" (1988, 24). She also adds: "Feminist history then becomes not the recounting of great deeds performed by women but the exposure of the often silent and hidden operations of gender that are nonetheless present and defining forces in the organization of most societies" (1988, 27).

4. One should stress the importance of New Historicism's skeptical rereading of history for the evolution of women's history and historical fiction. See in particular, Veeser 1994.

5. The theory of "entrustment" (*affidamento* in Italian) is the basis of the theoretical elaboration of the feminist group of Italian philosophers, "Diottima," and in particular, of Luisa Muraro's theory as formulated in the 1991 *L'ordine simbolico della madre.*

References

Banti, Anna. 1965. *Artemisia.* Milan: Arnoldo Mondadori.

Bellonci, Maria. 1989. *Rinascimento privato.* Milan: Arnoldo Mondadori.

———. 1995. *Private Renaissance.* Translated by William Weaver. New York: Morrow.

Cutrufelli, Maria Rosa. 1990. *La briganta.* Palermo: La luna.

de Certeau, Michel. 1984. *The practice of everyday life.* Berkeley: University of California Press.

Della Colletta, Cristina. 1996. *Plotting the past: Metamorphoses of historical narrative in modern Italian fiction.* Lafayette, IN: Purdue University Press.

Di Lascia, Maria Teresa. 1995. *Passaggio in ombra.* Milan: Feltrinelli.

Eco, Umberto. 1993. "Postille al *Nome della rosa*": *Il nome della rosa.* Milan: Bompiani.

Hutcheon, Linda. 1988. *A poetics of postmodernism: History, theory, fiction.* New York: Routledge.

La Capra, Dominick. 1985. *History and criticism.* Ithaca: Cornell University Press.

Lukács, György. 1965. *Il romanzo storico.* With an introduction by Cesare Cases and translated by Eraldo Arnaud. Turin: Einaudi.

La Spina, Silvana. 1994. *Quando Marte é in capricorno.* Milan: Bompiani.

———. 1995. *Un inganno dei sensi malizioso.* Milan: Arnoldo Mondadori.

Mancinelli, Laura. 1981. *I dodici abati di Challant.* Turin: Einaudi.

Manzoni, Alessandro. [1840.] 1966. *I promessi sposi.* With an introduction by Vittorio Spinazzola. Milan: Garzanti.

————. [1850] 1984. *On the historical novel.* With an introduction by Sandra Bermann and translated by Hanna Mitchell and Stanley Mitchell. Lincoln: University of Nebraska Press.

Maraini, Dacia. 1992. *Isolina: Una donna tagliata a pezzi.* Milan: Mondadori, 1985. Reprint, Milan: Rizzoli.

————. 1992. *La lunga vita di Marianna Ucrìa.* Milan: Rizzoli.

Marotti, Maria Ornella. 1995. Literary Historicism and Women's Tradition. *Italian Culture,* 13 : 261–72.

Morante, Elsa. 1974. *La storia.* Turin: Einaudi.

————. 1984. *History: A novel.* Translated by William Weaver. New York: Vintage.

Morazzoni, Marta. 1986. *La ragazza col turbante.* Milan: Longanesi.

————. 1988. *Girl in a turban.* Translated by Patrick Creagh. New York: Alfred Knopf.

Muraro, Luisa. 1991. *L'ordine simbolico della madre.* Rome: Editori Riuniti.

Romano, Lalla. 1957. *Tetto murato.* Turin: Einaudi.

Sanvitale, Francesca. 1993. *Il figlio dell'impero.* Turin: Einaudi.

Scott, Joan Wallach. 1988. *Gender and the politics of history.* New York: Columbia University Press.

Sereni, Clara. 1993. *Il gioco dei regni.* Florence: Giunti.

Spinazzola, Vittorio. 1984. *Il romanzo anti-storico.* Rome: Editori Riuniti.

Veeser, Aram H, ed. 1994. *The New Historicism reader.* New York: Routledge.

Veyne, Paul. 1971. *Comment on écrit l'histoire: essai d'epistemologie.* Paris: Editions du Seuil.

Viganò, Renata. 1974. *L'Agnese va a morire.* Turin: Einaudi.

White, Hayden. 1987. *The content of the form: Narrative discourse and historical representation.* Baltimore: Johns Hopkins University Press.

Part One
Toward a Definition of Women's Historical Fiction

Stranger Than Life? Autobiography and Historical Fiction

Carol Lazzaro-Weis

Any bibliographical review of women's writings in the past ten years indicates an increase in the production of historical fiction by women writers coming from diverse national, cultural, and literary traditions.[1] In *A Poetics of Postmodernism: History, Theory and Fiction*, Linda Hutcheon (1988) attributes the appearance of what she terms "historiographic metafictions" to postmodernism's questioning of official truths, master narratives, and the possibility of representation. It would appear that in historical fiction, feminism and postmodernism could unite to create "new and critical communal awareness of past and present errors of oppression, omission and commission" (93–94).

Yet attempts to theorize about women's historical novels, even along gender lines, are fraught with problems. One primary difficulty stems from the fact that given the extremely Protean nature of the form, it could be argued that there is no such thing as a historical novel—just historical referents appearing and functioning in a series of other, more clearly delineated and demanding forms. Occupying such a varied position, the historical novel has much in common with another unclear and contested "genre," that of autobiography, whose popularity also derives from postmodernism's interest in analyzing the study of self-representation as an ensemble of cultural, historical, and textual practices. Since all autobiographies must be representative of their times, they are as much historical as they are personal. Nineteenth-century German philosopher Wilhelm Dilthey (1833–1911) saw autobiography as the human side of history; German historian Leopold Ranke (1795–1886) proposed that history is nothing other than a distillation of participant subjectivities (quoted in Bruner 1993, 43). According to these two, History and autobiography were two sides of the same coin, one impossible without the other, and a great man and good autobiographer must bring them together.

Naturally enough for Dilthey and Ranke, this synergetic act seemed to involve primarily male mind and matter and major critical works in autobiography in this century focused primarily on male autobiographies. However, in recent years other volumes appearing in English on autobiography mark the renewed interest in the form for male and female critics, the common roots of their interest (postmodernism), and the main split between male and female *critical reaction* to the form. Although autobiography's popularity derives from postmodernism's dictum that all subjectivity is created in language and is therefore a fiction, fiction presents a problem both for contemporary female critics and female/feminist practitioners of autobiography, who nowadays are often one and the same.

The essays in James Olney's *Autobiography: Essays Theoretical and Critical* (1980) explore autobiography's relationship to literature. The autobiographical experience produced grist for the writer's mill; therefore, the act of remembering was strongly determined by the fictional impulse. Memory in autobiography, writes Olney, "can be imagined as the narrative course of the past becoming present" (214). In essays in the 1993 volume, *The Culture of Autobiography: Constructions of Self-Representation*, the fictional nature of memory and autobiography is treated as a given. Jerome Bruner, among others, reminds us that any narration of a life story is going to proceed along the lines of some sort of narrative plot that the autobiographer rewrites along different interpretive lines:

> I want to assert that an autobiography is not and cannot be a way of simply signifying or referring to a life as lived. I take the view that there is no such thing as a "life as lived" to be referred to. On this view, a life is created or constructed by the act of autobiography. (38)

These "interpretive lines" are guided not only by the author's intentions but also by the conventions and style appropriate to the form chosen.

Since critics such as Dominick La Capra (1985) and Hayden White (1984) have told us this is much the same for the writing of history, any comparison between autobiography and historical novels clearly does not define any real relationship to each other except that both are genres whose practitioners are more liable to be called liars and self-deceivers than writers of other genres.[2] And it is precisely this latter possibility that has traditionally posed more of a threat for women writers. Hence the articles in Estelle Jelinek's *Women's Autobiography: Essays in Criticism* (1980) stressed the marginal and adversarial status of women's autobiographies. Still today, most women critics insist on locating women's life writings in a primarily adversarial space, hostile to any (presumably male) fictional form or life pattern. Leigh Gilmore (1994) in her recent book *Autobiographies* concedes that certain narratives include structural or symbolic fictions to resolve problems they cannot solve thematically (xiv). However, according to Gilmore:

> Autobiographies are those elements of self-representation . . . which are *not* bound by a philosophical definition of the self derived from Augustine, *not* content with the literary history of autobiography, those elements that mark a location in the text where self-invention, self-desires, and self-representation emerge with the technologies of autobiography—namely those legalistic, social and ecclesiastical discourses of truth and identity through which the subject of autobiography is produced.[3] (my emphasis) (42)

Gilmore emphasizes correctly that in autobiographical writings, issues of truth versus lying are always at stake since all autobiographical writings draw on culturally dominant discourses of truth-telling even if there is no truth. She is equally right to be skeptical of following in male critical tracks. Robin Pickering-Iazzi (1993) tells us how "autobiographism" in Italian women's writings, an element presumed to be its defining characteristic, has been used to define and then bury women's writing far from literary fields. Critics, such as Croce and Gobetti—to name only two she mentions—generally conclude that men know how to make their private memories illuminate "universal" literary themes, whereas women remain mired in concerns specific to the female-gendered subject and its relationship to society. Succinctly (and sarcastically) put, if literary techniques served, according to these critics, to make men's autobiographies more "universal" and thus closer to the real truth, their presence in women's writings seemed only to exacerbate the latter's idiosyncratic and falsifying nature (Pickering-Iazzi 180).[4]

Scholars of Western literature trace its beginnings to auto-biographical or historical writings. Likewise, in the twentieth century, critics seeking to define nascent literary traditions such as African, African-American, or Caribbean writings locate the beginning of these traditions in autobiographical accounts of experience, which then begin to function as a collective history for the group.[5] In listing types of women's historical writings in the Western tradition, Gerda Lerner (1993) argues that women's autobiographical writings post-date their historical writings which were primarily biographies of women. Thus the genre, first practiced by female mystics such as Hildegarde of Bingen, Dorothea of Mantua, St. Teresa of Avila and St. Catherine of Siena, should be seen as part of the effort to document historically the lives of women. In her essay, *Writing a Woman's Life,* Carolyn Heilbrun (1988) claims that the return to autobiography by contemporary women writers is a necessary step in the birth of new traditions for women in fiction and history. Nineteenth-century fictional paradigms suppressed the female literary voice by suppressing its factual and literary memory. Autobiography, she writes, facilitates a rebirth of both types of memory to create the narratives from which women's fiction will emerge.

If Heilbrun is correct, critics will need to redefine the relationship between autobiography and fiction in contemporary women's writings. Indeed, this is the goal of the essays in the 1991 collection *Redefining Autobiography in Twentieth-Century Women's Fiction.* In her foreword, Molly Hite points out that women writers now find it difficult to evade the imputation that they are just "writing themselves," an activity presumed to require little creative mediation and even less historical consciousness. Significantly, although many essays in the collection deal with women's historical fictions, the term historical novel is eclipsed by that of fictional autobiography. Flora Schiminovich prefers to classify Isabel Allende's novel *House of the Spirits* as a fictional autobiography rather than as a historical novel since the autobiographical elements are more easily verifiable than the historical referents (1991, 103).

It is certainly difficult to speak of the historical novel to Italianists without evoking reference to Manzoni. Nonetheless, as the essays in this collection demonstrate, Italian women writers have long participated in the production of the various manifestations of the form. The return to the historical novel by feminist writers such as Dacia Maraini and Maria Rosa

Cutrufelli, among others, has invited comparisons between these writers and women writers of previous generations, as well as analyses of distinctions between a possible "male" and "female" historical novel.[6] In my own analysis of various manifestations of the historical novel in Italian women's writings, I have argued that the historical novel form offers a means to do what Rossana Ombres has called for, namely to create a "great women's literature (that) would be one where the female experience is absorbed to the point of non-recognition" (quoted in Lazzaro-Weis 1993, 150). Yet autobiographism still plays an important role in these novels. In several interviews (Fumagalli 1991; De Michelis 1990; Vigani 1990; D'Isa 1990), Maraini has emphasized that her most obviously literary narrative, *La lunga vita di Marianna Ucrìa*, is inspired by a personal motive, the desire to come to terms with her oppressive childhood in Sicily. Maria Rosa Cutrufelli also claims her relationship to her brother exerted a more formidable shaping force on *La briganta* than did her historical research. Much recent criticism on women's autobiographies and historical novels relates how these works construct matrilineal genealogies to create a personal history (Marotti 1994; Pickering-Iazzi 1994; Schiminovich 1991). In this paper, I would like to trace other genealogies that surface when we look more generally at the dynamics of autobiographism, history, and fiction in a few selected works by Italian women writers over an extended period of time. The contemporary historical novel may still function to disguise the female autobiographical voice and experience but with some significant differences especially as it relates to the creation of a female literary voice.

History has long functioned as a narrative space both to empower and disguise women's autobiographical and literary voices. Graziella Parati (1996) begins her study on Italian women's autobiographies with a chapter on Camilla Faà Gonzaga's brief "historical autobiographical narrative," written in 1622. In *Historia*, Camilla details and protests her forced divorce of convenience from duke Ferdinando Gonzaga and her subsequent seclusion in a convent. Gonzaga takes pen in hand to offer her *truthful* (italics mine) autobiographical account, which, on the basis of being more logical, factual, and certainly not "fictional," would perhaps succeed in writing her back into an official history poised to efface her. However, as Parati shows, when Gonzaga changes certain facts and adds fictional elements, these changes function to present the stereotype of

the wronged, virtuous woman, an act dedicated to gaining the
sympathy and support of her hypothetical (and future) readers.
Gonzaga's revisionist history is shaped by the structure of the
fairy tale: stereotypes such as the obedient daughter-princess
betrayed by a cruel father and then husband point to fiction's
shaping role in this purportedly factual treatise. Gonzaga's
collaboration with female stereotypes is a result of the fact
that for women writers, no tradition of secular self-exploration
existed to legitimate and validate their narrative—their only
hope was their claim to represent historical truth faithfully.
Ironically, fictionalization and not truth functioned to guarantee the life rather than the death of the text and author, since
until recently, knowledge of Gonzaga's text came from the fictionalized versions her writing inspired.

The disguising of the autobiographical voice as historical
fact and truth, an act necessary to assure both physical and
literary survival for Gonzaga and her text, has had both liberating and restrictive effects on the literary history of women's
writings. Although women writers seemed obliged to disguise
their fictional voice as autobiographical truth when writing of
themselves—to disguise their art as life so to speak—autobiography could and did provide a space from which they could
simultaneously denounce "fictions" about themselves. Certainly this is the case in Sibilla Aleramo's *Una donna* (1906),
where fictional plots, themes, and stereotypes concerning
women are pointedly demonstrated to be insufficient and are
ultimately rejected. *Una donna* reenacts the difficulty women
experienced while dabbling in stock fictional plots in their attempt to represent their own life.

This double bind is usually explained as a result of patriarchal domination in the spheres of both life and art. However,
even if Aleramo is denouncing literature's insufficiencies, her
text enters the hallowed halls of literature primarily by becoming the paradigm of the true history of woman kind and
their collective past (Bassanese 1990, 43). Heilbrun documents
this trend and argues for the primary role of women's autobiographical writings in establishing women's history as a shared
fate. She quotes Hannah Arendt's words that "if we do not
know our own history, we are doomed to live it as though
it were our private fate" (in Heilbrun 1988, 71). Nonetheless,
however empowering, the validation of women's autobiography through attachment to a collective identity and history
would also exercise its own tyrannical effect on the female

literary imagination. References to the collective past for women recalled other images of cancellation of the private, individualistic memory that was the stuff of the male act of transforming life into art.

Indeed, collective and personal amnesia due to collective and personal oppression is a common theme in Italian feminist literature of the sixties and seventies. Out of many examples, I refer briefly to the novels that constitute Dacia Maraini's first two fictional stages. The alienation and amnesia that characterize the protagonists of *La vacanza* (1962) and *L'età del malessere* (1963) are given comical, ironic and tragic treatment in the short stories in *Mio marito* (1968). Yet, if we look at the tradition of women's writings in Italy, most of which have been accused of being too overtly autobiographical, the theme of memory loss predominates. Clarice Tartufari's tale "A Life Story?" published in 1925 and recently translated by Robin Pickering-Iazzi, speaks of the cancellation of personal memory and of women themselves at the same time. The repetition and similarity in the universal female experience cancel memory so that it is unimportant, impossible even, to remember the names of those who went before. Tartufari's tale demonstrates how, in the process of becoming "woman," her personal memory progressively merges with and is obliterated by women's collective lot or history. Women's memory needed more space for what Graziella Parati (1996) calls, in speaking of Fausta Cialente's *Le quattro ragazze Wieselberger* (1976), a wider definition of personal memory. This kind of personal, individual and creative space that was canceled for many Italian women writers as they wrote their history was synonymous with their limited lot in life.

Cialente's work, like Grazia Deledda's *Cosima* (1937) and Ada Negri's *Stella mattutina* (1921), could be classified as "fictional autobiography." Fictional autobiographies are indeed collective in nature; they participate in the handing down of information, beliefs, and customs, and they assure cultural continuity in social attitudes and institutions that define people. Fictional autobiographies typically have a generic plot; most often, they describe the genesis of a writer. Fictional autobiographies are produced by a double consciousness. Writers usually focus on a common plight while, at the same time, they fix an historical reality. More importantly, these autobiographies in themselves create a literary tradition of autobiography (Olney 1990).

The common plight/plot in the fictional autobiographies mentioned above revolves around the material and psychological difficulties encountered by women seeking a public role other than that of wife and mother. The topos these writers share to express their protest is the separation of life and art for women.[7] In revolt against the dictum that for women, depictions of a female self resulted in the exclusion of their work from the literary realm, these women use their "fictional memory" to resist the conflation of women's personal memory with women's history. More precisely, as in all autobiographies, they practice what they theorize. While questioning why art and life are separate for women, they demonstrate the opposite through their use of literary memory.

Cosima's narrator brings the themes of memory and imagination immediately to the fore. The third-person omniscient narrator uses her flawless, untroubled memory to recreate Cosima's struggles in becoming a writer. A second type of memory operative here, and one that could be more correctly termed imagination, is practiced by Cosima as a young girl. At several points in the text, Cosima encounters her grandmother, who stirs unconscious, indescribable feelings of an archaic dream world in her. This imagination, we are told, is what enables Cosima to see reality and to color it, that is, to turn reality into the word (1988, 4). Descriptions of this transformation of reality through will (and form) are found throughout the text. For example, when Cosima is waiting to hear the gender of her new sibling, she imagines she has a little brother. The narrator comments: "As it happens, it was a girl; but she wanted a little brother and had invented him, name and all" (5).

The primary issue here is not truth versus lying, since the creation of memory in *Cosima* is done by writing stories: the stories Cosima hears and would spend the rest of her life writing and publishing in contempt of anyone who tried to stop her.[8] As in most fictional autobiographies, memory and imagination become coterminous as they assist the narrator in avoiding the patterned fate of (women's) history. Although the sight or the recollection of her grandmother arouses in her a sense of the "indelible memories ... that she later explained to herself as a surfacing and sudden resubmersion of her earlier life that remained or was reborn in her subconscious" (10) the text is a monument to a type of narrative imagination that is irrepressible and eminently expressible. If, in *Cosima,*

Deledda appears to be recounting the experiences that formed her, she is also creating her own personal memory from literature. Most importantly, this is the literature she has already written.

Precisely because many of the stories included in the "autobiography" appear elsewhere in Deledda's work, it is less relevant to draw parallels between life and work than to note how Deledda creates her own autobiography from her fiction and thus circumvents the tight link between women's collective memory and the collective history depicted in many life stories of and by women. Deledda stops her autobiography of becoming a writer when she leaves for Cagliari. She does not discuss her marriage and life in Rome since there is no need. *Cosima* is the story of the formation of a writer. When Deledda leaves for Cagliari this formation is indeed complete since *Cosima*, by repeating Deledda's fiction, is embodying what happened since Deledda left. At the end of her career, Deledda's life is at one with her art.

This is not the case in the historical novels of the first generation of women writers of the twentieth century. James Mandrell (1990) uses the examples of Elena Garro, Elsa Morante, and Isabel Allende to show how women's historical novels differ essentially from those of men: whereas the classical historical novel is essentially analeptic, or conciliatory toward the past, women's historical novels privilege prophecy, creativity, and the feminine to challenge the continuous fabric of history and predict change (229–31). Mandrell thus concludes that memory does not play an important role in these works that explore the possibilities for historical and social change (231). On the other hand, Neria De Giovanni (1989) argues that in Anna Banti's *Artemisia* (1947) and Maria Bellonci's *Rinascimento privato* (1989), to name only two of her examples from the first generation of twentieth-century Italian women writers, autobiography and official history are pitted against one another. Anna Banti and Maria Bellonci use the historical novel primarily as a means to know themselves rather than to know the outside world. Thus, historical figures and fact in these novels are blatantly changed and eventually eclipsed to signal the victory of the authors' private, individualistic struggles (107–9).

Although both Mandrell and De Giovanni view these different means of privileging autobiography over official history as the expression of a triumph for a woman-centered world and life the writers they discuss, for the most part, do not. In *Un grido lacerante* (1981), Anna Banti's angry fictional autobiographer protests the exclusion of women from the male literary kingdom where life and art can productively merge. Banti's fictional autobiography is a psychological inquiry into her own literary imagination—one whose experimentation with historical novels provides a good example of the art-versus-life conflict we previously noted in many women writers.

This conflict structures Banti's historical novel *Artemisia*, which was first published in 1947. Banti herself defines this version, a rewrite of the first version of her "historical novel" (which had been destroyed in the 1944 bombing of Florence) as a "historical-literary symbiosis" (1).[9] She casts her work in the form of a fictional autobiography to signal to the reader that the work will describe the genesis of an artist, one whom the narrator seeks to resuscitate and identify with across time. However, the form also assists in the dramatization of the longstanding conflicts between admixtures of history, fiction, and autobiographism in women's writings.

Banti claims to write *Artemisia* out of a desire to give a personal history to one of the few female artists that history had recorded and whose reputation was now on the verge of eclipse. Threats of Artemisia's erasure from history came not only from German bombings. Banti's own husband, Roberto Longhi, had begun the procedure in an article (1943) attributing some of Artemisia's paintings to her father Orazio.[10] Ironically, not unlike Gonzaga who reshaped her own life, Banti blatantly changes many of the facts to give Artemisia life. However, in many cases, the altering of facts is directly related to the troubled thematic relationship between autobiographism and women's collective history in the text, a relationship that, until resolved, causes the narrator here to consider abandoning the rewriting of the work and thus constitutes a serious threat to its completion.

In contrast to the third-person narrator in *Cosima*, Banti's first-person narrator speaks often of memory. Early in the text when the narrator questions her ability to reconstruct the lost manuscript, she states that Artemisia is "succumbing to the force of memory" (13). The meaning of memory here, as in Tartufari and later Maraini, is synonymous with effacement and forgetting, since the memory referred to is the collective memory of women's oppression and defeat. Whereas in *Cosima* memory functioned as a bridge between life and writing, here memory is the locus of the narrator's own (over)identification with Artemisia. It is this overidentification that causes her to attempt initially to take over Artemisia's story and try to write it as the perennial history of the wronged and subservient woman.

Although Banti's narrator tries to establish constant similarities between herself and the object of her writing, Artemisia resists becoming the alter ego of the narrator, first by forcing Banti to question if the narrator is telling the story correctly. Toward the middle of the narrative, an emboldened Artemisia pointedly demands that the narrator examine her personal motives for trying to tell her own story through Artemisia. Artemisia makes this request after a scene in which Artemisia is forced to recognize her daughter's difference from herself.[11] The narrator is then obliged to acknowledge that her "memory" of Artemisia is infested with stereotypes coming from fiction and women's history:

> Artemisia's obstinacy in making me remember her, my own obstinacy in remembering her according to my whims, is becoming a game. . . . I have grown accustomed, through contradicting her and even situating her in my own time, to feeling her stand beside me, present. (108)

The narrator admits to having recalled Artemisia "with memories of her unhappy motherhood, *the usual topic of a woman's conversation*" (111; my emphasis). Upon realizing this falsification of Artemisia's story and history, the narrator then changes her reasons for writing *Artemisia*. The text is not to be written as an apology for women's servitude and misfortunes but rather "to release my companion from her human errors and reconstruct for her an ideal freedom, the freedom that gave her strength and elation during her hours of work, of which there were many" (111).

It is precisely when Banti's narrator admits that she cannot truly recapture the essence of a woman who lived three hundred years ago, the text becomes both more fictional and more historical as Banti begins to practice her "art." Banti, a well-trained art historian, starts to paint verbal frescoes of the people, places and events Artemisia, in her search for artistic freedom, would have seen and experienced in her travels in the seventeenth-century. Despite the liberties taken with the known facts about the artist Artemisia Gentileschi's life in the second part of the text, Banti's knowledge of painting and her literary frescoes of seventeenth-century life are objectively verifiable. Released from the task of writing a collective history for women as her own story, Banti practices her art in fiction and thus negates in this way the defeat and erasure of female creativity.[12]

At the age of 81, Banti again turned to fictional autobiography in *Un grido lacerante* to protest the exclusion of the depiction of a female life from the literary domain. Again she challenged the separation by showing how she transposed the female self and experience into a variety of fictional types and plots. Thus, despite differences, her experimentation with the historical novel and fictional autobiography, is not totally dissimilar to the more recent historical fictions of Dacia Maraini and Maria Rosa Cutrufelli, which are also cast in the form of fictional autobiography. Maraini and Cutrufelli use the form to forge links to and create a women's *literary* history as opposed to their collective and oppressed one. To be sure, in *La lunga vita di Marianna Ucrìa*, Maraini revisits her own apprehensions and fantasies concerning her unhappy childhood in Sicily. Here, however, history and autobiography are no longer pitted against one another in a struggle between *autocancellazione* (self-annulation) and *autoaffermazione* (self-affirmation) as was the case for many first-generation writers.[13] Maraini's *La lunga vita di Marianna Ucrìa* is a literary rewrite of the paradigm of oppression, emancipation, and rebirth found in her previous novels, a paradigm that itself recalls the structure of Aleramo's *Una donna* (1906).[14] Yet Aleramo's autobiography reflects a constant preoccupation with the unreliability of memory and its inability to convey her experience. Despite the obvious differences, by casting a fictional life in a context that recalls her previous writings, Maraini uses fictional autobiography in a manner more reminiscent of Deledda. She has literary memory serve to fulfil the form's generic function of describing the genesis of a writer by re-presenting and re-narrativizing her previous works. In so doing, both writers affirm and validate a different story of women's relationship to writing.

Maria Rosa Cutrufelli's *La briganta* (1990) is also a historical fiction cast in fictional autobiographical form. The story of the revolt of an upper-middle-class southern woman at the time of Italy's reunification includes Aleramo and Maraini's emancipation paradigm, albeit to demonstrate its limits since emancipation has led here to violent revolt. The heroine, Margherita, becomes a brigand to express her feminist revolt, only to be defeated with the others in the band and imprisoned for life. Cutrufelli's most recent novel, *Canto al deserto: Storia di Tina, soldato di mafia* (1994), rewrites Margherita's revolt in a contemporary setting. Both Tina and Margherita dress like men and reject the subservient roles reserved for women. Tina, a more drastic example of *femminilità negata* (femininity denied), is no less doomed to failure. Although Tina manages to obtain some respect in the mafia, she is ultimately forced into a suicidal escape attempt when she tries to effect "a rise in the ranks" [un salto di qualità].

La briganta is a carefully researched historical novel set in the nineteenth century. Cutrufelli invites comparisons between her own feminist consciousness and that of Margherita by granting the heroine the consciousness and the speech of a twentieth-century feminist. In *Canto al deserto*, autobiographical parallels are more strongly invited by the narrative point of view. The narrator, a Sicilian woman writer in self-imposed exile (Cutrufelli, presumably), returns to Sicily to meet and write a book on Tina, a modern and even more violent permutation of the *briganta*. As in Maraini's *La lunga vita*, the search to understand another female figure facilitates a return in writing to a (Sicilian) past that the author had previously denounced and forgotten. Again in this text, autobiographism is a fictional device that allows Cutrufelli to review her previous fictional creation, Margherita, as well as many recurring themes in her works in a contemporary context, rather than offering a personal truth disguised or distorted by fictional stereotypes or history's demands. History and autobiographism do not result in fictional lies or historical cancellation; instead they reaffirm a literary memory with a history. Rather than stifling production, these elements allow Cutrufelli to continue her personal historical and sociological inquiry, which includes analyses of the socioeconomic condition of the south and its relationship to the creation of individual and organized violence. The search for Tina in *Il canto del deserto* is a continuation of the history of Sicilian women, with a focus on the effects of industrialization without economic growth on Sicily and its impoverished inhabitants. Tina's story forms another part of the intellectual autobiography of a writer struggling with *il problema del sud*, especially as it affects women and the practice of her own art.

In other words, Maraini and Cutrufelli return to the historical novel not primarily to condemn past practices against women nor to show a preference for a private, artistic yet isolated sphere, as was the case in many earlier historical fictions. Rather they use it to rewrite the script of the relationship of fiction to women's lives and their history. Their historical fictions enact a shift from collectivity to individuality. The medium of fictional autobiography allows them to exploit fiction to rewrite woman's history from a personal and critical point of view while reaffirming the existence of their own literary tradition. No longer strangers to life and art, historical fact and personal memory fuse in their works in a way to create new stories about women. To be sure, these stories and their plots are informed by the collective experience of the feminist movement. Yet, historiography, a technique that is prompted by its specific status to dissipate amnesia and cultivate memory, is preserving the individual autobiographical voice in women's writings, making it possible for them to continue to create and express an expanded personal memory in a fictional space.

Notes

1. Portions of this article have already appeared in "History, Fiction and the Female Autobiographical Voice," *Romance Languages Annual* (1995). I would like to thank the editors for allowing these portions to reappear here.

2. Recent debates among Italian feminist historians demonstrate concern for the relationship of narrative form to historical content. Just as narrative form can help define goals as well as impose limits, so can the method of recuperating a lost or forgotten female past determine the results of the inquiry. Thus, historian Gianna Pomata writes: "Our problem is not simply what to write (changing the content of history), but how to write: experimenting with new forms of historical narrative more adequate to the cognitive aims of women's history," (quoted in Bono and Kemp, 1991, 19).

3. Gilmore (1994) concludes, "if autobiography provokes fantasies of the real, then autobiographies explore the constrained 'real' for the reworking of identity in the discourses of women's self-representation" (239).

4. For example, in his complimentary review of Dacia Maraini's 1962 novel *La vacanza*, Walter Pedullà praises the work not only for its modernity of themes, language, and form but also for its "mancanza di autobiografismo." (Quoted in Grazia Sumeli-Weinberg 1993).

5. See, for example, Butterfield 1974, Blassingame 1973–74 and Ismond 1990.

6. See De Giovanni 1994. De Giovanni suggests that the acclaim received by women writers (e.g., Rosetta Loy and Dacia Maraini were awarded the *Premio Campiello* in 1987 and 1990 respectively) for their best-selling histori-

cal novels in the late eighties and early nineties is responsible for the increased production of historical novels in the last few years by male writers.

7. See Paola Malpezzi-Price 1990. Price argues that the main structuring theme in Cialente's novels that preceded her fictional autobiography was how "life in the world of art was irreconcilable with a woman's traditional role as wife" (110). Cialente desired to equate art (the life of the intellect) and life (political activism). In her fictionalized autobiography she first renounces fiction as a means of reconciling the two realms. This renunciation is later rescinded and Cialente reaffirms the separation of art and life in order to reclaim her writings as individual and fictional.

8. In this respect, Deledda's modernist approach (1988) is akin to that of Zora Neale Hurston's in *Their Eyes Were Watching God*, first published in 1937, the same year as Deledda's *Cosima, quasi Grazia.*

9. All quotes come from Shirley D'Ardia Caracciolo's translation (1988).

10. On this topic see Mary Garrard 1981.

11. It is of interest to note here that the descriptions of Artemisia's relationship with her daughter are highly fictionalized. Banti depicts the daughter as reluctant to imitate her mother's career or lifestyle. Historical fact contradicts this depiction since this daughter was also a painter and seems to have spent much time with her mother. See JoAnn Cannon 1994.

12. Other critics have noted that when autobiographism becomes less prominent, the text changes in tone. Heller (1990), for example, writes, "the dynamic interplay between the narrator and protagonist becomes less prominent as the novel gradually focuses more sharply on Artemisia's own story" (48). It is also in the second part of the story that Banti blatantly changes historical fact by writing that Artemesia's self-portrait was really a picture of another woman artist. It is tempting to discuss this scene using contemporary Italian feminist difference theory. However, in my interpretation it fits in perfectly with the thematics of her refusal to write women's history as repetitive loss.

13. These terms come from De Giovanni 1994. De Giovanni sees fiction and history as the two mediums through which women writers traditionally expressed their autobiographies because "L'autobiografia femminile è sempre sbilanciata tra autoaffermazione e autocancellazione, perché l'insicurezza del proprio genere porta (o almeno portava) alla difficoltà dell'autoriconoscimento" (82). "Women's autobiography always vacillates between self-affirmation and self annullation because women's insecurity about their gender results (or at least resulted in the past) in their difficulty in recognizing themselves positively." (my translation)

14. Merry (1990, 223) suggests that both *Donna in guerra* (1975) and *Il treno per Helsinki* (1954) can be read as updates of the archetypal story of women's oppression, emancipation, and rebirth told by Sibilla Aleramo in *Una donna.*

References

Aleramo, Sibilla. 1906. *Una donna.* Rome: STEN.

Banti, Anna. 1947. *Artemisia.* Florence-Sansoni.

———. 1981. *Un grido lacerante.* Milan: Rizzoli.

————. 1988. *Artemisia*. Translated by Shirley d'Ardia Caracciolo. Lincoln and London: University of Nebraska Press.

Bassanese, Flora. 1990. *Una donna:* Autobiography as exemplary text. In *Quaderni d'italianistica* 11, no. 1: 41–60.

Bellonci, Maria. 1939. *Lucrezia Borgia: La vita e i suoi tempi*. Milan: Mondadori.

————. 1989. *Rinascimento privato*. Milan: Mondadori.

Bono, Paola, and Sandra Kemp, eds. 1991. *Italian feminist thought: A reader*. London: Blackwell.

Blassingame, John W. 1973–74. Black autobiographies as history and literature. In *Black Scholar* 5, no. 4: 2–9.

Bruner, Jerome. 1993. The autobiographical process. In *The culture of autobiography: Constructions of self-representation*. Edited by Robert Folkenflik, 38–56. Stanford: Stanford University Press.

Butterfield, Stephen. 1974. *Black Autobiography in America*. Amherst: University of Massachusetts Press.

Cannon, JoAnn. *Artemisia* and the Life Story of the Exceptional Woman *Forum Italicum* 28.2:322–41.

Cialente, Fausta. 1976. *Le quattro ragazze Wieselberger*. Milan: Mondadori.

Cutrufelli, Maria Rosa. 1990. *La briganta*. Palermo: La Luna.

————. 1994. *Canto al deserto: Storia di Tina, soldato di mafia*. Milan: Longanesi.

De Giovanni, Neria. 1994. Le tendenze della narrativa femminile italiana del secondo novecento. In *Artemide sulla soglia: Donne e letteratura in Italia*, 75–90. Rome: Demian Edizioni.

————. 1989. La sfinge cantatrice: Realtà come specchio nella narrativa femminile del post-neorealismo. First published in *Romance Languages Annual* 1 (1989): 105–10. In *Artemide sulla soglia: Donne e letteratura in Italia*, 59–73. Rome: Demian Edizioni.

Deledda, Grazia. 1937 *Cosima quasi Grazia*. Milan-Treves. 1988. *Cosima*. Translated by Martha King. New York: Italica Press.

De Michelis, Cesare. 1990. *Il gazzettino* 23 June.

D'Isa, Dina. 1990. La liberazione attraverso la scrittura. In *Il tempo* 11 May.

Fumagalli, Fiorella. 1991. Marianna dei Miracoli. In *Tutto Milano* 31 January.

Garrard, Mary. 1981. Artemisia and Susanna. In *Feminism and Art History: Questioning the Litany*, edited by Norma Broride and Mary Garrard, 146–71. New York: Harper and Row.

Gilmore, Leigh. 1994. *Autobiographies: A feminist theory of women's self-representation*. Ithaca: Cornell University Press.

Heilbrun, Carolyn. 1988. *Writing a Woman's Life*. New York: Ballantine.

Heller, Deborah. 1990. History, art and fiction in Anna Banti's Artemisia. In *Contemporary women writers in Italy: A renaissance*, edited by Santo Aricò, 44–60. Amherst: University of Massachusetts Press.

Hite, Molly. 1991. Foreword to Morgan and Hall,

Hutcheon, Linda. 1988. *A poetics of postmodernism: History, theory and fiction*. New York: Routledge.

Ismond, Patricia. 1990. Another life: Autobiography as alternative history. In *Journal of West Indian Literature* 4, no. 1: 41–49.

Jelinek, Estelle, ed. 1980. *Women's autobiography: Essays in criticism.* Bloomington: Indiana University Press.

La Capra, Dominick. 1985. *History and criticism.* Ithaca: Cornell University Press.

Lazzaro-Weis, Carol. 1993. *From margins to mainstream: Feminism and fictional modes in Italian women's writing, 1968–1990.* Philadelphia: University of Pennsylvania Press.

———. 1995. "History, Fiction and the Female Autobiographical Voice." *Romance Language Annual* 7: 273–77.

Lerner, Gerda. 1993. *The creation of feminist consciousness: From the Middle Ages to eighteen-seventy.* Oxford: Oxford University Press.

Longhi, Roberto. 1943. Ultimi Studi sul Caravaggio e la sua cerchia. In *Proporzioni.* 1 p. 47 n. 38.

Malpezzi-Price, Paola. 1990. Autobiography, art and history in Fausta Cialente's fiction. In *Contemporary women writers in Italy: A renaissance,* edited by Santo Aricò. Amherst: University of Massachusetts Press: 108–22.

Mandrell, James. 1990. The prophetic voice in Garro, Morante and Allende. In *Comparative Literature* 42, no. 3: 227–46.

Maraini, Dacia. 1962. *La vacanza.* Milan: Lerici.

———. 1963. *L'età del malessere.* Turin: Einaudi.

———. 1968. *Mio marito.* Milan: Bompiani.

———. 1990. *La lunga vita di Marianna Ucrìa.* Milan: Rizzoli.

Marotti, Maria. 1994. Filial discourses: Feminism and femininity in Italian women's autobiography. In *Feminine feminists: Cultural practices in Italy,* edited by Giovanna Miceli Jeffries. Minneapolis: University of Minnesota Press: 65–86.

Merry, Bruce. 1990. *Women in modern Italian literature: Four studies based on the work of Grazia Deledda, Alba de Céspedes, Natalia Ginzburg and Dacia Maraini.* Townsville: James Cook University of North Queensland.

Morgan, Janice, and Colette T. Hall. 1991. *Redefining twentieth-century women's fiction: As essay collection.* New York: Garland Publishing.

Negri, Ada. 1966. *Stella mattutina: Tutte le opere di Ada Negri.* Milan: Mondadori.

Olney, James, ed. 1980. *Autobiography: Essays theoretical and critical,* 214. Princeton: Princeton University Press.

———. 1990. Autobiographical traditions black and white. In *Located lives: Place and idea in southern autobiography,* edited by J. Bill Berry, 66–77. Athens: University of Georgia Press.

Parati, Graziella. 1996. *Public history, private stories: Italian women's autobiography.* Minneapolis: University of Minnesota Press.

Pickering-Iazzi, Robin. ed. and translator. 1993. *Unspeakable women: Selected short stories written by Italian women during fascism.* New York: The Feminist Press.

———. 1994. The politics of gender and genre in Italian women's autobiography of the interwar years. *Italica* 71, no. 2: 176–97.

Schiminovich, Flora. 1991. Two modes of writing the female self. In Morgan and Hall, 103–16.

Sturrock, John. 1993. Theory versus autobiography. In *The culture of autobiography: Construction of self-representation*, edited by Robert Folkenflik, 21–37. Stanford: Stanford University Press.

Sumeli-Weinberg, Grazia. 1993. *Invito alla lettura di Dacia Maraini*. Pretoria: University of South Africa Press.

Vigani, Virginia. 1990. Tutta una vita da ribelle. In *Anno* 26 July.

White, Hayden. 1984. The question of narrative in contemporary historical theory. In *History and Theory* 23: 1–33.

Revising the Past: Feminist Historians/ Historical Fictions

Maria Ornella Marotti

Part of the evolution of women's historical novels in italy runs parallel to historical research based upon feminist premises. This research shares aims and themes with historical fiction. Literature tells the stories of the invisible, the stories that traditional historiography does not include and that feminist historiography strives to include. Fiction can inscribe the traces of those whose everyday rituals are erased by traditional historiography and that, although encompassed by cultural history, are without any individual specificity. More importantly, through the stratification of its codes, fiction addresses one of the dilemmas at the core of the word "history" itself, as indicated by Hayden White (1987, 55). Historical fiction draws attention to the ambiguous nature of the term "history," which designates both the events and their narration, and it does so by addressing the separation between historical and nonhistorical groups. If, indeed, this separation is based either on the existence of written records or on their lack thereof, historical fiction fills the gap between the two categories by constructing the missing links.

In the present paper I examine aspects of works by Italian feminist historians, working within and outside the *società italiana delle storiche*, Association of Italian Women Historians. These aspects are relevant for a better understanding of the evolution of women's historical fiction.[1] While the aims and methods of these feminist historians fall within the general trends of the new historicism, one of their main and specific concerns is the construction of women's history and the related need to delimit their field of inquiry and establish new methods of research.

One must acknowledge at this point that some of "the theoretical reference points which we still have are those drawn up by male historians," as Annarita Buttafuoco argues (1993b, 170). From an overview of the corpus of research done by Italian feminist historians, a connection with Carlo Ginzburg's work is certainly apparent, in particular in their search for the submerged voices of the marginalized multitudes who were erased by historical narration. Ginzburg's use of offical records for the purpose of reconstructing the lost voices and lives of the peasants, rather than the forms of the persecution that obliterated them, has been particularly influential in the handling of archival sources by female historians. For example, Ginzburg's influence can be traced in Margherita Pelaja's *Matrimonio e sessualità a Roma nell'ottocento* (1994) [Marriage and sexuality in Rome during the nineteenth century], in Angela Groppi's *I conservatori della virtú. Donne recluse nella Roma dei Papi* (1994) [The keepers of virtue: Recluse women in the Rome of the popes], and the all-encompassing cultural history *Le italiane dall'unità a oggi* (1992) [Italian women from the unification to the present] by Michela de Giorgio.

Despite this debt to male social historicism, the female historian's own work acquires nonetheless its specificity in being predicated on the historian's own gender perspective and her feminist political affiliation. It is from this composite and present standpoint that the historian takes either side of a twofold path: she can focus on women's status either as victims or as rebels. In other words, she can either consider the "wiping out of women due to oppression" or "perceive in the female historical experience pockets of resistance and of refusal of imposed roles," as Buttafuoco puts it (1993b, 176). In this work to reconstruct lost voices, the female historian operates through a memory as selective as male historiographers' amnesia.

As feminist historian Anna Rossi Doria (1993) argues, a distinction is necessary from the outset between two different historiographical methods: one is based on the codification of women's history, while the other is based on women' s memory. The former aims at recording the history in a systematic mode and, often, from a nonfeminist perspective both in the method of research and in the form of the narration, while the latter re-creates the past, through a clearly political orientation and a subjective narration. Italian women's historical texts, including either fictional or nonfictional forms of historical narration, exemplify both historicist methods.

It is the approach to women's history, based on subjective memory, that prevails in the documents recording the initial phases of the recent feminist movement.[2] The feminist movement of the 1970s represents the first phase of openly feminist historiography. However, the reconstruction of the movement of those years, done by its protagonists, is tainted by the tendency to rely solely on memory with a strong ideological bent, as both Buttafuoco (1993a, 23–24) and Rossi Doria (1993, 156) argue. In order to celebrate the novelty of the movement, the historiographers of the movement focused on the present and immediate past, forgetting to search for roots and sources in the more remote past. Their purpose was to reconstruct a memory that is at the same time an instrument of self-recognition and a means of empowerment for women, as Rossi Doria puts it (1993, 156–58). This kind of ideological history, instead of rediscovering women of the past in their specificity and with their differences from contemporary women, sees them as mirrors of present-day female reality. Buttafuoco points out that the post–World War II women's movement performs a similar erasure of female ancestors from the pre-Fascist period (1993a, 23–27).

For the purpose of establishing, at the same time, a history and a tradition of women, Rossi Doria sees the need for a fusion of subjective, that is memory-based, historicism and scientific methods of historiography. In other words, she fosters a historical method that is based on both the historian's empathy with her subject and historical research. One needs to construct a tradition for women, she argues, so that women can first reappropriate their forgotten illustrious female ancestors and then reclaim those who disappeared without leaving a trace (1993, 159). This work of recovery is aimed at reclaiming a heredity from the women of the past. At this point in her essay, Rossi Doria discusses the paradoxical reality of the maternal heritage on which the female tradition is based. It is as hard for the mother to bequeath a heredity that she is not sure she owns as it is for the daughter to accept such a heredity from her mother without perceiving it as something threatening to her own autonomy (1993, 160). Through the fusion of subjective and scientific historicism, however, it is possible to create a tradition in which the women of the past, by providing both protection and autonomy, play a role that our real mothers cannot play. In order for this to happen, Rossi Doria concludes, the female historian needs to reclaim the lost heritage from our foremothers and write the never-written will through which such a heredity was handed down (1993, 161).

I have taken the time to summarize Rossi Doria's argument because many facets of the subjective historicism that she fosters are already present in many nonfictional and fictional historical texts by women. Among others, Luisa Muraro's *Guglielma e Maifreda: Storia di un'eresia femminista* (1985) [Guglielma and Maifreda: history of a feminist heresy] is an interesting example of this kind of feminist historicism, combining feminist thought with historical research. Muraro makes apparent the communality between Guglielma's late medieval heresy and feminist difference theory. In claiming her divine feminine nature, equal in nature and different in gender from Jesus, Guglielma and, after her death, her follower Maifreda, refuse to accept women's inferiority while they also claim women's difference. Even though Muraro does not explicitly point out the nexus between the late medieval heresy and her own feminist thought, she clearly finds in Guglielma and Maifreda the ideological foremothers who can ensure both protection and autonomy, and she establishes a tradition of illustrious women, dating back to the Midddle Ages, who believed in women's inherent greatness and were ready to bequeath such a heredity to other women. However, in this case, the heredity never reached its addressees because the message was intercepted by the Inquisition. The work of a historian like Muraro, who has unearthed the documents and then narrated the story of the Guglielmite heresy, has recovered a missing link in the tradition of women.

In establishing a method of research, two very important issues arise, the rereading of historical periods according to a different perspective than the one adopted so far and the problem of the sources on which to base the rereading and rewriting of women's history. According to some of the authors of the collection, *Le donne e la storia* (Pelizzari 1995) [Women and history] one of the major problems that feminist historiography has to deal with is the historical periods that were set up by nineteenth-century historiography. As Anna Maria Rao argues, historical periods were set up in compliance with a historical vision based on the belief in the triumphant affirmation of national states, the bourgeoisie, capitalism, and liberalism (1995, 100). Feminist historicism needs to formulate new historical periods that would no longer be based on the above mentioned perspectives but rather on the evolution of gender relations. It is important, in this respect, to avoid re-writing women's history following the blueprint of general history, that is, simply by replacing male protagonists with female protagonists while leaving historical periods untouched. Women's history needs to challenge the use of sources as well. Most available archival sources are of an institutional, administrative, and juridical nature and were established for the purpose of supporting the existing governmental power. It is necessary for women's historiography on the one hand to use different non-archival sources, while on the other hand to reread archival sources with a different outlook—that is, a nonphilological and, instead, critical approach that takes into account the specific context in which the sources were formulated. This approach, which is used in other areas of nontraditional historiography, emphasizes the interconnection with other related disciplines, such as anthropology, economics, and sociology (89).

A related tendency among feminist historians—one that is followed in particular by both Annarita Buttafuoco (1993) and Gianna Pomata (1993)—is to give preference to women's biographies as sources for research. There is already a rich tradition in that sense both among nineteenth-century emancipationists and women protagonists of the Risorgimento, who left memoirs, diaries and letters. During the second half of the nineteenth century, there was also an equally rich tradition of catalogues of illustrious women destined to the education of young women, as Buttafuoco argues (1993a, 28). Pomata traces the origin of women's history to Plutarch's *Mulierum virtutes*, in which an egalitarian principle prevails (1993, 68). This tradition, which Plutarch inaugurates, later becomes a way for women to vindicate their participation in wider spheres of action than the traditional ones. Because of this biographical tradition, women in the Italian Renaissance could look back to a lineage of formidable women. However, by the end of the nineteenth century, with the rise of positivist historiography, whatever tenuous links women still maintained with this biographical tradition were severed because positivism rejected biographies, regarding them as unreliable sources for historical research, while insisting, instead, on a more general emphasis in writing history. This bias erased both the private sphere and the presence of women and their contributions to economic, social, and religious history, as Pomata argues (1993, 77–79).

If biographies are rediscovered by feminist historicism, whose biographies should be employed in rewriting history, and how? Issues concerning the method and the object of research are interconnected. As important as it is to recognize the origin of women's history in the biographies of illustrious women, it is also important to avoid the iconic, atemporal tendencies of some of these texts. Their greater importance lies in the shift in their emphasis from general to particular history. Instead of recording wars and battles, women's memoirs and biographies record the rituals of everyday life and the personal feelings of women, who are both objects and subjects of these texts (Pomata 1993, 75).

A central concern among feminist historians is the emergence of women's subjectivity through historical research.[3] Moving away from a too intense focus on women's victimization, historians now tend to unearth the voices of women and discover their identification in their gender and their becoming active protagonists of their lives, despite victimization by patriarchy. Just as women's biographies, memoirs, and epistolaries provide sources for the study of the past, oral history is the preferred method for the study of women's history in the present and recent past. It is also a method through which women's subjectivity speaks out in the most uncompromising terms, as Luisa Passerini's and Paola Di Cori's dedicated research in this field have proven. The focus of oral history, just like that of any historiography based on personal writings, is the particular rather than the general. This is not to say that women's history is not also part of general history. However, while women take active part in the various phases of human history, they are eventually excluded from the decision-making process, in other words, from power. More importantly, women are underrepresented in the narration of those events, while male power is not only inscribed in the actual unfolding of the events, but also in their interpretation, as Collin argues (1993, 33, 35).

One of the crucial dilemmas of feminist historicism in Italy is, therefore, how to include in women's history the unrepresented together with the representative. If, on the one hand, there can't be general history of the invisible, on the other hand, accepting the full implication of such a statement means that feminism would become part of the logic of power, as Collin puts it (1993, 38). A space must then be created for those who are condemned to repetition, those who don't have a visible history. Cultural history, with its attention to the rituals of everyday life, proves to be a useful method for reclaiming the life of those who were erased from general history. However, although helpful in dismissing the image of women solely as victims and "subordinate to male domination," the study of "women's culture" is fraught with dangers, Buttafuoco argues. "Women's culture" can foster an improbable image of a perfect and separatist world, totally unpolluted by the intervention of male culture and history—an image that is historically untrue (1993b, 179).

Gianna Pomata's deconstructive work shows the marginality and even absence of women in history books—a disappearance that becomes gradually more and more noticeable with the advent of positivist historiography, on the one hand, and with women's increased access to education, on the other. For women, studying history is a humiliating experience, Pomata argues (1993, 67). It means the contemplation of one's own erasure. The revision of historiography is therefore based on both a revision of the method of research and a revision of the method of narration.

One may wonder at this point: what does the work by contemporary feminist historians in Italy share with the texts by female historical novelists? Feminist historiography has certainly no prescriptive value for the novel. While some of the historical novelists, like Bellonci and Cutrufelli, are historians in their own right, it would be highly questionable for us to trace a direct influence from feminist historians to historical novelists. Yet, as we will see in a moment, similarities between the two fields abound.

In their effort to reread history, women novelists parallel, and sometimes forerun, tendencies that are evinced by various streams of feminist historiography. Challenging conventional historiography as an aspect of that power-knowledge that has construed "woman" and invented a specific space for her, while it has also devalued women's agency, some women's novels point to the presence of women in the making of the historical process. Finally, as feminist historiography challenges the universality of history that excludes women's particularity, women's fiction works in the same direction by creating narratives about women that encompass subjective experiences. Just as feminist historians suggest that one needs to rewrite general history if women's presence is to be inscribed, novelists seek to revisit history through a different perspective.

A recurrent feature of women's historical fiction is also the frequent use of personal forms of narration, either autobiographical, diaristic, or epistolary. While this narrative structure draws from the very origin of women's fiction—that is, personal writing—it also demonstrates that the specificity of women's historical writing is based on the blurring of the boundary between private and public spheres.

If women's historical fiction, just like feminist historicism, follows a somewhat different evolution from its male counterparts, can we claim for this aspect of the genre a different origin as well? Both Manzoni (1850) and Lukács (1965) trace the origin of the historical novel in the epic. Even without discounting the influence of Manzoni's masterpiece and of other nineteenth century texts on the evolution of women's novels, I advance here the idea of women's personal writings as a possible and more likely origin for at least part of women's historical fiction. If, indeed, the evolution of the epic toward the historical novel is the expression of the formation of a national identity, such an evolution cannot account for most of women's historical fiction, in which the themes of national identity, if present at all, are ancillary to other more personal themes. Here again, it is possible to hypothesize a common origin for the writing of women's history and at least a substantial section of women's historical fiction. Moreover, the awareness of women's position displayed by historical women writers is at the base of the construction of a tradition for women in the forms identified by Rossi Doria (1993, 156–58). A large number of fictional and nonfictional historical texts by Italian women do tend toward the construction of a women's tradition. Given this perspective, it is indeed possible to read Italian women's historical novels as a revision of Italian history from a gendered perspective.

The proliferation of studies on literary women during the Italian Renaissance is paralleled by novels with a Renaissance setting that by celebrating illustrious women from the past attest to the origin and persistence of women's greatness.[4] Maria Bellonci's and Anna Banti's historical fictions are the most well-known examples. The authors' respective backgrounds in historical and art historical research create foundations for their fictions. Both novelists work within the biographical tradition that Pomata claims as the origin of women's history.

Bellonci's *Rinascimento privato* (1985) is narrated as Isabella d'Este's journal. The choice of a personal form of narration allows Bellonci to penetrate the individual consciousness and to illustrate the private side of politics. Through Isabella's penetrating insights, the novel develops a gender conscious discourse on power, on what constitutes and creates it, and on what undoes it. Isabella's intimate thoughts show her awareness both of the gender-related aspects of power and of her own limitations due to her gender. In order to acquire power she appropriates forbidden spheres and claims her own male side. In the upbringing of her children she gives herself to the males, neglecting the females. Isabella's awareness as well as her ability in expanding her political domain do not lead, therefore, to a substantial change of the status quo for women, even though they lead to her own political empowerment. Even though she joins the short list of those exceptional individuals who, due to both their outstanding qualities and special circumstances, rise above their gender and their contemporaries, Isabella d'Este personifies Bellonci's skepticism toward the possibility of radical societal change. The novel creates, however, a form of cultural history from a woman's perspective.

If, due to its diary form, narrator and protagonist are fused in Bellonci's novel, in Banti's *Artemisia* (1947) narrative voice and authorial voice are combined in an experimental form, which breaks down the fictional narrative to allow space for the author's discussion of her own writing within the novel. *Artemisia* is thus both Artemisia Gentileschi's fictional biography and the story of the writing of the novel. The character emerges from a previous novel, allegedly lost by Banti during the World War II's bombing of Florence, and establishes a dialogue with the author/narrator. In discussing her writing, Banti consciously deviates from the historical records, and allows, instead, a more intuitive form of knowing to emerge: her response as art historian and emancipated woman to another talented and independent woman. Artemisia's gender-based marginalization is Banti's as well. The self-referential and dialogic structure of *Artemisia* points toward a new form of historical fiction that fuses scientific documentation and the author's empathy with her subject.[5] The prioritizing of the process of writing over the research shapes the narrative. The narrator's soliloquies, which are addressed to her character, and the focus on the character's consciousness highlight both Banti's own dilemma and Gentileschi's isolation as an exceptional and "virile woman" in a society where the construction of femininity follows rigid codes. The historical past mirrors the present and offers a spiritual ancestor for the writer.

Both Bellonci and Banti deal with illustrious women, and therefore work within a limited sphere of women's historicism, that is, the history of the representative. A much more extensive group of contemporary novelists construct the stories of the underrepresented. One must note, however, that, if themes and ideological tendencies differ, a common narrative structure prevails in both groups of historical writers, that is, the use of a confessional and personal mode of narration—one of the original forms of women's history.

The creation of a tradition of women serves to repair the injustice perpetrated against those who disappeared without a tangible trace. Both through cultural studies and through fiction, women historicists rewrite the stories that were never written and give voice to the disinherited. In particular, Maria Corti's *L'ora di tutti* (1962) [*Otranto*, (1993)] , Elsa Morante's *La Storia* [History: A Novel (1984)], Toni Maraini's *La murata* [The Immured Nun (1991)], Dacia Maraini's *La lunga vita di Marianna Ucria* [The Silent Duchess (1990)], Maria Rosa Cutrufelli's *La briganta* [The Woman Bandit (1990)], work within this thematic framework. Lastly, some texts at the border between biography and autobiography, such as for example, Fausta Cialente's *Le quattro ragazze Wieselberger* (1976) [The Four Wieselberger Girls], and Clara Sereni's *Il gioco dei regni* (1993) [The Game of the Kingdoms] reclaim the foremothers by mapping a female genealogy against a well-defined historical setting that interacts as a motif in the biographer's act of reappropriating her female ancestry.[6]

In the historical novel the confessional mode has the function of emphasizing the particular over the general, thus letting female subjectivity emerge. Toni Maraini's *La murata* (1991) and Maria Rosa Cutrufelli's *La briganta* (1990) are centered around fictional characters set in a historical setting. The protagonists of both novels are also narrators of their stories, which they recount in a confessional mode. However, while Toni Maraini's protagonist is a pure observer of the mores of her time, Cutrufelli's character is an active participant. "La murata" is a French immured nun during the Middle Ages. Her decision to be immured at the border of the cemetery is meant as a protest against the violence and inequality of society. In becoming a silent observer, she chooses "to place the inside outside and the outside inside" [mettere il dentro fuori e il fuori dentro (21)] , thus reversing in her inner self the usual order of things. The narration reflects both the separation of the inside from the outside and their interconnection: while the outside is narrated in the third person, through constantly shifting centers of consciousness, the inside consists of the protagonist's interior monologues. The violent convulsions of the outside contrast with the tragic although calm determination of the inside. While the inside observes and interprets the motives of the world outside, the outside world is unable to decipher the real motives of the immured novice living inside her cell. Not only does the spatial symbolism of the text epitomize women's isolation from history, but it also alludes to the willing refusal by many women to be part of a violent power. *La murata* thus affirms, just as some streams of feminist historicism do, that women in an apparently passive role throughout history have often achieved active goals, as Accati argues (1990, 98).

Revising Italian history calls for the reformulation of categories and periods that have formed the basis of earlier canonical writing. Besides the Renaissance, another crucial turning point in Italian history is the Risorgimento. Maria Rosa Cutrufelli's *La briganta* (1990) revisits the aftermath of the wars that liberated Italy from foreign invasions. The Piedmontese government, which led the country in the liberation process, afterward imposed a heavy taxation system on the south, thus causing an uprising in which peasants and fallen aristocrats united. *La briganta* revisits the Risorgimento by pointing to the gender bias of its narration. Rather than focusing on the victorious battles for the liberation of the country, the novel deals with its less than glorious aftermath—the Southern uprising known as *brigantaggio*. The Sicilian writer develops the theme of female subjectivity resulting from an active participation that, nonetheless, never leads to decision-making power. Margherita, condemned to a life sentence for her participation in *brigantaggio* in the newly unified Italy of 1861, writes her memoirs, at the request of a scientist—a follower of Lombroso—who is studying the criminal mind and who considers her "History's extravagance" [una stravaganza della Storia (7)]. Because her narration is a response to the scientist's male gaze, that tries to frame her, it bears deep gender implications: she is trying to place herself outside male power-knowledge—outside positivist science. She understands the full liberating implications of her autobiographical act, which

allows her to address her presumably male audience as a peer.
In order to write, she feels that she needs her courage, which,
according to the societal and patriarchal construction of femaleness, places her outside her gender. "Writing one's own
memoirs is for a woman, perhaps, even a more daring thing
than being a bandit in the mountains," [scrivere le proprie
memorie è per una donna cosa ardimentosa, forse ancor piu'
che l'andar briganteggiando per i monti (8)] she writes; she is
aware that claiming one's own life marks the entrance into
history—not necessarily the traditional history of history
books, but the construction of women's history. The protagonist of *La briganta* is a Southern aristocrat who reminds one
of contemporary terrorist women, who like Margherita, desired "to share the destiny of so many children of poverty"[7]
[condividere la sorte di tanti figli della miseria (9)]. In addition, her female subjectivity unfolds through solidarity with
other women—an experience that again reminds us of the experience of women involved in the Resistance as recorded by
oral historians (for instance, Passerini 1991, 23–27). Her final
act of self-preservation—baring her breasts in front of the ca-
zabiniere who is going to shoot her—is the recognition of her
own femaleness, despite her attempt to appropriate male
spheres of action. Her ambivalent relationship with male attire—alternating feelings of uneasiness and liberation—signifies her conflictual attitude toward both gender and history.
Playing either male or female roles, Margherita is excluded
from the decision-making process during the southern rural
uprising as much as she is eventually excluded from the historical narration of the events. Only women's history and fiction reclaim her traces and in so doing inscribe a noncanonical
rereading of an important period of Italian history.

In fostering the fusion of memory and history through a
method combining subjective and scientific historiography,
Rossi Doria refers to a new method of historical narration
rather than to the historical events. Through a deviation from
male standards, women's historical fiction provides innovative
models for a feminine historical narration. In *L'ora di tutti*
(1962), Maria Corti entrusts the narration of the 1480 siege
and sack of Otranto by the Turks to five characters.[8] All of
these characters/narrators, with the exception of one, are protagonists of the siege and sack who narrate the events from
their graves. Three of these are Otrantini belonging to the
working class—two fishermen and a fisherman's widow—

while one is a minor historical figure, the city's governor, Francesco Zurlo, a Neapolitan aristocrat and intellectual anointed by the Aragonese king. The narrators' individual stories are intertwined with their recording of the exceptional events that alter their lives and give them the opportunity to prove their personal worth while meeting their death with dignity and even heroism. Their language and style of narration betray class and gender differences as well as different perspectives on history. The siege brings a new awareness to the fishermen who realize their positions as subjects of history: they are the unwilling victims of the power games between the dominant nations occupying Italy and the Ottoman empire. They fight valiantly to defend their community and their beliefs, and those who survive the siege are eventually executed by the Turks because, on the one hand, they are not willing to give up their beliefs and, on the other hand, they do not have the financial ability to pay for their own lives. The final character/narrator, Aloise de Marco, comes to Otranto with the Spanish army, which eventually liberates the city, one year after its conquest by the Turks. His testimonial is particularly revealing becase it foreshadows the author's own perspective on history as a fraudulent narration by the powerful—the military and the church in this case.

During the celebration of the city's liberation, the newly appointed bishop gives an account of the maryrdom of the Otrantini that does not correspond to the one given in the previous sections by the protagonists of the events. Not only does the bishop's narration alter the events themselves, but it also diminishes the actual import of the Otrantinis' heroic struggle and human valor by mystifying their actions and turning them into miraculous occurrences. By giving voice to the actual protagonists of the siege, Corti suggests a new historical method of narration that values the individual lives of people who are either erased by the official recording of history or are misrepresented and placed in a context that has no relation to their actual experiences. Fiction in Corti's narrative becomes a way to retrieve the unrepresented by exposing the fallacy of power and its modes of narration. It is also a way of deconstructing official archival sources, in a way similar to the one suggested by Anna Maria Rao (1995), while rereading and replacing them with more individual forms of narration that suggest the existence of a different and deeper historical truth.

The only woman narrator of the group is particularly successful in demonstrating the exclusion of women as subjects
from the historical process as well as in claiming such subjectivity through the expression of female desire. Not only are
Otrantini women excluded from the narration of their struggle
for the preservation of their community, but they are further
marginalized by gender construction that demands their exclusion from the battle area, just as it demanded their imprisonment within the domestic enclosures during peacetime. The
only female narrator breaks down her assigned roles by claiming the legitimacy of her desire, which violates class and gender barriers.

The five narratives also highlight another central issue.
Otranto is about the "other." The Turks play this role unequivo-
cally during the Italian Renaissance because of their ethnic
and cultural difference. However, a number of other "others"
emerge in the narration of the siege and sack of the town: in
particular, the fishermen and peasants marginalized by class
and the women construed by gender. In one of the final narrations, relating the events after the collapse of Otranto, the in-
vading Turkish soldiers are finally recognized by the narrating
fisherman, Nachira, as similar to them, the working-class
Otrantini. Ethnic and cultural differences appear, therefore, as
surmountable while class still remains a barrier that prevents
salvation for the impoverished fishermen who eventually sacrifice their lives to hold onto their beliefs, whereas upper-class
inhabitants of Otranto are allowed to buy back their freedom.
The ultimate "other" is, however, woman: other for the Turks
as she is for the Otrantini, other for the fishermen as she is for
the aristocrats—a nonexistent object, a cultural construction.
To this purpose, the female narrator's section is particularly
significant because the character/narrator challenges the construction of woman at all social and cultural levels, both in
its Neoplatonic formulation by her aristocratic admirer, don
Felice, and in its less refined connotations.

World War II, the Resistance, and the antifascist movement
are some of the preferred topics of Italian historical novels. A
number of women's texts propose a gendered rereading of that
historical period. Elsa Morante's tragic anti-epic, *La storia*
(1974) deals with history in ways that anticipate some of the
more recent formulations of feminist historians. Morante combines an objective method of narration with a subjective one.
For Morante the creation of the missing written record of the

nonhistorical groups, of the disinherited, of the ones without a voice, calls for the creation of a structure where the narration of history, as the stories of the common people, is juxtaposed to the narration of history as a scientific record of events. While the latter narration consists of impersonally recounted historical documentation, the former is told with a narrative voice that is, at the same time, inside and outside the events, limited and omniscient. Through the breaking up of the diegetical mode—omniscient and external narration—not only does Morante signify the rupture between history and story, but also between prevalent historiography and the only possible historiography for the nonhistorical groups. Here again fiction breaks the silence of official history and expands the narration by including a myriad of voices that are usually excluded from historical narrative: those of children, animals, prophecy, dream, and madness. More importantly, Morante deconstructs historical fiction itself by problematizing the status of the narrator who is, in turn, marginal and central to her own narration. The inconsistencies in the narrator's voice, at times limited in her knowledge of aspects of the story and as participant as if she were a character personally involved in the story, and at times omniscient and external to the events, emphasize the rupture in Morante's historical fiction, which both parallels and relates to the opening up of the narration to voices and languages that are external to the historical process.

While most critics consider Morante's work nonfeminist, in a recent article (1993), Lucia Re traces aspects of La storia to feminist thought. Re bases her illuminating observations on philosopher, Aldo Gargani's definition of the "feminine voice" as the subtext of androcentric history (361), and on Julia Kristeva's concept of the semiotic chora "linked to the pre-Oedipal mother figure, whose discourse is opposed to the discourse of the Father, and to its symbolic order based on difference and the Law" (363–64).[9] Morante's deconstruction of official history—both its narration and the events—as a game of power, her objection to power as exerted by the patriarchy, and her embracing of maternal love as the only antidote to the male violence of history implicitly link her work to feminist thought in its wider meaning. While it is undeniable that Morante did not identify with the feminist movement, I think that I can safely suggest that, although it may not have been Morante's intention to contribute to the construction of a tradition of women, La storia marks a turning point in women's historical novels because it provides a mode of historical narration that is later explored and expanded by more contemporary writers.

Traces of both Morante's experimental historical narration, and Banti's self referential and dialogic mode, can be found in Clara Sereni's *Il gioco dei regni* (1993). Like *La storia*, Sereni's text combines history and story, as well as different modes of historical narration. Yet Sereni's text moves one step forward in the construction of a new historical feminine text. History, memory, documentation (excerpts from diaries, memoirs and letters), and fiction are not simply juxtaposed but rather fused in her narration. Moreover, the choice of official excerpts includes for the most part documents that are at the same time public and private—as for example, private letters found in public archives. Although most of the text is what one could classify with some approximation as a very original form of biography, the epilogue clarifies that indeed the motivation for the entire project is autobiographical. As in Banti's *Artemisia*, the writer's empathy with her subject is inscribed in the text. Not only is a fusion of subjective voice and historical research achieved in this kind of historical narration, but the intention to create a tradition of women is made explicit by the narrative structure itself, which is clearly focused on the foremothers and their heritage. However, both Alfonsa and Xenia, Sereni's grandmothers, are unable to bequeath their heritage. Sereni's text becomes then that lost legacy, and the act of reappropriation of the long-lost lineage.

In a truly experimental mode, *Il gioco dei regni* crosses over the boundaries of genre, combining biography with autobiography, and historical narrative with fiction. By including a variety of documents, personal perspectives, and narrative focuses, she creates a polyphony of voices—a dialogic text as theorized by Bakhtin. Moreover, in opening up the text, Sereni increases the stratification of its codes, thus expanding its theoretical potential. Sereni challenges, indeed, one of the tenets of one of the social and political movements that she recounts, that is, the neat separation between private and public as one of the iron rules of conduct for the most devoted Communist party members. In telling from inside the history of the Italian Communist party, as reflected in her parents' lives, she uses personal documents—letters, notes, diary entries, poems— thus transgressing both a long standing practice of Communist historicism and her father's wish. Through this act of transgression she constructs both a private history of her public family and a form of female historicism. To this purpose, one must note that the kind of genealogy that Clara Sereni is constructing in her text is not solely a line of female ancestry, and therefore, not only a female family line. Her form of historicism goes even deeper in the direction of creating a women's literary historicism by reclaiming her father's feminine side, the publicly unacknowledged side of his personality, and thus giving him back his lost voice, which was buried in his love notes, poems, and Judaic religious background. This is a particularly poignant act of recovery, because as Sereni indicates, during the last years of his life, Emilio Sereni withdrew in silence. Once a very eloquent speaker, he gave up communicating when faced with the tremendous changes in world Communism. Through fiction, she gives life to her ancestors by placing them in their family setting, much dominated by matriarchal rule; through the insertion of private documents she places them back in history, not in the place that they traditionally occupied in it, but in a different space created for them by her own female historicism.

In restoring a private voice to her parents, she reclaims their ancestry, as well as her own. Submerged, repressed, and misplaced by Marxist ideology, Sereni's Judaism surfaces both in the author's reclaiming of it for herself and in her inscribing it in the text through the narration in fictional form of her parents' childhood and youth. Here again, in claiming her religious ancestry, Sereni gives voice to a marginalized group in Italian culture: the Jewish community.

In reclaiming her foremothers, Sereni constructs a tradition of illustrious women. The formidable career of her maternal grandmother, Xenia Panphilova Silberberg, as anarchist terrorist, political agitator, and, finally, as one of the founders of the state of Israel certainly places her among women of the past who can inspire other women, giving them protection and autonomy on a symbolic level. A similar role is played by the Jewish paternal grandmother, a stoic matriarch, who survives the deaths of her sons and persecution. However, if placing the grandmothers in the place they deserve in women's history is a rather uncontroversial act, dealing with her own mother—also named Xenia—is for Sereni quite a different matter. Although, because of her relentless political activity, her self-sacrifice, and her courage, the younger Xenia herself deserves a place in the Parnassus of illustrious women, her actual position is much more problematic. Her ambivalent personality is epitomized by her three names Xenia, Marina, Loletta: Xenia, her given name, places her in the shadow of a mother who, although inspiring for other women, allows her very little autonomy; Marina, the battle name, the pseudonym that she uses in her political writings, marks her entrance into the Parnassus of communist women and mummifies her in a rigid although heroic role; Loletta, the playful name that her husband calls her by, signifies her most private and loving self. Sereni's mother personifies in her controversial relationship with her own mother the dilemma at the core of the construction of a women's tradition. Unwilling to accept the heredity that her own mother intends to bequeath her, she is unable to pass it on to her own daughters. Moreover, her own premature death interrupts her own lineage. For the biographer the writing of her text becomes then an act of recovery that includes both the grandmothers and her own mother. In order to recreate the interrupted line and restore the intercepted message, Clara Sereni needs to recreate her own lost mother in all the complexity of her three distinct identities. More importantly, in exposing the dilemma in the controversial relationship between her mother and her grandmother, Sereni alludes to her own dilemma as autobiographer—one who is caught in the juggling act of claiming from her own mother a heredity that she cannot accept.

Nonhistorical groups enter history when the written record of their past is produced, as Hayden White puts it (1987, 56). Through historical narration, both in fictional and non-fictional forms, Italian women have joined history. However, their entrance is problematic. Not only is the reappropriation of women's submerged past a long and laborious process still underway, but also the forms in which such a reappropriation is carried out through literature are marked by deep ambivalence. Giving voice to the submerged and to those who haven't spoken, women writers tend to reverse the law of the father and the symbolic order that has commanded their exclusion in the first place. In creating new forms of historical narration, they question patriarchal order, while they also create a space marked by female difference and subjectivity.

In their effort to fill the interstices of history—the unrecorded and the invisible—women historical novelists parallel the efforts of the feminist historian. Yet as similar as the work of the historian and that of the novelist may appear, they occupy in reality adjacent, sometimes overlapping, but ultimately different fields. While the historian transforms memory into history, the novelist works toward the construction of a new fictional and symbolic feminine world.[10] Both, however, create a new female narration of history.

Notes

Parts of the present article already appeared in two articles published and forthcoming in *Italian Culture* 13 and 14, respectively entitled, "Literary History and Women's Tradition" and "Feminist Historians/Historical Fiction."

1. The *Società Italiana delle storiche* was created in 1989 for the purpose of coordinating the works of Italian women historians. My study is based in particular on the following collections of essays produced by the society: *Discutendo di storia: Soggettività, ricerca, biografia* (1990) and *Generazioni: Trasmissione della storia e tradizione delle donne* (1993). Other important sources of information for my study are *Donne tra memoria e storia* (Capobianco 1993), which collects papers from a 1990 meeting organized by the University of Naples and other Southern Italian historical associations, and *Le donne e la storia* (Pellizzari 1995), which collects the proceedings of a symposium on women's historiography held at the University of Salerno in 1993. In her article "Sulla storia delle donne in Italia," Andreina De Clementi (1995) points out that the "marriage" between feminism and historical research was originated at a multidisciplinary conference that took place in Modena in 1982, the proceedings of which were published in 1987. She also argues that, due to the imposing presence of the Communist Party and in reaction to it, feminist historiography in Italy had already broken loose from Marxism in the early eighties. Up to a few years ago, reviews such as *DWF.Donna/Woman/Femme* and the now defunct *Memoria* provided the major contributions and sources for feminist historicism (Pellizzari 1995, 17–21).

2. In this respect, some of the collectively compiled historical records by the women of *la libreria delle donne*—the women's bookstore—in Milan are particularly relevant. In some of these documents the need to construct a feminist identity and to announce the absolute novelty of the political and societal transformation underway prevail over the need to reevaluate women's past. I am referring in particular to *Non credere di avere dei diritti* (1987) by the Libreria delle donne in Milan—a publishing/editing feminist group.

3. The issue of women's subjectivity in historical research is developed in particular in *Discutendo di Storia* (Società Italiana delle Storiche 1990).

4. For a good bibliography on works on Renaissance women available in Italian see *Leggere Donna* 36 (1992): 4–5. Among works that have appeared in the United States, a particularly noteworthy book is *Refiguring Woman: Perspectives on Gender and the Italian Renaissance* (Migiel and Schiesari 1991).

5. JoAnn Cannon comments: "To suggest that the facts of Artemisia's history are on a par with the Punic War is to reconceive our view of what is historically relevant. Banti's exercise in historical-literary symbiosis is

part of a larger enterprise—the reconceptualization of Western history from the perspective of marginalized subjects" (1994, 326).

6. In *From Margins to Mainstream* (1993, 143–50), Carol Lazzaro-Weis devotes a chapter to women's historical novels in which she also takes into account the autobiographical impulse that motivates some of these fictions. I would like to suggest here that some autobiographical texts are at the borderline of historical narration and even historical fiction and should, therefore, be taken into consideration when dealing with historical narratives.

7. For a possible comparison of Margherita and contemporary Italian terrorist women see in particular, Silvana Mazzocchi's *Nell'anno della tigre. Storia di Adriana Faranda* (1994) ["During the Tiger Year: The Adriana Faranda Story"].

8. Lazzaro-Weis points out similarities between Carlo Ginzburg's historiographical method focused "on expressing the experience of people lost by history's quantifying process" (1993, 134) and Maria Corti's *L'ora di tutti*. She also explores similarities between "weak thought," as theorized by Gianni Vattimo, and feminist redefinitions of experience (138).

9. Morante's displeasure with feminism is a well-known fact, well-documented by Sandra Petrignani (1984, 119). However, her interpretation of the historical process, her refusal of strictures and categories, and her rereading of conventional values are close to some of De Lauretis's definitions of feminism in *Feminist Studies/Critical Studies* (1986, 14–15).

10. From a philosophical perspective, the feminist philosophers Luisa Muraro and Adriana Cavarero also work in a similar direction when they propose respectively the creation of a new symbolic order based on the maternal and the rethinking and reinterpretation of the mythical categories, which are the foundation of Western world philosophy. Nonetheless, notable differences exist between the feminist revisions embraced by Italian feminist philosophers and those supported by Italian feminist new historians.

References

Accati, Luisa. 1990. La sposa in prestito: Soggetto collettivo, soggetto individuale e conflitto politico (1566–1759), 77–102 Società Italiana delle Storiche.

Banti, Anna. [1947], 1994. *Artemisia*. Milan: Bompiani.

Bellonci, Maria. 1985. *Rinascimento privato*. Milan: Arnoldo Mondadori Editore.

Bono, Paola, ed. 1993. *Questioni di teoria femminista*. Milan: La Tartaruga.

Bono, Paola, and Sandra Kemp, eds. 1993. *The lonely mirror*. London: Routledge.

Buttafuoco, Annarita. 1993a. La politicitá della storia delle donne, 19–30 In Capobianco.

————. 1993b. On "mothers" and "sisters." Fragments on women/feminism/ historiography. In Bono and Kemp.

Cannon, JoAnn. 1994. *Artemisia* and the life story of the exceptional woman. *Forum Italicum* 28, no. 2, (fall): 322–41.

Capobianco, Laura, ed. 1993. *Donne tra memoria e storia*. Naples: Liguori Editore.

Cavarero, Adriana. 1995. *In spite of Plato: a feminist rewriting of ancient philosophy*. Foreword by Rosi Braidotti. Translated by Serena Anderlini-D'Onofrio and Aine O'Healy. New York: Routledge.

Cialente, Fausta. 1976. *Le quattro ragazze Wieselberger*. Milan: Mondadori.

Collin, Françoise. 1993. Storia e memoria: La marca e la traccia. In Capobianco.

Corti, Maria. [1962], 1977. *L'ora di tutti*. Milan: Feltrinelli.

————. 1993. *Otranto*. Translated by Jessie Bright. New York: Italica Press.

Cutrufelli, Maria Rosa. 1990. *La briganta*. Palermo: La Luna.

De Clementi, Andreina. 1995. Sulla storia delle donne in Italia. 17–26 In Pelizzari.

De Giorgio, Michela. 1992. *Le italiane dall'unità ad oggi*. Bari: Editori Laterza.

De Lauretis, Teresa. 1986. *Feminist Studies/Critical Studies*. Bloomington: Indiana University Press.

Di Cori, Paola. 1987. Dalla storia delle donne a una storia di genere *Rivista di storia contemporanea*, 4.

Ginzburg, Carlo. [1966] 1992. *The night battles: witchcraft and agrarian cults in the sixteenth and seventeenth centuries*. Translated by John and Anne C. Tedeschi. Baltimore: Johns Hopkins UP.

————. 1989. *Clues, myths, and the historical method*. Translated by John and Anne C. Tedeschi. Baltimore: Johns Hopkins UP.

Groppi, Angela. 1994. *I conservatori della virtù: Donne recluse nella Roma dei Papi*. Bari: Editori Laterza.

Lazzaro-Weis, Carol. 1993. *From margins to mainstream: Feminism and fictional modes in Italian women's writing, 1968–1990*. Philadelphia: University of Pennsylvania Press. First published in *Leggere Donna* 36 (1992).

Libreria delle donne di Milano. 1987. *Non credere di avere dei diritti*. Turin: Rosenberg & Sellier.

Lukacs, Gyorgy. 1965. *Il romanzo storico*, with an Introduction by Cesare Cases, and translated by Eraldo Arnaud. Turin: Einaudi.

Manzoni, Alessandro. [1850] 1984. *On the historical novel*, with an Introduction and translation by Sandra Bermann. Lincoln: University of Nebraska Press.

Maraini, Dacia. 1990. *La lunga vita di Marianna Ucria*. Milan: Rizzoli.

Maraini, Toni. [1976] 1991. *La murata*. Palermo: La Luna.

Marotti, Maria Ornella. 1996. Feminist historians/historical fictions. In *Italian Culture*: 14: 147–160.

————. 1994. Historicism and women's literature. Presentation at the 1994 AAIS meeting in Madison, Wisconsin.

————. 1995. Literary historicism and women's tradition. In *Italian Culture* 13: 261–72.

Mazzocchi, Silvana. 1994. *Nell'anno della tigre: Storia di Adriana Faranda*. Milan: Baldini & Castoldi.

Migiel, Marilyn, and Juliana Schiesari, eds. 1991. *Refiguring Woman: Perspectives on Gender the Italian Renaissance*. Ithaca: Cornell University Press.

Morante, Elsa. 1974. *La storia*. Turin: Einaudi.

————. 1984. *History: a novel*. Translated by William Weaver. New York: Random House.

Morazzoni, Marta. 1986. *La ragazza col turbante*. Milan: Longanesi.

————. 1988. *Girl in a turban*. Translated by Patrick Creagh. New York: Alfred Knopf.

Muraro, Luisa. 1991. *L'ordine simbolico della madre*. Roma: Editori Riuniti.

————. 1985. *Guglielma e Maifreda: Storia di un'eresia femminista*. Milan: La Tartaruga.

Passerini, Luisa. 1991. *Storie di donne e femministe*. Turin: Rosenberg & Sellier.

Pelaja, Margherita. 1994. *Matrimonio e sessualità a Roma nell'ottocento*. Bari: Editori Laterza.

Pelizzari, Maria Rosaria, ed. 1995. *Le donne e la storia: Problemi di metodo e confronti storiografici*. Naples: Edizioni Scientifiche Italiane.

Petrignani, Sandra. 1984. *Le signore della scrittura*. Milan: La Tartaruga.

Pomata, Gianna. 1993. Storia particolare e storia universale. In Capobianco.

————. 1993. Premiss: a figure of power and an invitation to history: Epilogue: to room nineteen. 155–169 Bono and Kemp.

Rao, Anna Maria. 1995. Medioevo al femminile? Le sfide mancate della storia delle donne. 87–106. In Pelizzari.

Re, Lucia. 1993. Utopian longing and constraints of racial and sexual difference in Elsa Morante's *La storia*. In *Italica* 70: 361–75.

Rossi Doria, Anna. 1993. Memoria, storia e tradizione delle donne. In Bono.

Sereni, Clara. 1993. *Il gioco dei regni*. Firenze: Giunti.

Società Italiana delle Storiche, ed. 1993. *Generazioni: Trasmissione della storia e tradizione delle donne*. Turin: Rosenberg & Sellier.

————. 1990. *Discutendo di storia: Soggettività, ricerca, biografia*. Turin: Rosenberg & Sellier.

White, Hayden. 1987. *The content of the form: Narrative discourse and historical representation*. Baltimore: Johns Hopkins University Press.

Unsigned History: Silent, Micro-"Technologies of Gender" in the Narratives of the Quotidian

Giovanna Miceli Jeffries

For me history was not a large stage filled with commemo-
ration, bands, cheers, ribbons, medals, the sound of fine
glass clinking and raised high in the air; in other words,
the sound of victory. For me history was not only the past;
it was also the present. I did not mind my defeat, I only
minded that it had to last so long.

(Kincaid 1996, 138–39)

We have to tell stories to explain ourselves although we can
never, in however many tellings, get it right.

(Orr 1986, 13)

THE TWO QUOTES ABOVE INDICATE THE DIRECTIONS INSPIRING AND
guiding this study. The first understands "history" as a fluid
and flexible category encompassing the official and collective
narrative of past and contemporary events as well as individual stories embedded in the official and collective memory.
With this definition comes the notion that in women's narratives, woven around biographical and collective historical
memory, the representation of the "quotidian," with its indisputable economic, social, and gender ramifications and operations, constitutes the basis of any history that might still aspire
to be called inclusionary.

This concept of history assumes a nonexclusionary style and
practice of reading, remembering, telling, and writing about
life experiences; it considers current and past official history
deficient and incomplete and seeks to reclaim all the missing
parts. More than a replacement, it is a critical correction and
completion of history as it has been passed on. As we read
women narratives embedded in historical passages, whether
biographical or fictionalized, we become aware that a dimension of life, of what makes history, is represented, and this

71

dimension is material life, the "bricks and mortar" of any history. Women's practices and productions of the everyday life—biological reproduction, care taking, making of devices, tactics, and decisions—are all factors taken for granted. All are unrecognized pillars as well as gears moving history. Such a vision and understanding of history implies that one remains critically involved in and with official history and operates within it as in a breeding process that will eventually shed official history of its "deficient" and gender-biased interpretations and representations.

Inclusionary, corrective history originating in and advanced by practitioners of New Historicism is very useful to feminist writing and criticism since traditional diachronic historicism can only chronicle the historical absence of women. The synchronic and organicistic approach of New Historicism allows for a gathering of stories, of genres (biographies, autobiographies), and of fields of knowledge (anthropology, sociology) all involved in the interpretation of texts by women and about women's lives. History and literature reestablish their dynamic, close relationship, which was severed by what Linda Orr calls the "epistemological break" of positivistic philosophy, itself interested in giving history a more scientific stand and a closer association with social sciences (1986, p. 12). In her article "The Revenge of Literature," Orr argues about how intrinsically compromised history and literature are (have been since classical times), feeding from each other because both are narratives displaying linguistic and rhetorical processes and creations: "Neither language nor history is self-constituted once and for all. . . . Literature appears a condition for history and history cannot but 'speak' as discourse" (1986 p. 14). In the feminist project of recovering the presence of women and unveiling their cultural constructions and productions, the novel offers, according to Orr, the most consistent critique of dominant, linear history, since "fiction evokes the other history that history refuses to write, preferring its traditional fictions" (p. 19).

In contemporary women's writings one can see a proliferation of books blending history and fiction and offering alternative views of "historical truth." They are hybrid texts, commonly catalogued as historical novels, and they display subgenre affiliations with biographies, autobiographies, diaries, or fictions embedded in what we can call a collective historical context. Writings encompassing mythological figures, traditional biographies, autobiographies, and diaries are generated by women writers while a growing number of women historians are also examining these narratives and proposing new possible ways to read and interpret history.[1] The task facing the woman historian is double: reading history from a feminist and gender perspective as it has been transmitted and styled, and also giving proper collocation and historical legitimacy to writings that do not fit the category of "historical" but are reconstructing and documenting women's presences.

Although the Foucauldian equation of knowledge, power, and deployment of unaccountable technologies of control has provided gender theory with a powerful tool for unmasking multiple constructions meant to disfranchise and discriminate against women in all epochs and cultures, one of its unavoidable facets is its tendency to lose track of the historical presence of an individual woman and of women as a group.[2] In the process of merging postmodernist, deconstructionist, and postdeconstructionist theories, a historical perspective has been at times sidestepped. What do women's experiences tell us about the systems and subsystems women produced and developed? Does a hegemonic, all encompassing discursive system of knowledge and power neutralize all human agency? How did women get by in marked gender-divided environments?

There is a danger of dehistoricizing women when feminist theory succumbs to the temptation to perceive the subject "hollow."[3] It is too risky to dematerialize a subject that is just emerging: we are not yet done with assembling and figuring out the historical presence of women. Neither are we done with understanding the mechanisms—psychological, economical, biological—that generate gender differences and create unequal power systems. Carried to the extreme, such a position could lead to an understanding and representation of women that undermines and possibly erases female agency as well as minimizes the historical importance of "personal and social life—family, sexuality, sociability—the areas in which women have been visible participants" (Scott 1988, 24).

There is a "radical potential" for women's history in the writings of "histories that focus on women's experiences," remarks Scott (1988, 27). In these experiences one can analyze how "the private sphere is a public creation" and how nonactors—women—partook in the making of history by revealing "the meanings and uses of power" (24). Scott recognizes the contradictions inherent in establishing women as "historical actors": the generalization of broad categories that leads to an "exclusionary concept of history," and, on the other hand, the unreachable goal of ascribing specificity to all human subjects in a historical project. Scott nevertheless does advance the category "women" as subject of historical investigation and does not seem to indicate how otherwise such an investigation could proceed outside of a framework of the group "women." She proposes gender as an "analytical, useful tool for historical analysis," which means that relations between the sexes are "a primary aspect of social organization" (25) and that these relations are political as long as they involve unequal distribution of power between the sexes.

There cannot be any argument that the majority of women's writings, whether fictional, autobiographical, or history-based, have been or are still concerned predominantly with women's areas of action and production—the family, the house, women's emotional and physical investment in the care of others, reproduction of the species, maintenance and providing of goods, food, household, preservation; in short, women's domestic intelligence, creativity, and pseudohegemony of the domestic. It is therefore important to examine and historicize the areas in which women have articulated knowledge and agency, albeit gender determined. This type of analysis has the advantage of tracing a well-documented referentiality in women's writings—not only fictional narratives but also journals, shopping lists, home budgets, letters— that provides a complementary historical narrative of women's activities. In order to build a historical narrative inhabited by women, the mimesis of the quotidian needs to be reconfigured first in our understanding and secondly in the reimagining of history. Our awareness of the subjectivity of history—of which we become progressively convinced thanks to decades of feminist and nonfeminist-oriented deconstructive critique and new historicistic-oriented reading of historical and para-historical texts—has collapsed history's pseudoscientificity and its claim for unquestionable truth.

The deconstruction of "history," legitimized by the realization of history's partiality, needs to be preceded by diagnoses that take into account the evidence of partiality and the incompleteness of history as well as the interconnected factors that concurred and concur in the production and authorization of such history. And when these factors are human agents, they need not be interpreted or anticipated necessarily as passive or docile. As Michel de Certeau (1984) sees them in his analysis of the politics of everyday life, they are tacit users and at times subverters of the dominant discourses and culture (those who can "escape the dominant power without leaving it," XIII). In adopting and adapting to a reading of women's historical fiction de Certeau's theory of everyday practices as sites of secondary productions of meanings, goods, and culture super-imposed on the official cultural production, [it is] possible to identify the microtechnologies and tactics of women's experi-ences as well as the macrotechnologies of power and control that necessitate the former. If the narratives of the macrotech-nologies represent dominant, linear history, the narratives of the nondominant groups' silent tactics of everyday life consti-tute horizontal history, the invisible support of official history without which the story of the past as we know it would not exist. De Certeau uses the same optics as Foucault's analysis of power structures by focusing on the mechanisms distilled by the institutions and their work to reorganize power (disci-pline). The difference is in their goals. While Foucault is inter-ested in how these technologies reorganize power and discipline, de Certeau looks at all the secondary productions of meanings and forms that constitute an antidiscipline (1984, xvii).

   de Certeau's observations on the tactics of everyday life dis-played by marginal groups bring to the fore a series of unoffi-cial, second level actions superimposed on the dominant, recorded systems. What he says about North Africans living in Paris, who "insinuate" their own ways of operating in the officially imposed system of space by using low income hous-ing and the language (French) is applicable to women's ways of operating in patriarchal cultural systems in which women do not fully participate either politically or economically. While functioning and performing within the rules of the sys-tem, the subalterns of history develop "a second level" of actions, of ways that follow other rules—opportunity, neces-sity—that are superimposed on the generalized system of so-cial living and behavior. Like the North African immigrant who, "without leaving the place where he has no choice but to live and which lays down its law for him, establishes within it a degree of *plurality* and creativity" (de Certeau 1984, 30), women stake their presence within the dominant culture. They

perform an "operational logic" that triumphal history and ex-
pansionistic, spectacular production typically shadow and do
not take into account.

In a sample of contemporary history-based narratives by
Italian women writers, we can follow a pattern of silent technologies involving the use of spaces, goods, and rituals that
deflect institutional structures without defeating or neutraliz-
ing them, and that at the same time tend to reinforce them.
These are operations that go hand in hand with power appara-
tuses and discursively redistribute "a generalized discipline"—
women's reproduction, housework, care. But some writers also
articulate a series of "tactics" in the execution of these practices that are strong enough to manifest clandestine forms and
make-to-do modes of operating. With these practices, women
resist the expected socioeconomic, gender order and "compose
a network of antidiscipline" (de Certeau 1984, xv), an alternative culture. In the tactics that women develop to circumvent
crises and meet needs, one can see at work "the ingenious ways
in which the weak make use of the strong" (xvii) and how,
consequently a political dimension punctuates everyday life.

Two novels published in the last two years, one more properly definable as historical fiction than the other, are particularly fit for this type of analysis because women's tactics and
practices vary and have different impacts according to class,
geo-economics, and education. Even though a common project
is at the center of these practices—the fashioning of human
masterpieces both female and male—women differ in how
they utilize, respond to, and challenge the macro systems such
as education, aesthetics, economics, and politics. Both *Il gioco
dei regni* (1993) by Clara Sereni and *Passaggio in ombra* (1995)
by the late Maria Teresa Di Lascia display a family saga, a
female genealogy, and an array of characters articulating with
richness and ambiguity the experience of living in different
environments in this century's Italy and of directly and indirectly processing historical and social changes. While Sereni's
book is a montage of biographical memory, historical research
and reconstructive narrative, Di Lascia's book (which won the
Strega Prize for fiction) is more easily classifiable as a novel
in the fashion of an autobiography spanning the period from
World War II to the present.

In both works, the histories of the various characters—and
there are many—open into large pictures: they introduce complex stories of whole families and public events where one

would be hard pressed to find a real protagonist, since all the characters seem equally complementary to one another. In this sense, both novels have a choral style of representation. The various histories move in and out of the general cultural milieu of a country and of a period to a more distinct nuclear culture defined by class, geo-economics, family, nongeneralizable customs. They thus unveil the cultural models regulating or subordinating life and the mechanisms of its functioning and disfunctioning.

The novels also reveal different levels of gender consciousness by narrators and characters, varying appropriately according to age, educational background, and agendas. While they offer a macro view of how gender molds and affects the lives of three generations of women, they also signal and represent various degrees of ambiguity in the way these women process, live with, and manipulate their gender identities. Both narratives are concerned in part with the construction of destinies by women invested, "interpelled" as mothers and aunts—in the Althusserian sense of having absorbed as their own and recognized as real the social representation of themselves with such a mandate. These women's class, education, and geo-economics determine and affect the mechanisms used as well as the outcome of their efforts and investment. At the center of *Il gioco dei regni* is an upper-middle-class, highly educated Jewish-Italian family dedicated to the education and upbringing of three sons (there is also a daughter who does not seem to be the object of much attention) who are going to be instrumental in the development of Zionism and Italian Communism. Their mother, Alfonsa, and their childless aunt, Ermelinda, take turns within their own fields of expertise in securing the boys' education and advancement in life. Alfonsa operates from her practical and highly ethical formation and beliefs while Ermelinda transmits her artistic inclinations and knowledge of music, literature, and art.

Alfonsa's silent technologies include a no-nonsense lifestyle for all: she oversees and organizes meals, study, and outings. Thanks to her husband's positivistic trust in science, she makes sure, together with her sister, that her children lead a life that can only make them successful and accomplished: care of the body in all its aspects, and, especially, care of the mind. In addition to formal education, she exposes them to arts, languages, and a moderate dose of religious training to preserve their Jewish roots. Everything is indulged properly and never-

excessively. Both Alfonsa, Ermelinda, and their male counterparts invest enough efforts in the upbringing to create a new
class of intellectuals who will become devoted leftist activists.
They will carry on the hopes and goals of the Bolshevik revolution, Zionism, and other liberational causes. In this sense, Alfonsa (with her sister) works in the construction of the sons'
destinies, and by extension, indirectly participates in affecting
history. Her tactics are different from those of her husband
and the other men in the family; she works in silence with her
antennae always alert, scanning dust, moods, and danger all
at once. When crises and tragedies shake her projects of happiness, security, and greatness for her sons, she makes sure that
the cracks are repaired with care, sustenance, and generosity.
Even when facing the death of her children, she does not vacil-
late in her self-imposed rule of "being strong and constant and
of even temperament to all" [essere forte e costante e uguale
d'umore con tutti (Sereni, 1993, 271)].

While Alfonsa's practices are rooted in her domestic science
and conducted with the zeal and exactitude of a scientist orga-
nizing and administering material and spiritual comfort to
the young and to adults, her sister Ermelinda transgresses the
limits of the domestic. Thanks both to her contacts with high-
powered political figures and to her commitment to the Jewish
cause, her interventions for the successful development and
placement of the young men are studied and crafted. She at-
tends to all details and misses no opportunity for their learning. In fact, even the stories the young boys adore listening to
are wisely dosed and conducive to her final goal. Only on special occasions or to keep their attention would Ermelinda tell
"real" stories from the Jewish imaginary and wisdom reper-
tory; as the boys grow up, most stories are taken from the
"canon" of literature and history. These accounts, substantial
as the first two courses of a meal, are followed only on special
occasions by the dessert of fairy tales. Such an education and
stimulation could not fail: all three Sereni boys become competitive scholars and devote themselves to higher causes that
are not necessarily fulfilling their own and their mother's projects of happiness and satisfaction. One commits suicide; another dies in a Nazi laager. The third does not die prematurely
but lives a life of self-imposed order dedicated to an ideology
he cannot control or change, and he closes himself up to the
world and to life. The micro technologies of the mother under-
estimated the power of the macro systems of racial politics,

the blinding ideologies, and the patriarchal order of things that would eventually disable them. In and out of the house that Alfonsa creates both as a real entity and as a point of reference, her sons make history, the history of regime changes and political orientations. With the movement and actions of the history resonating inside and around her house, Alfonsa's sons—brought up in rectitude, in liberality of spirit and body, and in the cult of knowledge—all become casualties of intransigent ideologies, of self-righteous beliefs in oppositional categories of behavior and values, and of the subordination of love and affection to a rigid system of cause and effect. Triumphal history becomes suspect from the beginning of this book: too many signs and premonitions are floating around alerting Alfonsa's intelligence and preparing her for the unexpected and the subsequent tragedies. These same signs are invisible to the driven, goal-oriented, competitive men of this story.

If in *Il gioco dei regni* the target of women's tactics and practices is the success and happiness of the male lineage, in *Passaggio in ombra* the entire scenario changes. In planning for the future, the focus is a young girl, Chiara, who is also the narrator of the story. Although there is not a visible "history" to consign Chiara to, the tactics to protect and secure her advancement in life—her success as a "woman" first of all—are more transgressive than in Sereni's story, and the results are as tragic. Here again, a mother and a succession of aunts take it upon themselves to bring up the girl in an extended family environment. They display the same determination and mission as Alfonsa and Ermelinda but on a different playground. Chiara, the child of a single mother but reclaimed by her father and his family, grows up in an environment diametrically opposite to that of the Sereni brothers, who are a generation older. Chiara's is a world of smothering southern Italian peasants where love and hate are equally and freely poured down rather than rationed as in the other book. What is singular and little expected is the magnetic attraction the child exercises on members of a family for whom she would have been an ordinary bastard. Unsolicited, actually discouraged by Chiara's mother who has resolved to live and raise her child as a single, independent woman, the father and subsequently his childless aunt and sister claim stakes in the fashioning of Chiara's life and future. For the father, this project is short-lived and ends before Chiara enters adolescence; in the women's lives this goal remains central. If the Sereni brothers were wisely and scientifically dosed with comfort, security, and family warmth—intellectually challenged and even overstimulated—Chiara's anomalous family situation is compensated for by ebullient and smothering love coming from all directions; it is both her beauty and the promise of her intellectual potential that mark her difference and design her destiny: she is expected to become a doctor and marry well and thus start a new course for the future generation of women of her family. Both aunts, after Chiara prematurely loses her mother, direct their efforts toward that end with calculated maneuvers. Their tactics consist of artful management of the environment—social, economic, material, emotional, and gendered—to reach their goal. Their movements are in and out of gendered identities. While they subordinate to prescribed external roles and mores, they at the same time carve "other interests and desires that are neither determined nor captured by the systems in which they develop" (de Certeau 1984 XVIII). Besides providing Chiara with abundant and incessant love and admiration, they also work in instilling a firm conviction of her worthiness and her call for greatness. This they do by defying the laws of reality and common sense, and by undertaking extraordinary sacrifices. They steal, lie to others and themselves, and pretend.

But Chiara, unlike the Sereni brothers, does not respond to the programmed destiny. The young men have been nurtured to their destiny of greatness by generations of males before them, and by a gendered culture that saw this success as possible. Chiara's development and projected success are built on unprepared grounds of disillusions, insecurities, and fears. She becomes a casualty not of competition and blinding ideologies, but of nihilism and self-dissolution. While her aunts fight against reality and construct for her a world that is in collusion with reality, Chiara, after one aunt's death, lets herself be invaded and conquered by all the unacceptable reality she had not previously known. In the end, she acts out, albeit of negative volition, by letting reality invade her and take her over.

The women's genealogy in *Passaggio* does not renew itself with Chiara; their investment did not pay off with the young woman who, devoided of the clear life purpose of her aunts and mother and programmed in a gender mold, recycles the same tactics—lying and pretending—pretending is a way of getting by—by imitation. (But) This time, it is conscious. The break, for good or bad, occurs with her generation, and she rebels in the only way that requires the least effort and action upon life: letting life happen to her.

If the practices and tactics of the southern women in *Passaggio*, driven by bovarism and unmediated passions, seem doomed to fail, the outcome is not more successful in the more controlled, upper-class, educated women of Sereni's story. With their means and culture they operate at a more "sovrastructural" level. Ironically and paradoxically, the women in *Passaggio*, culturally marked by more exacerbated and unexamined gender roles, develop more radical and clandestine tactics of opposition to patriarchal rules than their presumably more democratic and emancipated upper-class counterpart. Sereni's matriarch, Alfonsa, as well as her sister Ermelinda are more compromised in the construction of a male dynasty of power and influence. Through their use of available knowledge and culture, they take seriously and almost scientifically their roles of educators, while the uneducated women of *Passaggio* are more involved in offsetting and destabilizing patriarchal power with their daily subversive tactics, which they have developed not through appropriation of scientific knowledge but by proven make-do, unobservable acts.

In the postscript to *Il gioco dei regni*—called "After the history: why/because"—which also functions as a type of narrated acknowledgment, Sereni talks about her motivations for writing the book, the various channels of people's memories, and the extensive archival materials consulted that confirmed what she already knew about her family. Thus in these pages we learn about the method she adopts for writing a historical novel: letting the characters tell the stories while she is fully responsible for selecting, cutting, mounting the materials according to her point of view.[4] We also learn that in constructing a biographical history of people known to her, Sereni is both drawn to find out and to present how people "really were" as well as to speculate fictionally how they could have been in a given circumstance. As she becomes hungry for "written things with an appearance of truth and certainty" [cose scritte con apparenze di verità e certezza (1993, 442)] she also realizes that rereading what one used to consider truth offers the possibility of discovering falsehoods and omissions previously unnoticed. She finds this state of affairs in her mother's autobiographical book *I giorni della nostra vita* [*The Days of Our Lives*], meant to be a sort of gospel for a new generation of Italian communist women. Compelled to investigate the reasons for the many omissions and censored parts in the book, Sereni thus reconstructs another story, and we are alerted to distinguish and appreciate through "her" story the limits of traditional historical inquiry: a method unable to fully account for the richness of emotions, motivations, and life's multiple contradictions.

Feminist theory and especially gender theory have long explored and denounced sexual politics first and then gender politics that support history's partiality and women's unaccounted presence and productions. In the spirit of pioneers—that is, in the eagerness to create representations in a new territory, women's writing—feminist writings have positioned women at the center of their representations even if these positions were marginal, obscure, taken for granted, or modeled after previous models. Simultaneously with and subsequent to the first impetus to chronicle or fictionalize the "exemplary" women, there has also been the necessity to give voice to ordinary female characters and portray their experiences, which occupy a point of reference in the collective imaginary, as well as in the individual memory. Women's culture (cultural history), far from being exhausted as acritically self-serving, remains the indisputable ground of women's historical presence and therefore of feminist analysis, historical and otherwise.

Notes

Quotes in English from both *Il gioco dei regni* (Sereni 1993) and *Passaggio in ombra* (Di Lascia 1995) are my translations from the original Italian.

1. I refer here mostly to the works of Italian historians Gianna Pomata and Anna Rossi Doria. For Pomata, it is in women's individual stories that one acquires a sense of women's history, and one learns and imagines from the specificity and exemplariness of these stories "other identities" as well as those that "power has imposed upon us" (1993, 168). Rossi Doria sees in the prevalent memory-based narratives of women their need to reconstruct a tradition, to legitimize their existence while exposing patriarchal systems of oppression. Because the "heredity" that mothers can transmit to their daughters is a negative one—that is, a suspect identity or one they are not sure to possess—the challenge for the feminist historian is to make a bridge between past and present by being both the inheriting daughter and the bestowing mother (1993).

2. In their efforts to "skirt" the slippery generalized and essentialistic valence of "woman" and "women," Denise Riley and Mary Lydon propose similar, virtual definitions for the individual/s we still call "woman" and "women." Riley argues that while there is not such a firm, historical category

responding to the name "woman," one can instead talk of "peculiar tempo-
ralities of 'women'" (1988, 98). Woman as category and women as collectivity
are shifting historical characterizations that are not innate but precipitated
by social, economic, biological factors. Lydon borrows Foucault's distinction
between an "event" and a "state of being" to further her argument on the
"unsubstantiality" and transiency of the terms "woman" and "women": "Being a woman is not simply an attribute, hence a constant of any woman's life,
but is rather something that occurs, as an event. . . . It is its very intermittent
nature [once one thing, once another, according to who the caller is] . . .
that makes 'being a woman' an event" (1995, 224). Although in theory one
immediately recognizes the traps of constructionism inherent in any group
categorization or generic definition, in practice there are serious structural
problems with the notion or persuasion of women as "shifting" and "eventual" in attempting an historical analysis of such groups. How do we account
for a group and a gendered-effected group? What is the responsibility toward
the historical, material reality exercised in the life experiences of women
who did not think of themselves as "events," who played their part in the
only stage and script they knew? I can only talk of "a woman" as an event
and a series of events from my theoretical framework, but I am afraid that
I am not representing "that woman," since she did not think of herself as an
event. I am superimposing on that entity (called woman) another construction, another definition among others. I am presuming all along. However,
since there cannot be "going back to the innocence of 'biology,'" as De
Lauretis says (1987, 20), having "apprehended" gender consciousness, any
historical analysis of/about women will necessarily include or project a self-
evident gender critique of the articulation of women's practices in individual, clan, family, societal daily experiences.

Gender theorists have also discounted and cautiously dismissed some culturally oriented approaches to women's agencies as essentialist and reduc-
tionist. Both Joan Scott and Annarita Buttafuoco, for instance, recognize the
importance for women's historiography of the proliferating literature on
female culture that focuses on the valuation and distinctiveness of women's
experiences (personal, family, domestic life). But both critics distance themselves from the ideological "separatism" and acritical interpretation of such
historical experiences (Buttafuoco, 1993). Scott is particularly critical of
Carol Gilligan's work on female moral development, which, in her opinion,
espouses an essentialistic notion of woman hypothesizing "a universal female
preference for relatedness," and therefore exacerbating even more binary
oppositions and a "hierarchical construction of the relationship between
male and female" (Scott 1988, 40–41).

3. Attacks to subject formation come from New Historicistic quarters,
claiming as Stephen Greenblatt (1994) does, that one cannot talk any longer
of "pure, unfettered" subjects, makers of their own identity. The human subject seems unfree, the ideological product of relationships of power in particular societies and given epochs: "a cultural artifact" with no "free choices"
since these are determined by "the range delineated by the social and ideological system in force" (1994, 76). At the same time, emerging historiography is concerned with the disempowering effects of discourse theories that
convey to the subaltern groups the "fatal inability to act" and thus erase
agency and resistance as well as revolutionary potential (1991, 4). Maurizio
Viano also echoes feminists' objections to some postmodern tendencies to

84   GIOVANNA MICELI JEFFRIES

disqualify the subject just when women (and other emerging groups), coincidentally, are engaged in their affirmation as subjects (1989, 417).

4. The wide use of montage technique in this novel reveals Sereni's past experience of work in the film industry and television.

References

Bono, Paola, and Sandra Kemp, eds. 1993. *The Lonely Mirror: Italian Perspectives and Feminist Theory*. New York: Routledge.

Buttafuoco, Annarita. 1993. On "Mothers" and "Sisters." In Bono and Kemp, 170–85.

de Certeau, Michel. 1984. *The practice of everyday life*. Berkeley: University of California Press.

De Lauretis, Teresa. 1987. *Technologies of gender*. Bloomington: Indiana University Press.

Di Lascia, Maria Teresa. 1995. *Passaggio in ombra*. Milan: Feltrinelli.

Greenblatt, Stephen. 1994. The improvisation of power. In *The New Historicism reader*, edited by H. Aram Veeser, 46–87. New York: Routledge.

Kincaid, Jamaica. 1996. *The autobiography of my mother*. New York: Farrar, Straus, Giroux.

Lydon, Mary. 1995. *Skirting the issue*. Madison: University of Wisconsin Press.

Orr, Linda. 1986. The Revenge of literature: A history of history. In *New Literary History* 18: 1–22.

Pomata, Gianna. 1993. Premiss: a figure of power and an invitation to history. In Bono and Kemp, 155–69.

Riley, Denise. 1988. *"Am I that name?" Feminism and the category 'women' in history*. Minneapolis: University of Minnesota Press.

Rossi Doria, Anna. 1993. Memoria, storia e tradizione delle donne. In *Questioni di teoria femminista*, edited by Paola Bono, 156–62. Milan: La Tartaruga.

Scott, Joan Wallach. 1988. *Gender and the politics of history*. New York: Columbia University Press.

Sereni, Clara. 1993. *Il gioco dei regni*. Florence: Giunti.

Veeser, H. Aram. 1991. Remembering the deformed past: (New) New Historicism. In *M/MLA* 24: 3–13.

Viano, Maurizio. 1989. Sesso debole, pensiero debole. In *Annali d'italianistica* 7: 394–422.

Part Two
The Representative

"Uno sguardo acuto dalla storia": Anna Banti's Historical Writings

PAOLA CARÙ

IN ITALIAN ANTHOLOGIES, ANNA BANTI IS OFTEN EXCLUSIVELY "labeled" as a writer of historical fiction. Indeed, she did occupy herself with history both in her fiction and in her nonfiction works. Titles featuring historical characters run through her whole literary production from *Artemisia* (1947) to *Noi credevamo* (1967) and *La camicia bruciata* (1973), to her numerous short stories, "Lavinia fuggita," "Joveta di Betania," "I porci," and others. Banti's concern with the past and its interpretation was a long-standing interest that had its origins in her initial training as an art historian according to the school of Roberto Longhi.[1]

Banti theorizes her approach to writing history in a series of essays that appeared in the literary magazine *Paragone* and were later collected in a volume entitled *Opinioni* (1961). She is critically interested in the field of concerns defined by Manzoni in the essay *Del romanzo storico* (1850); in it Manzoni renounces the historical novel as a genre, after having written *I promessi sposi* (published first in 1827), a masterpiece of this genre. Manzoni highlights the gap that exists between history and invention, and reserves his approval for the writing of history proper. This essay marks Manzoni's abandonment of fiction and his devotion to nonfiction. Banti regrets this stance on the part of one of her greatest literary models; she argues against it by adhering to Manzoni's earlier position, as a believer in the verisimilar, and she explores its potentials in relation to female figures.

Manzoni's understanding of the verisimilar—that which is invented but historically verifiable—is explained in his theoretical work *Del romanzo storico*. This text marks a turning point in the author's stance vis-à-vis the complex relationship between historical and fictional writing. Though published in

1850, *Del romanzo storico* represented the result of years of meditation on (and practice in) this particular literary field. Manzoni had analyzed the tension between invention and historical fact, hinting at a possible reconciliation of the two as early as 1823 in his "Lettre à Monsieur Chauvet." Manzoni justifies therein the literary dignity of historical poetry, that is, of those works that mix history and fiction. As Banti shows, his historical novel *I promessi sposi* puts theory into practice, yet marks at the same time the beginning of the author's final period, in which he abandons the writing of fiction to concentrate on nonfiction. The essay *Del romanzo storico* reflects Manzoni's overall intellectual development and justifies the conclusive position that he reaches concerning the question of the relationship between history and poetry.[2]

In "Romanzo e romanzo storico" (1951), "Ermengarda e Geltrude" (1954), and "Manzoni e noi" (1956), Banti focuses on her relation to Manzoni and her departure from his theory of the novel. She disagrees with his final defense of the "historical fact" [fatto avvenuto] against the "traps" of the "invented fact" [fatto inventato], which leaves no room for the "hypothetical fact" [fatto supposto], that is, for the verisimilar (1951b, 5). Banti regrets Manzoni's programmatic scruples; she asserts that they served the cause of history too much to the detriment of the cause of the novel. Banti pursues her analysis of Manzoni's works in other essays: she chooses for herself the vantage point of the "hypothetical fact"; she justifies her desire for a plausible picture of history, namely, for a representation of what she referes to as the "animated scene" of history that includes both "historical characters" [personaggi storici] and "characters who lack a history" (1955, 79) [senza storia].[3] Banti considers the historical novel a high challenge for a writer because at its best, it must re-create the complexity of the past by intertwining "official" facts with probable hypotheses.

Banti's declaration of poetics vis-à-vis Manzoni's last stand is reconfirmed at the end of her writing career in *Un grido lacerante* (1981), her last novel and a sort of veiled autobiography. In this text Banti meditates upon her professional choices at various stages of her career and her progressive orientation toward a reinterpretation of history through writing. She needs distance from her subject matter and sees in historical writing an artistic opportunity: to recover "impulses and thoughts" of women and men whose lives have been effaced by the darkness of unrecorded time (114).

Banti's approach based upon the verisimilar allows her to define the historical novel as a "hypothetical interpretation of history" (120). It privileges the narration of minor details, those that can be told by assuming they could be "true" even if they remain unrecounted by historiographers. When writing historical novels and short stories, Banti favors the depiction of the contingent aspects of history, that is, the depiction of events that are not recorded but are probable. However, they are always embedded in Banti's accurate research of historical documents. She aims at revealing a complex tableau that includes both established facts and the thoughts and emotions of her characters. She attempts to retrace the traceless, to illustrate the quotidian that sustains people and their deeds and yet is not remembered, as it is taken for granted. Banti sets out on a search for the "fleeting signs neglected by time" [segni labili che il tempo non ha raccolto] that indicate "voids to be filled, mending to be done with the threads of apparently endless days" (1973, 9) [lacune da colmare, rammendi da tessere coi fili delle giornate apparentemente senza eventi]. Since "official" history does not account for "eventless days," those who lived and acted on such days are doomed to remain historically voiceless. Traditionally, this has been the lot of women. Therefore Banti accepts a "bet against the verisimilar" whenever she chooses women as her privileged subject.[4] It is Banti's own phrase in her novel *Un grido lacerante* (1981, 110). From this point of view, Banti aligns herself with Virginia Woolf, a writer she much admired. Upon assessing the situation of the contemporary novel, Woolf stressed its basic deception as far as its depiction of the "infinitely obscure lives" was concerned. She wrote:

> For all the dinners are cooked; the plates and cups washed; the children set to school and gone out into the world. Nothing remains of it all. All has vanished. No biography or history has a word to say about it. And the novels, without meaning to, inevitably lie. (1957, 93)

In Banti's historical novels and short stories, the past is seen mostly through female eyes, eyes that look at reality from a different perspective since they are off-center in relation to it. Banti's female characters live on the borders; they strive to participate in both worlds, that is, the external male-dominated society and the internal realm of the domestic where they have been confined. Some of them stand out because they move from one area to the other while trying to assert themselves in values other than those determined merely by sexual function. These characters are extraordinary individuals—artists, abbesses, queens. Among them are real historical figures such as Artemisia (1947), Joveta (1971a), Marguerite Louise d'Orléans (1973), and imagined characters, such as Lavinia (1952) or the various female protagonists whose stories are set by Banti in the period following the fall of the Roman empire.[4] The women of the first group existed historically. Those of the second group did not, but could have existed in the historical period described by Banti. Both groups were active in the past, and both have been misrepresented or completely erased by history. Banti makes them into representable subjects. She investigates the void left by the silence of historiography on history. Her relationship with Manzoni's tradition centers around the "knot" of the relationship between history and invention. Banti takes up Manzoni's heritage from its most representative example of historical fiction, *I promessi sposi*, and develops its potential by having her own works branch out into two, complementary directions: she depicts undocumented women (Lavinia, the Roman youth) in their documented historical setting, and, conversely, she portrays historical characters by exploring the untold aspects of their daily lives and their links to others (Artemisia, Joveta, Marguerite Louise). These two approaches to women's positions in past history function interactively. They both aim at reappropriating from a female perspective the submerged areas of the past—everybody's past.

Banti's female protagonists are characterized by their desire to leave the confinement of silence and practice strategies of self-assertion. Although they pay a high price, they succeed in being vocal. They must prove themselves in a hostile world and, in addition, they have to face the reactions of those from their original environment who do not understand their ambitions. As a result, they are often doubly marginalized—as women and as outstanding women. Nonetheless, they rebel against the constraints of convention and try to break away from the sidelines to which they have been confined.

In their efforts to define their own independence, they embody the rebel type, a recurring figure in the Bantian corpus. Besides misunderstanding and marginalization, Banti's rebels, in fact, also experience empowerment. They can draw courage from their relationships with other women, especially older ones. Another characteristic Bantian theme, the courage of women in of the eponymous collection of short stories, is widely represented in her historical writings. Banti traces non-biological female family trees by stressing the importance of female bonding, a relevant topic in her works.

Female bonding is one of the topics that Banti explores most thoughtfully, especially in her depiction of outstanding women and their relationships with the outside world; such women are most immediately in need of understanding and support, including professional recognition and guidance. The more a talented woman is exposed to external pressure, the more she requires a model she can use as a point of reference. She can most likely find such a figure in a woman from a previous generation. The best example of this type of powerful communication is offered by *Artemisia* (1947), Banti's best-known novel. In one of the key episodes of the text, the seventeenth-century painter Artemisia Gentileschi meets with Pietra Spinola on her way to England. Spinola, an old and influential noblewoman from Genoa, acknowledges Artemisia's talent and encourages her choices. Artemisia discovers in her the authoritative support and the emotional closeness that she had not found in either her family or in her professional environment. She finds herself talking without reticence about herself in a way she had not experienced in many years, as Spinola's attentive listening "inspired her with new words" (1965, 164). In their first and last meeting, Artemisia opens her heart and mind to this elderly lady who is both "tough and compassionate" [cruda e pietosa], and who can see beyond the meaning of Artemisia's words [mostrava d'intendere oltre la parola (165)].

Banti's interest in female bonding is especially evident in the way she varies her exploration of the topic in *Artemisia*. On the one hand, the protagonist as a relatively young artist is seen in her revealing encounter with the elderly and powerful Spinola; on the other, Artemisia herself, as a mature *maestra*, is recurrently shown as she interacts with her female pupils. Banti emphasizes one such relationship in particular: Artemisia's tutoring of Annella De Rosa, a promising and beautiful younger painter. Both Spinola and Artemisia, in their roles as mentors, are interested in their interlocutors and actively support them; they are not afraid of competition or misunderstandings on the part of those whom they teach. The strength of these relationships, in which she functions respectively as the receiver and the giver of authoritative counsel, helps Artemisia define herself both personally and professionally, a difficult task for a female artist in the seventeenth century. Artemisia would like to find an exemplary personality that could assist her in "recognizing" herself, yet she cannot find one, at least not until the moment when she encounters Spinola's authoritative presence. Artemisia needs a female "model" because she cannot identify with the male artists who surround her. She is a woman "who would like to find inspiration for all her actions in a decent, noble role model of her own sex and time" (110). Conversely, *maestra* Artemisia is proud of those female artists such as Annella De Rosa who become famous under her guidance: "If a woman is honored, it is her honor" (210).

Banti's characters draw psychological reinforcement from their participation in a system of bonding that is determined by sex, and by intellectual or professional relationship, rather than by a traditional genealogical system. The ties among them are all the more powerful precisely because they are based upon nonbiological bonding. The symbolical connotation of these affiliations is highlighted, by contrast, whenever they are juxtaposed with biological relationships. Banti's novel *Artemisia* provides a telling example of this difference by presenting Artemisia herself in her role as mentor for the painter Annella, and as a mother to her daughter Porziella. Artemisia's tutoring of Annella is marked by affection and pride; it falls short of full success and fails to achieve independence and fame as an artist for the pupil only because of a tragedy in Annella's household: Annella lets herself be killed by her jealous husband. Artemisia's relationship to Porziella is twisted and unsatisfactory: the mother tries to communicate with her daughter, but her attempts are unsuccessful. Communication between the two is painful and marked by misunderstandings and regrets on both sides. As a consequence, it is Artemisia's symbolic maternal tie to her pupil rather than her biological tie to her daughter that remains most significant. It allows female empowerment to be transmitted among generations; it does not require lengthy association; in fact, it can develop from short but intense encounters, as the one experienced by Artemisia with Pietra Spinola. The painter in search of recognition knows that Spinola handles "the weapons of authority" (166). Conversely, in her tutoring relationship with Annella, Artemisia is eventually paid an homage of gratitude by her talented yet moody pupil: "There are dozens of male painters, yet there is only one woman painter, you, *Maestra*" (210). Banti's women recognize themselves in the strength of other women.

Banti's consistent highlighting of female value and female bonding sets her in a pioneering position with respect to later developments of feminist theory in Italy. In the 1980s, a group of Italian feminist philosophers called *Diotima* explored the idea of mediation among women who, by virtue of their differing ages, skills, or privileges, have arrived at different levels of status in society. The experience of disparity can lead to a consequent recognition of female authority, engendering in turn the practice of "entrustment" [*affidamento*]—a kind of fostering of other women carried out by women who are older and more established. Within such a system, the former can be helped to negotiate their own empowerment. This process is meant to reenact the relationship between mother and daughter, and should lead to a symbolic female order that parallels the dominant male system. Banti, who always refused the label of "feminist," had in fact proposed a similar practice of empowerment through female bonding four decades earlier. Banti actually went beyond the mere representation of it in her fiction; she tried to practice it in her own profession by encouraging younger talented women in need of guidance and support. One of them, Grazia Livi, a writer herself, acknowledged her debt of gratitude in an autobiographical short story significantly entitled "Maestra e allieva" and dedicated to Banti.

Artemisia also demonstrates Banti's concept that female bonding leads to the discovery of genealogies that in turn—leads to empowerment. It is also exemplified by the short story "Lavinia fuggita" (1952), in which a character finds support among her peers. Its protagonist, Lavinia, is an abandoned child who lives in a Venetian orphanage in the early years of the eighteenth century. She secretly composes music and tries to have it performed by substituting her own scores for the official scores written by the school's maestro, Vivaldi. Once discovered by the director of the institute, she is publicly humiliated and driven to despair. She throws away her score book and decides to escape, thus apparently falling again into the mist of anonymity. Orsola and Zanetta, Lavinia's friends, are instrumental in her survival. They save her score book and keep alive her memory after her escape. Banti writes "Lavinia fuggita" as a narrative flashback, in which Lavinia's story lives because her friends retell it. Their voices give her a voice. Even while at the orphanage, Lavinia is aware of the importance of their solidarity. Before running away she entrusts what she calls her "portrait" to Orsola; she asks Orsola to learn and perform for her one of her pieces; she means it as a token of their friendship. Orsola recalls that moment for Zanetta: "'This is my portrait,' Lavinia said, while giving her the sheets of music. 'You'll learn it and then you will remember me as if it were my picture.'" ['Questo e il mio ritratto' le aveva detto Lavinia porgendole i fogli 'lo impari e poi ti ricordi di me come fossi dipinta'. (1952, 116)][5]

In addition, female relationships overcome the disruptive intrusion of time that shortens women's chances for self-affirmation. It is the peculiar relationship of women to time that relegates them to reproductive roles and excludes them from social or political power. For centuries women have been identified and stigmatized by their relationship to their own bodies, by their link to motherhood, and by the expectation that they perform the maintenance tasks of daily living. They have evolved as ostracized creatures, having to live and provide for the lives of others within the alien frame of male-defined time. Hence their historical invisibility. By writing historical fiction Banti is doubly involved with the issue of time: she lengthens the life span of her historical characters by drawing them out from the fragmentation of the past, and she extends her own time by finding her ideal predecessors. This mutual benefit vis-à-vis the power of time is fictionally represented by Banti in the intertwining of narrative voices featured especially in her historical writings.

Banti is aware that, in order for a woman to be recognized as a source of authority, she needs to be part of a net of relationships where she can refer to other women; this is particularly true for women artists. Being one herself, Banti actively seeks to bring to light her female precursors so as to break her sense of historical and professional isolation. She maps out her female genealogy both in her historical fiction and in her nonfiction. A significant example of Banti's practice is given by "Amiche remote," an article she wrote for *Paragone* in 1983 and dedicated to her "companions whom she longed for" (1983a, 92). It is a tracking of female figures from the past, mostly well-known but some anonymous, that gives a general picture of women's presence in various sectors of society through the centuries. The final sentence of the article is particularly significant: Banti asks herself whether she is satisfied with her depiction of "older friends." She answers [by twisting an Italian proverb] she cannot content herself with what she has found; therefore, the search for her companions must be kept up.

Banti focuses on time, role definition, and the detention of power in many of her works, both in her fiction and in her nonfiction. Possibly her most explicit statement on this issue is given by her 1954 novel *Allarme sul lago*. The text offers the tale of three miserable families encapsulated within a futuristic and dystopian frame: three women are obliged to stay at a hotel on a lake because of an unspecified "alarm." They recount their lives to a fourth one, Eugenia, who eventually declares:

> I believe that the whole difference lies in this: women are afraid of not having enough time to live, of having too little time—only a few years in which to have the things that are necessary and desirable: now or never. (217)

Banti's historical characters are well aware of having a short time, which they must not waste. Banti shows them engaged in the effort to conquer it. They need particular determination as they must overcome anxiety about male responses in relation to their work as artists and about their male artist forerunners. According to Harold Bloom (1973), the male writer feels anxious when he compares his own achievements to those of his predecessors, and compares himself to the tradition that those predecessors represent. This "anxiety of influence" is caused by his uncertainty concerning his ability to compete successfully with the past. In their study of nineteenth-century literature (1979), Sandra Gilbert and Susan Gubar revise Bloom's theory by focusing on the female writer who is discouraged from writing by the scarcity of female predecessors rather than by their overbearing presence.

The female writer is troubled by an "anxiety of authorship" that complicates her situation: she must affirm her role of young female artist within the male tradition (3–92). Such is the case of the female artists depicted by Banti: they need to express themselves through art, and know they are capable of so doing; yet, the overwhelming presence of a male tradition, combined with male dominance of the artistic scene in general, involves the female artist in a stressful fight for her artistic survival.

Both Artemisia and Lavinia are aware of their talents and struggle to affirm them. Throughout her father's life, Artemisia strives to win his recognition both as a paternal figure and as a master painter. Her art is for her a means of survival because it gives her a way to live independently and lets her overcome the trauma of her adolescence: Artemisia had been repeatedly raped by her drawing teacher, one of her father's friends, and had been tortured during the lengthy trial that eventually proved her "innocent." The double function of her painting is made clear in the crucial scene in which Artemisia paints Holofernes' decapitation. It is a moment of relief and pride:

> An enormous pride fills her breast, the awful pride of a vindicated woman who harbors, despite her shame, the satisfaction of the artist who has solved all problems of art, and can speak the language of her father, of the pure ones, of the chosen. (1965, 54)

This episode apparently marks Artemisia's entrance into the realm of the symbolic order characterized by the "law of the father."[6] It is a moment in which Artemisia vanquishes her "anxiety of authorship" by distancing herself from her previous roles as dejected daughter and unacknowledged artist. This is a first step in her personal and professional development: her awareness of her father's absence and the lack of his explicit recognition of her talent will stop troubling her only later on during her eventful encounter with Pietra Spinola. Artemisia's meeting with Spinola determines Artemisia's approach to an alternative female symbolic order that provides her with the proper authoritative frame of reference.

Lavinia also strives to assert her talent. She can enjoy her work only illicitly: she secretly composes and substitutes her own scores for Vivaldi's. She is willing to run the risk of being discovered because she needs to hear the sound of her own "voice." She confesses to Orsola: "I must . . . hear the sound of my own voice: the more I listen to it, the more I realize that [both] my song and the sound of my voice are different" ["Io devo . . . sentire il suono della mia voce: più ne ascolto e piu so che il mio canto e il mio suono sono diversi" (1952, 107)]. It is this "different" song, this voice, that Banti is interested in recovering, the presence of distinct female voices heard in the faint noise of unrecorded history.

Banti finds the idea of "ransoming" marginalized figures intriguing. In writing historical fiction she intends to challenge the traditional interpretation of documented "facts." "Facts— yet which ones really matter?—those that are imperceptible" ("Europa 1606" 1961, 15). She questions the somber presence of some characters in history by taking for herself the role of gambler: she means to fill the gaps left by historiography by renewing "the anonymous fascination of lives crushed by dark centuries" [l'incanto anonimo delle vite schiacciate dai secoli bui (1981, 114)].[7] It is interesting to notice how the image of the gambler appears very early in Banti's literary career; in one of her "articoli di costume," her socio-political articles combined with fictional elements she describes the research job of scholars in dusty archives as a combination of risk, excitement, and tenacity, that is, as the equivalent of gambling: "Archival research is not at all boring or routine; on the contrary, it is exciting and intriguing, like predicting the numbers in a lottery or game of chance, with the risk and the prize thrown in for good measure" (*Documenti*, 1939, 6). By extension, the same image fits Banti herself. As a passionate writer of historical fiction, she tries to offer alternative clues to the interpretation of reality by focusing on marginalized characters. Banti is induced to do so by the pleasure she finds in curiosity, in discovery—the same pleasure she perceived in the attitude of Marguerite Louise d'Orléans, the seventeenth-century protagonist of her last historical novel:

> Marguerite abandons herself to the pleasure of imagining this obscure character's life: in the same way, as a child she enjoyed going inside the workers' huts to uncover their pots and see what was boiling inside them. (1973, 111)

Writing allows one to get a better hold on the past, and therefore on the present. It can temporarily halt time by dilating it through the practice of memory. It allows one to investigate the past and to obtain a key for interpreting the present. Banti explores all these topics in her only historical novel that has a male protagonist, *Noi credevamo* (1967). Written midway between *Artemisia* and *La camicia bruciata*, her earliest and latest historical novels, it is a fresco of Italian nineteenth century history seen through the eyes of a disappointed Italian patriot, a rebel and an outsider.

Domenico Lopresti, the protagonist of *Noi credevamo*, is an elderly Calabrese who recollects his youth and middle age when he fought the oppressive regime of the Bourbons and suffered in their prisons. His old age finds him once again a free man, but he is disappointed in the "new Italy," having been let down by his old comrades, many of whom are discovered to have been traitors. At the opening of the novel, Lopresti lives with his family in Turin in a sort of voluntary exile. He feels himself to be a stranger in that northern city, and, to a certain extent, feels the same strangeness in relation to his own family. He is tired of life and begins writing his memoirs almost by chance but continues with them in order to find a reason to go on living.

Precisely because of his marginal position, the old Garibaldino Lopresti can offer a disenchanted perspective of "official" history. *Noi credevamo* can be read also as a statement of Banti's poetics: it elaborates the "birth to writing" as a means of exploring the interplay between the time of history and the time of the individual. In the novel, the act of writing is considered by the narrator to be essential because it allows him to gain some degree of distance and to analyze the present from the perspective of his past and vice versa. Domenico Lopresti is engaged in a sort of "game" with the passing of time, in which he himself is the potential gambler; he must examine his own past within the broader context of the general course of history. Furthermore, the protagonist of *Noi credevamo* is a member of the Bantian cluster of "anonymous" voices that should be recorded: a political and social outcast, his voice would be forever lost without the action of writing.

The precondition for "salvaging" the voices of minor characters from the obliteration of historiography, suggests Banti, consists in having a sharp focus; the practice of attaining artistic distance leads, paradoxically, to closeness. It gives insight. Banti believes that authors should attain objectivity and detachment by distancing themselves from the present. Only from a distance can the writer afford to depict the verisimilar.

Banti's stance, based on the need of "looking over one's shoulders," emerges in her early works. Her first published long fiction, *Itinerario di Paolina*, appears in 1937; in 1947, Banti becomes well-known with her acclaimed historical novel *Artemisia*. In an interview with Grazia Livi, (1971b) Banti declares: "After writing [*Itinerario di Paolina*] I understood that you need a certain distance in order to write fiction, and I have chosen the path of historical fiction."

The concept of *sguardo acuto*, or sharp vision, which allows the writer to engage in a reinterpretation of history, is also an expression of the writer's fascination with her subject matter. The "bet against the verisimilar" implies an attitude of dissatisfaction with known depictions of the past, as well as an openness, vis-à-vis the unexplored realms of "history" that derive from curiosity. It is a combination of detachment—the analysis of history through the study of official documents—and passion—the desire to explore the lives obscured by those documents—that lies at the core of Banti's writing. It aims at understanding the importance of the invisible female presence throughout the past and intends to reevaluate that presence by means of a gendered perspective.

Notes

1. Longhi devoted great care to the language he used to write his art criticism. He also placed great importance on the accurate analysis of details. Pier Paolo Pasolini, who also was one of Longhi's students, comments on the influence of Longhi's style on Banti's writing in an article entitled "Il cammino di Anna Banti dalla semplice stima ai primi posti," *Tempo*, 6 May 1973, 74–76.

2. For a thorough discussion of Manzoni's poetics, see Sandra Bermann's introduction (1984) to the translation of *Del romanzo storico*.

3. This remark comes from a review written in 1955, precisely in the middle of the years in which Banti exposes her critique of Manzoni. In it, Banti praises Cecchi's biography of Tiziano Vecellio for his ability to recreate the painter's life through the depiction of his relationships to a variety of people, not just historical characters. Unless otherwise indicated, all translations are mine.

4. Artemisia is the Caravaggist painter Artemisia Gentileschi (1598–1652?); Joveta of Betania (also referred to under other names in documents) was the youngest daughter of King Baldwin II, and her story is set by Banti in eleventh century Palestine at the time of the Latin kingdom of Jerusalem; Marguerite Louise d'Orléans (1645–1721) was the French wife of Cosimo III de' Medici. The female characters set in the period of the fall of the Roman empire are the protagonists of some of the short stories collected in *Campi Elisi* (1963) and *Je vous écris d'un pays lointain* (1971a).

5. This short story was reprinted in *Campi Elisi* 1963; in *Il coraggio delle donne* 1983; in *Lavinia fuggita* 1996. This shows the importance of Lavinia fuggita.

6. According to the revisionist view of the Oedipal complex advanced by the French psychoanalyst Jacques Lacan, the child enters the domain, i.e., the social institution of language, by acknowledging the power of prohibition inherent in the paternal role. In Lacan's notion of symbolic order, paternal

law consists in particular in the power to establish relationships through speech. A detailed analysis of the Oedipal aspects of *Artemisia* lies beyond the scope of the present essay, but for an analysis of the implications of the Oedipal and castration complexes in Artemisia Gentileschi's actual painting, *Judith Beheading Holofernes*, see Mary Jacobus, 1986, 110–36.

7. Two relevant sources for an understanding of Banti's position of writer of fictional history "as gambler" are her essays on Manzoni (1951b, 1954b, 1956) and her last novel, *Un grido lacerante* (1981). It is interesting to notice, however, that Banti does not discuss her theoretical reasons for this "bet with history" in any organic body of criticism. On the one hand, Banti's fiction demonstrates a desire to give "lost voices" the opportunity to be heard; yet on the other, she appears to offer only fragmented expressions of the theory that lies behind this desire. To explore why this is so, a detailed analysis of Banti's nonfictional corpus—with special attention to articles in *Paragone*—would have to be undertaken.

References

Banti, Anna. 1937. *Itinerario di Paolina*. Rome: Augustea.

———. 1939. Documenti. *Oggi*, 3 June: 6.

———. 1951a. *Le donne muoiono*. Milan: Mondadori.

———. 1951b. Romanzo e romanzo storico. *Paragone* 20: 3–7.

———. 1952. Lavinia fuggita. In *Le donne muoiono*. Milan: Mondadori. 85–119.

———. 1954a. *Allarme sul lago*. Milan: Mondadori, 1954.

———. 1954b. Ermengarda e Geltrude. *Paragone* 52: 23–30.

———. 1955. Dario Cecchi. *Paragone* 68: 78–79.

———. 1956. Manzoni e noi. *Paragone* 78: 24–36.

———. 1961. Europa 1606. In *Opinioni*. Milan: Il Saggiatore. 13–23.

———. 1963. *Campi Elisi*. Milan: Mondadori.

———. [1947] 1965. *Artemisia*. Milan: Mondadori.

———. 1967. *Noi credevamo*. Milan: Mondadori.

———. 1971a. Joveta di Betania. In *Je vous écris d'un pays lointain*. Milan: Mondadori. 89–125.

———. 1971b. Tutto si è guastato. Interview by Grazia Livi. *Corriere della sera*, 15 April.

———. 1973. *La camicia bruciata*. Milan: Mondadori.

———. 1981. *Un grido lacerante*. Milan: Rizzoli.

———. 1983a. Amiche remote. *Paragone* 396: 92–97.

———. 1983b. *Il coraggio delle donne*. Milan: La Tartaruga.

———. 1996. *Lavinia fuggita*. Milan: La Tartaruga.

Bermann, Sandra. 1984. Introduction to *On the historical novel*, by Alessandro Manzoni (18) translated by Hannah Mitchell and Stanley Mitchell, 1–59. Lincoln: University of Nebraska Press.

Bloom, Harold. 1973. *The anxiety of influence: A theory of poetry*. New York: Oxford University Press.

Diotima. 1992. *Il cielo stellato dentro di noi: L'ordine simbolico della madre.* Milan: La Tartaruga.

Gilbert, Sandra M., and Susan Gubar. 1979. *The madwoman in the attic: The woman writer and the nineteenth-century literary imagination.* New Haven and London: Yale University Press.

Jacobus, Mary. 1986. Judith, Holofernes, and the phallic woman. In *Reading woman: Essays in feminist criticism.* London: Methuen. 110–36.

Lacan, Jacques. 1977. *Ecrits: A selection.* Translated by Alan Sheridan. New York: Norton.

Livi, Grazia. 1989. Maestra e allieva. *Racconti.* Milan: La Tartaruga. 17–25.

Manzoni, Alessandro. [1827 and 1840] 1965. *I promessi sposi.* Edited by Pietro Nardi. Milan: Mondadori.

Pasolini, Pier Paolo. 1973. Il cammino di Anna Banti dalla semplice stima ai primi posti. *Tempo* 6 May.

Woolf, Virginia. 1957. *A room of one's own.* New York: Harcourt, Brace & World, Inc.

Rinascimento privato: A Historiographic Carnival

GERDA REEB

MARIA BELLONCI'S NOVEL *RINASCIMENTO PRIVATO* (1985) IS A NOVEL of "self-knowledge" [autoconoscenza] of a possible maturation of the female self from within the margins of a masculine socio-symbolic order. This growth is accomplished both by Bellonci's female authorship, which calls into existence a plausible version of the past, and by her self-aware historical heroine's symbolical appropriation of her own place in history when she engages in her carnivalesque derision of that place. The subversive strategy endemic in the carnival, I suggest, is a crucial tool of a feminine appropriation of both history and the genre of the historical novel.

While the novel respects the succession of historiographically documented events, the narrative voice recounts the very personal history of Isabella d'Este as it merges with or diverges from the "official" version. Throughout this (sub)version of her self-authorized history, Isabella d'Este emerges as a protagonist constantly divided between a theatrical, fictional self employed for public purposes and an inner self aware of and resistant to this carnivalesque public performance. She thus subverts and mocks the sociohistoric role assigned to her. In this analysis, I will discuss the way in which Isabella d'Este's carnivalesque derision of her role as a historical heroine within a male canon is achieved and the positive and negative implications such an act of subversion entails.

In her essay "Displacement and the Discourse of Woman," Gayatri Chakravorty Spivak argues that in literature and philosophy, "unobtrusively but crucially, a certain metaphor of woman has produced a discourse that we are obliged 'historically' to call the discourse of man. Given the accepted charge of the notions of production and constitution, one might reformulate this: the discourse of man is the metaphor of

102

woman" (1983, 167). Hence, Spivak indicates we are faced with a female persona displaced in the male discourse, lacking an identity of her own and having the ability to dissimulate as the only way to define self. Thus she must fake a nonexistent identity to fill in for a genealogical and existential lack.

With the same definition of woman as displaced, misrepresented and lacking, Judith Butler in *Gender Trouble* (1990) elaborates on the concept of womanliness as masquerade, as performative production geared at subverting the female misrepresentation within a male-dominated discourse. Butler refers to Joan Riviere's 1929 essay "Womanliness as Masquerade" in which Riviere argues that femininity is a form of masquerade taken on by a woman who actually wishes for masculinity and the privileges associated with it, but "fears the retributive consequences of taking the public appearance of masculinity" (1929, 53). The mask donned by the women wishing for masculinity (or the Phallus) consists in the apparent effort to renounce the "having" (or owning) of the phallus. They act thus to avert retribution and to protect themselves against being punished for such inappropriate desires to occupy the position and the space of traditional male dominion. According to Riviere, women would mantle their attempts at occupying the male space with femininity in order not to threaten overtly the male subject-position. This denial of the masculine by feigning femininity is, in Riviere's view, a dissimulation of a fundamental, but illicit masculinity.

Lacan, according to Butler, argues that while the masculine subject has the phallus, it requires the other to confirm it, and by this validation and confirmation to be the "Phallus in an 'extended' sense" (1990, 44). Hence, "the symbolic order creates cultural intelligibility through the mutually exclusive positions of 'having' the Phallus (the position of men) and 'being' the Phallus (the paradoxical position of women)" (44). Women, in Lacan's economy, come to actually "be" the Phallus because they signify it, they embody it, they confirm its identity, and they provide the so-called "reality" on which the masculine subject can engender its subject-position. However, it is an imaginary reality, for women are presupposed to be the lack that conceals itself in a pretense of being a subject-position existing vicariously through their projection of the Phallus. According to Lacan, woman appears to be the Phallus through masquerade, a façade that woman constructs to cloak the fundamental lack of the Phallus as the transcendental signifier, the absence of which she nostalgically deplores and decries.[1]

From such positions as Riviere's and Lacan's, Judith Butler infers that "masquerade may be understood as the performative production of a sexual ontology, an appearing that makes itself convincing as a 'being'; on the other hand, masquerade can be read as a denial of a feminine desire that presupposes some prior ontological femininity regularly unrepresented by the phallic economy" (1990, 47). Either way, womanliness is dissimulation of either lack of masculinity or the presence of a potential feminine libido that is unacceptable in a phallic economy. As Luce Irigaray puts it, "masquerade . . . is what women do . . . in order to participate in man's desire, but at the cost of giving up their own" (Butler, 1990).

The subject positions for women thus have to be seized in the existing symbolic order by means of subversion of identity, dissimulation of one's self, and one's desires and intentions. Along these lines, Maria Bellonci's representation of the (female) heroine of a male-dominated and male-populated historiography subverts and appropriates a male domain through female agency. Bellonci lets her fictional persona, enacted and authorized by a woman, speak for herself to fabricate a view of history internal to but subversive of the male version.

Isabella d'Este's functioning within the novel is accompanied by a whole range of dissimulations that conceal her inner life. As a Renaissance persona carrying an ethical and political burden, she has to embody a role predetermined for her from birth. Due to her rank and her lineage, virtually no freedom of will and decision are granted to her. She has internalized the rules of public conduct and appearance, but she frequently appears to be a divided person watching herself perform a certain role: "I observe myself: I am proceeding along two parallel lines, one quite alert and controlled, the other all fire and distraught grief, bursting from the depths of my soul" (Bellonci 1989, 22) [mi osservavo: procedevo su due linee parallele, una attentissima e vigilata, l'altra focosa (1995, 33)]. Isabella d'Este is defined by the tensions that mark the struggle between her visible persona and her inner self: "I seem divided in two. One speaks and acts; the other coldly watches and judges everything, myself included" (1989, 88).[2] This condition is exacerbated by her searching of the mirror for self-confirmation and self-scrutiny: "and at the same time in the double mirrors I studied the effect, carefully flattering myself"

(1989, 166) [con un doppio effetto de specchi mi osservavo nell'uno e nell'altro, attentamente vagheggiandomi (1995, 205)]. "The mirror reflected my image. . . . My God, was I really begging for the mirror's approval?" (1989, 89).[3] The mirror is the (non) space that she can safely and exclusively inhabit, a condition that accentuates her fragmentary sense of self.

Isabella possesses a wide range of roles and costumes to better enact the theatrical persona that she chooses to impersonate. Her attire is extremely important since it reflects her moods and dispositions and is thus the most tangible tool for veiling and unveiling her inner self in a carefully tailored public display: "The awareness of dress is a habit of mine, and I do not believe it can be called vanity, at least not entirely. It is a science of appearing in harmony with the beauty of nature and the order of thought. And it may be that I express too much, or not enough" (1989, 35).[4] Her clothes are strategically donned to impress, stupefy, silence, amaze, impose, or pose. Isabella is always reinventing herself by changing her style, but always within the range of a breathtaking femininity. The minute textual examples of her wardrobe are echoed in the manneristic decor of her house; both serve as background props in front of which she can stage herself.

Isabella's movements are also studied and always geared to deceive the audience watching her. They are never spontaneous: "I had to be careful; sudden impulses are forbidden to us, surrounded as we are by people who can expose us to any suspicion" (1989, 42) [i moti subitanei non sono consentiti a noi circondati da gente che ci puó esporre ad ogni sospetto (1995, 55)]. She is aware of the vigilant eyes that monitor and penetrate her privacy and scrutinize every motion or gesture, and she grants them the voyeuristic spectacle they long for. Isabella knows that femininity is what she is supposed to represent, and she does it to an extreme, parodying with her hyperbolized feminine behavior the very tradition that requires her to play the part that she is playing. She manipulates and defeats a series of strategists, popes, husbands, and sons, by employing against them the very tools that were bestowed upon women to silence and handicap them in their struggle for public power and acknowledgment.

Her masquerade is, as previously defined by Joan Riviere, a protection against a potential retribution from the male whose power and judgment she contests. But at the same time, her strategy ridicules the powers that intend to keep her confined to a predetermined gender role. Riviere's concept of masquerade as defense lacks this dimension of masquerade as subtle offense and subversion. By feigning ostentatious femininity, Isabella manipulates events in her favor and practically disarms the ones who try to oppress her. Isabella uses masquerade techniques to achieve power and dominance in an environment hostile to the female ascent to power.

However, while her masquerade might subvert, boycott, and ridicule, it is not entirely liberating since it insufficiently questions or opposes the forces that induced it. Isabella does not seek to comprehend the causes of her need to dissimulate and, therefore, finds no generally viable solution to fight them. Through the effects of her masquerade, however, she demonstrates that man himself falls victim to his own fantasy of woman. Isabella thus emerges as a heroine who manages to highlight the vicissitudes of male dominance and misogyny ultimately detrimental to both sexes.

Isabella knows that in the system in which she lives, only a few exceptional individuals are able to successfully live an inner life[5] and at the same time wear a public mantle consciously employed to conceal it. Bellonci's heroine liberates her own private space by creating both a mental hideout in her masquerade and a physical one, spatial analogues to the divided self: the privacy of the *grotta* (cave) and the *stanza degli orologi*, (room of the clocks) her *studiolo*, (little study) secluded "loci amoeni" in which she can unfold and reflect upon herself apart from the gaze of others.

Isabella however, does not grant this potential of self-knowledge and self-scrutinizing strength that mocks any imposition to all women: "when I bore girls, I was disappointed, not because I loved them less, . . . but because I was afraid and almost repelled when I considered the great suffering that lay in store for them unless they managed to rank among the leading women of the world. Those fragile creatures put my own privileges in doubt; I felt threatened by their future state and the unhappiness of submission that would befall them, as it did all other women" (1989, 99).[6] Isabella, I suggest, is aware of how difficult it is to retain consciousness of one's masquerade, that is, to wear the mask and to comprehend it, too. In other words, there is a high risk of contamination from the mask one has to don in order to successfully perform in Isabella's society, and one might easily end up losing awareness of the mask itself.

Masquerade thus guarantees and preserves Isabella's inner self and dignity but cannot be advocated as a solution for women in general, since it takes critical and analytical awareness to preserve this acute sense of a fragmented self without despairing or being contaminated by the mask adopted. Although her disguise renders Isabella—and only Isabella—in a limited sense autonomous, it can hardly serve as a militant device for women's liberation; but then, such symbolism would have overburdened her role as a historical figure of the Renaissance with a claim to authenticity.

In Lacanian terms, Isabella's impersonation of the eternal feminine against the backdrop of the masculine, where the male discourse engenders itself can be interpreted as her becoming the Phallus in a symbolic sense. Thus the mask represents both the Phallus itself and the internalization of the discourse it gives rise to. Lacan believes that masquerade is an effect of the melancholy essential to the feminine position as such, marked by a loss or lack. In the last chapter of the novel, entitled "Rather Than Die of Melancholy" [per non morire di malinconia], Bellonci's Isabella does not succumb to melancholy, but counters it with a sense of self, unfinished and unstable, caught in a process of self-definition not paralyzed by a sense of lack: "I am driven to seek out the reasons that have made me the way I am, between one occasion and the next in the course of my days. Time flows by, and it is worth thinking. I have discovered that my woman's condition is not absolutely predominant; it does not prevent me from becoming a complete person, provided I am not deceived by myself" (1989, 450).[7]

Isabella does not manage to fully comprehend the mechanisms or the dialectics by which she has become the masked subject that she is. She is aware, however, of herself as a process of becoming, a site of ambiguity, marked by the perpetual masquerade enacted.

The concluding letter of Robert de la Pole—her admirer and historiographer—stands for the intrusive and judgmental male discourse that takes advantage of the female body to vicariously glorify the male self. De la Pole and his male tradition of historiography is indebted to figures like Isabella's that they exploited. The male implicitly established in a role of dominance and control has to master the female body to ensure its own existence and validity.

De la Pole has adored Isabella since her childhood; he writes her innumerable letters, interpreting her lack of response as silent consent to his advances and obsessive worship. He bombards her with advice and compliments and constructs a myth around her for which he had no realistic basis since he saw her only once when she was a child. Isabella was and is a figment of his fantasy, and it is this simulacrum that he addresses in his letters. Although she never responds to these letters or confirms his ongoing speculations about her inner life, he feels entitled to judge her, patronize her, and voice his apparent comprehension of her female nature: "having discovered in you one of the very rare creatures that live in a freedom invented day by day, according to the lights and shadows of your own truth" (1989, 459).[8] Isabella is, indeed, reinventing herself repeatedly, but Robert de la Pole obtrusively reinvents his version of her as well. While Isabella is comfortable with her sense of an unfinished and always varying self, de la Pole is relentlessly trying to find her final essence, upon which he can rely and rule as a historiographer.

Linda Hutcheon's remark that "Those in power control history" (1988, 196) seems to describe adequately de la Pole's gesture of seizing control over Isabella's historical persona and her representation in historiography. His epistolary account of Isabella evokes the annals of official history (and his-story— as both ideologic and patriarchal discourses of hegemony) that portrayed women, if at all, in a rather speculative and superficial manner.

Along these lines, Maria Bellonci's attempt at rewriting history from a female perspective goes against the grain of a male tradition that did not leave space for a female voice, but rather proliferated a distorted image of woman. Bellonci's female protagonist both resists and mockingly subverts this tradition by entering precisely into the unseizable blindspots that the oppressive discourse leaves open. Her persona can never be seized because she perpetually fluctuates and cannot be pinned down. She takes her ability to alter and masquerade to an extreme, leaving the male scrutinizer frustrated and aghast. Isabella's performative personae and implicit carnivalesque derision of the oppressive force and discourse of his-story contests and denounces such a concept as male-fabricated fantasy and renders it obsolete.

We face in *Rinascimento privato* an example not only of an attempt to remold a unilateral and monolithic account of history, but also a case study of a maturation of the female self from within the margins of a masculine sociosymbolic order. *Rinascimento privato,* as a novel of *autoconoscenza,* does not offer an explicit unraveling, but rather a process of awakening and self-discovery—even though the self must first be intuited under the armors of masquerade. The understanding of the contingencies of her subject-position is a crucial step toward the heroine's strategic contesting of male authority and territory.

Notes

1. Cf.: "How does a women 'appear' to be the Phallus? According to Lacan, this is done by masquerade, the effect of a melancholy that is essential to the female position as such" (Butler 1990, 46).
2. "mi divido in due: una parla e agisce, l'altra freddamente guarda e giudica tutto, me compresa" (Bellonci 1995, 111).
3. Lo specchio rifletteva la mia immagine. . . . Dio mio, davvero mendicavo il consenso dello specchio? (1995, 112).
4. Questa coscienza del vestire è una mia abitudine e non credo che si possa definire vanità, almeno non per intero. È una scienza dell'apparire in sintonia con la bellezza della natura e con l'ordine del pensiero. E può darsi che io dica troppo o che non dica abbastanza (1995, 47).
5. Esisteva in me qualche cosa che nessuno avrebbe mai conosciuto . . . uno spazio mio segretissimo a tutti i miei . . . (1995, 108).
6. ero delusa quando mi nascevano femmine: non perché le amassi poco, . . . ma perché avevo paura e quasi ribrezzo del gran patire che le aspettava a meno che non riuscissero a contare tra le prime donne del mondo. Quelle creature fragili mettevano in dubbio i miei privilegi: mi sentivo minacciata dalla loro condizione futura (1995, 126).
7. Sono sospinta alla ricerca delle ragioni che mi hanno resa come sono tra un'occasione e l'altra delle mie giornate. Scorre il tempo e vale pensare. Ho scoperto che la mia condizione di donna non è predominante in assoluto e non me impedisce di diventare un essere compiuto, purchè io non sia ingannata da me stessa (1995, 543).
8. avendo scoperto in voi una delle rarissime creature che vivono una libertà inventata giorno per giorno, secondo i chiari e scuri delle proprie verità (1995, 555).

References

Bellonci, Maria. [1985] 1995. *Rinascimento privato.* Milan: Arnoldo Mondadori.

Bellonci, Maria. 1995. *Private Renaissance.* Translated by William Weaver. New York: Morrow.

Butler, Judith. 1990. *Gender trouble.* New York: Routledge.

Hutcheon, Linda. 1988. *A poetics of postmodernism.* New York: Routledge.

Irigary, Luce. 1977. *Ce sexe qui n'en est pas un.* Paris: Minuit.

Lacan, Jacques. 1985. The meaning of the Phallus. In *Feminine sexuality: Jacques Lacan and the ecole freudienne,* edited by Juliet Mitchell and Jacqueline Rose and translated by Jacqueline Rose. New York: Norton.

Riviere, Joan. Women's Lives as Masquerade. In Butler, Judith. *Gender Trouble.* 1990. New York: Routledge.

Spivak, Gayatri Chakravorty. 1983. Displacement and the discourse of women. *Displacement: Derrida and after,* edited by Mark Krupnick. Bloomington: Indiana University Press.

"Ma cos'è questa verità storica? . . . Una favola convenzionale": Francesca Sanvitale's *Il figlio dell'impero*

DAVIDA GAVIOLI

IN AN INTERVIEW (PETRIGNANI 1993) GIVEN SHORTLY AFTER THE PUB-
lication of *Il figlio dell'impero* (1993), Francesca Sanvitale
explains the genesis of her latest text, a "romanzo storico"
which is ostensibly new and different in the context of her
literary production but is instead coherent and in synchrony
with it:[1]

> With this *Figlio dell'impero* I went through different stages. First I
> thought about writing a psychological novel; then I considered a
> biography that reads like a novel, . . then moved on to the tradi-
> tional historical novel. You cannot write the story of that boy with-
> out narrating the period, the fall of a certain Europe, and the reflux
> of the Napoleonic ebb. But, at a certain point in my research, it
> could not be even a historical novel, that is, fictionalized history.
> I knew too much about those real life characters to be able to
> allow myself to betray the supposed truth. I felt that those worlds
> that no longer exist had to be thoroughly respected.[2]

The result of four years of painstaking archival research is
thus a new kind of narrative form, variously defined by critics
as "historical reconstruction in fictional terms," [ricostruzione
storica in chiave narrativa (Grande 1994, 142)], "report-novel"
[relazione-romanzo (146)], and "biography of the king of
Rome" [biografia del re di Roma (Mazza 1994, 125)]. Sanvitale
defies these definitions and questions the possibility of a viable
encoding and interpretation of the historical past within the
boundaries of a traditionally conceived generic form.

Il figlio dell'impero thematizes, on the one hand, the author's
concern with a historical figure who, reduced to a footnote in
history books, was born as Napoleon II, king of Rome. Later
demoted to duke of Reichstadt, he was a romantic figure whose

111

life was ruled by the good of the State, which reduced him to
an icon, "pure nothing" [puro nulla (Sanvitale 1993, 538); all
subsequent page references will be given in parenthesis in the
text]. He was first a creation of his father and then a creation
of the Hapsburgs and, as Maria Antonietta Cruciata pointed
out, "The history of the son of the Napoleonic empire thus
becomes the metaphor for a human condition violently eradi-
cated and destined to succumb in a constant succession of
memories of grief."[3] On the other hand, the text is also a sample of Sanvitale's profound self-consciousness about history,
which she sees not as an objective recording of the past but as
a reconstruction and conscious reordering of past events into
a narrative. This narrative does not question the veracity of
events but "reminds us that, while events did occur in the
real empirical past, we name and constitute those events as
historical facts by selection and narrative positioning. And,
even more basically, we only know of those past events through
their discursive inscription, through their traces in the present" (Hutcheon 1988, 97).

In the choice of its main focus, Sanvitale's text seems to
distance itself from the renewed interest in historical writing
expressed by Italian women writers in the eighties. As Carol
Lazzaro-Weis (1993) pointed out, these authors "have returned
to the historical novel to portray women's private histories
and protest their exclusion from official History" (120). Works
like Dacia Maraini's *La lunga vita di Marianna Ucrìa*, Maria
Rosa Cutrufelli's *La briganta*, or Marta Morazzoni's *La ragazza
con il turbante* reinscribe women in history as subjects, as active agents, filling in the gaps and voids that characterize patriarchal historical discourse. And "despite differences among
these works, the re-creation of historical fact parallels the creation of a female authorial viewpoint that experiences history
in both personal and general terms" (Lazzaro-Weis 1993, 143).[4]
I believe that, in her narration of the story of the son of Napoleon Bonaparte and Maria Luigia of Austria, Napoleone
Francesco Carlo Giuseppe Bonaparte, *l'aiglon*, Sanvitale employs the strategies that these writers developed to "analyze
the innovations and permutations caused by the ongoing feminist cultural revolution" (Lazzardo-Weis 1993, 150). She employs these strategies not to "add" women to history but to
more radically criticize the notion of an objective historical
discourse. She also wishes to inscribe within it a voice that
had been erased, marginalized, and silenced for the "good of

the State," which saw in *l'aiglon* a potentially disruptive force of the reestablished status quo after the congress of Vienna in 1815.

The text is thus the story of the betrayal and erasure from history of a child who had been revered as a "dono celeste" [gift from heaven (28)], as the omnipotent embodiment of the continuity of the Napoleonic empire, "The anointed one sent by the gods . . the human prolonging of the arm of his father, the flower born of his sword" [l'eletto, mandato dagli dei . . . il prolungamento umano del braccio del padre, il fiore nato dalla sua spada (25)]. It is also the story of the existential drama of a child who loses everything when he turns three: his country, a father he will never see again, a mother who will move to Parma to a new life and a new family, his native tongue, and all the points of reference that had anchored his identity to the reality that he knew. Uprooted, forcibly inserted into a world that requires radical changes—from his education, to the food he eats, to the people with whom he will have to share his space, to the very language he speaks—"he was continuously subjected to contradictions, loneliness, and fears. His certainty of affections crumbled without warning, and through a series of sudden changes . . . having Bonaparte's blood was the burden he should have forgotten and helped others forget for his own good" (211).[5]

Il figlio dell'impero then is also the story of a metamorphosis, since the young Bonaparte has to reinvent himself, become a "piccolo duca austriaco" [a young Austrian duke (298)] with a new name (Franz, like his maternal grandfather), a new behavioral code, a new way of relating to those around him and to life itself. Since he is Napoleon's son, he experiences "the devastation of an annihilation, an irretrievable loss of self . . [he becomes] an utterly useless man who could serve no purpose for the state . . because what he represented was too big" (Cruciata 1995, 151).[6] As Franz himself says in the closing pages of the book, "My birth and my death: here is my life story" [La mia nascita e la mia morte: ecco tutta la mia storia (614)]. Sanvitale thus takes us on a journey to unearth the details of the life that unfolded between those two dates and to which history has denied all importance and recognition, since "according to the good of the State what had taken place between these two dates was not relevant and therefore of no importance. What interest could a life have if it did not fit into a political design?" [secondo la ragione di Stato ciò che era intervenuto tra queste due date risultava inutilizzabile e quindi senza importanza: che interesse aveva una vita che non rientrava in un disegno politico? (614)].[7]

In its effort to reinscribe into history one of its forgotten figures, a formerly excluded "ex-centric" (Hutcheon 1988, 95) silenced by the forces of official history, *Il figlio dell'impero* becomes also a self-conscious reflection on the act of historical writing. It also problematizes the issues of representation and "objective" historical truth traditionally identified as constitutive of the genre. The examination of this silencing highlights the ideological subtexts and power frameworks that influence our knowledge of past events:

> those who are seized by the desire, which cannot be fulfilled from the outset, to recover History—people, places, even feelings—contend with one another in a vast contradiction, in a constant manner that obsessively insinuates the refusal to deal with the past except as a capricious fantasy, and end up by re-creating the nothingness out of which they seem to appear. The past is this nothingness, and yet the truth lies only in the facts that took place and then vanished.[8] (5)

From the very opening section of the narrative, Sanvitale's text presents us with an overt narrator who does not claim for herself the omniscience, impersonality, and objectivity of canonic historical discourse, but emphasizes the "constructed nature of . . historical configuration" (Della Colletta 1994, 100). Thus the text concerns itself with the story of its own writing and of its relationship with "la Storia," stressing the subjective nature of the narrator's reconstruction of the past. In a way, the narrative becomes a vehicle for a metahistorical reflection upon the fictionality of historiography and the constructed nature of historical representations. It questions the supposed objectivity of historical and partially historical reconstructions, while explicitly pointing to their susceptibility to subjective interpretations and problematizing the entire question of historical knowledge.

As Sanvitale again points out, "*Il figlio dell'impero* is a novel that denies itself when it strays into similar or different genres. It is true: the formula for this book does not exist" [*Il figlio dell'impero* è un romanzo che nega se stesso nel momento in cui sconfina in generi affini o dissimili. E' vero, la formula di questo libro non c'è (Cruciata 1995, 148)]. The narrator weaves a careful web of letters, diary entries, official documents, and anecdotes to subtly undermine the traditional notion of an objective official history based on undisputable facts. She thus enters the current debate on the relationship of fiction and history, which are no longer seen as mutually exclusive systems but rather as dynamically and dialogically intertwined in the process of apprehending and encoding reality and the past; the rethinking of this relationship renders problematical the categories of referentiality, representation, and "objective truth" that previously constituted the foundations of historical fiction. Sanvitale stresses the process of subjective filtering, selection, and construction that organizes the plotting of historical events. She emphasizes that

> it is impossible to reconstruct the past in the conviction that one is narrating history in its objective wholeness. . . . In a way, my latest book is the product of a crisis of the historical novel. I found myself facing a genre in a state of crisis, because the idea of history was in a state of crisis. There were no more certainties because facts could no longer be believed. (149)[9]

This self-awareness is mirrored in the narrative structure, which is "innovative" since it refuses to hide the "unreliability" of the documents that the narrator analyzes. The text makes continuous references to the impossibility of finding "the truth" in contrasting accounts of the same event. For example, the account of the arrival of the conquering armies in Paris in 1814 is followed by an immediate disclaimer:

> When writing about a historical fact of this importance, it would be exciting to be able to reconstruct a detailed scene, with meaningful gestures and faces, sentences, arguments, cries and expressions of happiness, or uncertain and hidden gestures of pain—to at least cultivate the vain certainty that "something similar, with several accurate details" really happened, but the accounts we have are contradictory. (Sanvitale 1993, 68–69)[10]

Or again, "no piece is ever perfectly aligned" [mai nessun tassello combacia perfettamente (71)]. The divergences that are pointed out among the documented sources also point to their status as subjective interpretations of the events recorded, and thus cannot claim a "higher" truth status. It is the narrator's task to choose one version of the events over another, even without proof ("senza documenti di prova," 585). This process does not deny the "reality" of past events but "focuses attention on the act of imposing order on the past, of encoding strategies of meaning-making through representation" (Hutcheon 1989, 67). As Sanvitale observes:

> The first scene of this canvas, painted again so many times by history, by historians, and by biographers, was immediately erased with new subjects and new backgrounds and plots; betrayals and cowardly actions were mixed with instances of honesty and heroism. It is impossible to recover the original version, the threads that linked such intricate facts, to choose certain hypothesis instead of others. (59)[11]

The awareness of the unavoidable selectivity that limits our perspectives on the past is yet another element weaved throughout the narrative to undermine the assumption of official history's claim to objectivity.[12] The reader's attention is drawn to the act of reconstructing the past and to how these reconfigurations of the past depend on the subjective views and historical positions of those who "put the pieces of the puzzle back together":

> In what puzzle would we ever be able to render coherent or to place in preassigned slots the pieces of a human life or of grand epic deeds, or a series of causes and events that have changed the history of the world and have vanished? Of which map would we be able to draw the boundaries and the interlacings in the conviction that we will establish an order that is as valid as the old obliterated reality? A crazy arrogance guides the hand confident in its choice of the pieces or in the stroke of the pencil, and there seems to be a shifty mirroring, at a distance, of global events in the individuals, and in their suffering erased in an instant. (471)[13]

The closing part of this quotation questions and denounces the omissions and silences that have been part of ordinary historical chronicles: historiography's selectivity is political, as it traditionally relates only the stories of those who have achieved some measure of political success and have thus inscribed their names in the records; those who have suffered, rather than made history, are erased from our historical memory. Sanvitale acknowledges the need to denounce the biases of official versions of history that have been exclusively geared to uphold and maintain the existing power structures and the worldviews to which they subscribe. So, whose truth gets told? How can any historical account be checked against past empirical reality to test its validity if, as Hayden White (1978b) states, "facts are not given but are constructed by the kind of questions we ask of events" (43)? Perhaps the answer lies in Napoleon's words to LasCases, which frame the novel and recur at different times in the text as a reminder of the "polyinterpretability of historical records" (Wesseling 1991, 74). These words foreground the intimate connection between versions of history and the legitimation of political power:

> [T]he *real truths* are unlikely found in official history. Luckily, most times they do not possess actual import; they only amount to curiosities. There are so many truths! .. The historical truth that is so often called upon, to which everybody makes an appeal, is often only an empty word; it is impossible to know historical truth when events happen, when passions are still burning; and if the disagreement later ceases, this happens only because the debates no longer exist. Then, what is this historical truth that is so praised? A conventional fairy tale. . . . (71)[14]

Il figlio dell'impero thus questions the accessibility of the historical referent; the past as it really was remains elusive, an absence, since "the privileging of a certain textual tradition enforces a specific version of (historical) reality at the expense of rival versions. Those who do not benefit from the canonized tradition, therefore, have to subvert its monopoly on the construction of (historical) reality by wrenching radically new meanings from the privileged texts" (Wesseling 1991, 194) and by engaging in a self-conscious analysis of their own construction.

In her effort to reinscribe into history a figure that has been refused a place in official History, Sanvitale has exposed the ways in which "versions of history are used as instruments of power" (Wesseling 1991, 193). She has explored official records from the new perspective provided by new texts such as diaries and unpublished correspondence as well as by intertextual references to other novels, paintings, and even musical pieces. These sources have represented an era and have thus questioned the objective and "higher" truth status of the historical events recorded, more radically criticizing the notion of an objective history. As Sanvitale herself said, "Even the historical novel has evolved; one cannot write it from a partisan point of view anymore. When writing today, one cannot trust the facts, but only the very vitality of the narrative," [Anche il romanzo storico si è evoluto, non si può più scriverlo all'in-

terno di un punto di vista partigiano delle cose. L'unica fiducia
che oggi ci si può concedere scrivendo non è nei fatti, ma nella
vitalità stessa della narrazione (Petrignani 1993, 124)].

Notes

Unless otherwise noted, all translations from Italian are my own.
1. In her analysis of the novels and short stories Sanvitale published
before *Il figlio dell'impero*, Maria Teresa Giuffrè (1994) points out the elements that characterize Sanvitale's literary production and that, I believe,
are an intrinsic part of her latest novel as well: "Romanzi e racconti della
Sanvitale non seguono regole tradizionali di struttura. Il tempo all'interno
della narrazione è rotto e instabile, va indietro e avanti, ritorna su se stesso,
si aggroviglia; la storia non è mai in primo piano come in un romanzo
d'azione, trapela attraverso le maglie più o meno fitte di un discorso altro,
pacato e stringente. Lei conduce il discorso, trovando posto all'interno
dell'opera, quale componente non meno essenziale dei personaggi, accanto
a loro gomito a gomito, alla ricerca di un equilibrio delicato per una convi-
venza difficile" (46) [Sanvitale's novels and short stories do not follow traditional structural rules. Within the narrative, the temporal sequence is
broken and unstable, it moves as in an action novel, it seeps through the
more or less closely woven meshes of a different, forceful discourse. The
author directs the discourse, and she finds a place for herself within her
work as an element that is as essential as the characters, side by side with
them, in search of a delicate balance for a difficult cohabitation].
2. Con questo *Figlio dell'impero* ho attraversato varie fasi. Dopo l'idea
del romanzo psicologico, c'è stata quella della biografia che si legge come
un romanzo, . . . poi sono passata all'idea di scrivere un romanzo storico
vero e proprio. Non si può raccontare la storia di quel ragazzo senza narrare
anche l'epoca, il crollo di una certa Europa, il riflusso della marea napoleo-
nica. Purtroppo, a un certo punto delle mie ricerche, non poteva essere più
nemmeno un romanzo storico, ovvero storia romanzata. Sapevo troppo ormai di quei personaggi realmente vissuti per potermi permettere di tradire
la presupposta verità. Ho sentito che quei mondi che non esistono più anda-
vano rispettati fino in fondo (Petrignani 1993, 123).
3. La storia del figlio dell'Impero napoleonico diviene così la metafora
di una condizione umana violentemente sradicata e destinata a soccombere
in un susseguirsi incessante di memorie del dolore (Cruciata 1995, 147).
4. While rewriting women into history and, in a way, producing a new
knowledge about women, these texts also join the works of feminist historians in a critique of history "that characterized it not simply as an incomplete
record of the past but as a participant in the production of knowledge that
legitimized the exclusion or subordination of women. . . . Feminist history
then becomes not the recounting of great deeds performed by women but
the exposure of the often silent and hidden operations of gender that are
nonetheless present and defining forces in the organization of most societies"
(Wallach Scott 1988, 26–27).
5. veniva sottoposto di continuo a contraddizioni, solitudine e paure, si
smantellava senza preavviso e a colpi di scena la certezza degli affetti. . . .

Aveva sangue dei Bonaparte, la tara che bisognava dimenticare e far dimenticare per il suo bene (211).

6. la sconvolgente esperienza di un annientamento, di un azzeramento senza ritorno . . . un uomo del tutto inutile e inutilizzabile dal punto di vista ufficiale e istituzionale . . . perché ciò che egli rappresentava (per il suo passato) era troppo grande (Cruciata 1995, 151).

7. Sanvitale's statement that "Power does not recognize and does not have any other culture than its own: it grows on what has been decided or has to be decided" [Il potere non conosce e non ha altra cultura che se stesso: si nutre di ciò che è stabilito o da stabilire (78)] is an underlying commentary on the erasure of this character from history as anything but a silent instrument of political propaganda. In an interview, the author further explains that "the purpose of those who hold power is always to confirm their power. This is the first survival law of the same power. This is the reason why all actions converge to an ultimate purpose that has to do with power. This is the reason why any action, whether good or bad, has the purpose not just to keep but to reenforce power. No man in power uses power for others, if not for himself . . . (he) will never suggest acts or laws that could in any way reduce or damage his power. Power can't show itself to be fragile, weak or undecided" [Il fine di chi ha il potere è sempre quello di confermare il potere. Questa è la prima legge di sopravvivenza del potere stesso. Ecco perché tutte le azioni convergono ad un fine ultimo che riguarda sempre il potere. Ecco perché qualsiasi azione, buona o giusta che sia, ha la funzione non solo di conservare, ma anche di radicare il potere. Nessun uomo di potere usa il potere per gli altri, se non per se stesso. . . . Non verranno mai suggeriti atti o leggi che in qualche modo possano danneggiarlo o semplicemente ridurlo. Il potere non può mostrarsi fragile, debole o insicuro (Cruciata 1995, 152)].

8. per chi è preso dal desiderio, già in partenza incolmabile, di ritrovare Storia, personaggi, luoghi, persino sentimenti, essi vengono a misurarsi uno con l'altro in una capillare contraddizione, un basso continuo che insinua ossessivamente il rifiuto a occuparsi del passato se non in forma di libera fantasia, e finisce per far riemergere il nulla dal quale essi sembrano venire. E' il passato il nulla, eppure la verità è solo nei fatti accaduti e svaniti" (Sanvitale 1993, 5).

9. "ricostruire il passato con la convinzione di narrare la storia nella sua obiettiva integrità è impossibile. . . . In un certo senso questo mio ultimo libro è il prodotto di una crisi del romanzo storico. Mi sono trovata dinanzi ad un genere in crisi, per la semplice ragione che era in crisi il concetto di storia. Non vi erano più sicurezze, perché era venuta meno la credibilità dei fatti (Cruciata 1995, 149).

Sanvitale's statement echoes what has been identified by Linda Hutcheon as the postmodern attitude toward and representation of the past: "The postmodern situation is that a 'truth' is being told, with 'facts' to back it up, but a teller constructs that truth and chooses those very 'facts' . . . In fact, that teller—of story or history—also constructs those very facts by giving a particular meaning to events. Facts do not speak for themselves in either form of narrative: the tellers speak for them, making these fragments of the past into a discursive whole" (1989, 58).

10. Di un fatto storico del genere sarebbe appassionante ricostruire una scena arredata, precisa, con gesti significativi e fisionomie, frasi, alterchi, grida ed espressioni di felicità o moti incerti e nascosti di dolore; coltivare

almeno la certezza illusoria che qualche cosa di simile, con molti particolari esatti accadde davvero, ma le relazioni che abbiamo sono opposte (Sanvitale 1993, 68–69).

11. Di questa tela, tante volte ridipinta dalla storia, dagli storici, dai biografi, il primo quadro fu cancellato subito con nuovi soggetti e nuovi sfondi e si confusero i complotti, i tradimenti, le vigliaccherie con i casi di onestà e di eroismo. È illusorio ritrovare la stesura originale, i fili che legarono fatti tanto intricati, scegliere alcune ipotesi piuttosto di altre (Sanvitale 1993, 53).

12. Paradigmatic is the narrator's intense self-consciousness of the status of documents (either memoirs, eyewitness accounts, or official reports), none of which can any longer claim "to be a transparent means to a past event; [they are] instead the textually transformed trace of that past" (Hutcheon 1989, 87): "Eppure tutti gli avvenimenti, confermati da testimoni, relazioni, atti ufficiali, gazzette, all'improvviso li troviamo spostati di stagione e di anno nelle 'memorie' del maresciallo Savary . . . Svista. Memoria che tradisce. Ma il testo di Savary si considera una fonte attendibile per alcuni fatti storici . . . Molti autori hanno attinto o trovato conferma 'anche' nelle memorie di Savary. È un particolare poco significativo? O si tratta di uno degli innumerevoli indizi che fanno barcollare l'impalcatura attraverso la quale ci illudiamo di ripercorrere il tempo che non c'è piú?" (Sanvitale 1993, 104) [And yet all the events, confirmed by witnesses, reports, official documents, gazettes, are suddenly shifted to a different season and year in marshal Savary's memoirs. . . . Oversight. Memory lapse. But Savary's text is considered a reliable source for several historical events. . . . Several writers have drawn on or have found confirmation "also" in Savary's memoirs. Is it a meaningless detail? Or is it one of the countless signs that shakes the framework through which we illusorily believe we can recover the time that has passed].

13. In quale puzzle riusciremmo mai a rendere coerente o ad assegnare in posti che sembrino preparati, i tasselli di una vita umana o di una grandiosa epopea, serie di cause e di casi che hanno trasformato la storia del mondo e sono scomparsi? Di quale mappa potremmo disegnare i confini e gli intrecci nella convinzione che stabiliremo un ordine valido quanto la vecchia realtà cancellata? Una pazza superbia guida la mano sicura nella scelta dei pezzi, nel tratto della matita, e pare esistere un subdolo specchiarsi, a distanza, degli avvenimenti globali nei singoli, nelle loro sofferenze cancellate da un soffio del tempo (Sanvitale 1993, 471).

14. [L]e *vere verità* si trovano assai difficilmente nella Storia. Per fortuna, il piú delle volte, esse non hanno effettiva importanza, non hanno che un valore di curiosità. Vi sono tante mai verità! . . . Quella verità storica tanto invocata, alla quale ciascuno fa appello, spesso non è che una vana parola; essa è impossibile nel momento in cui si svolgono gli avvenimenti, quando le passioni sono ancora accese; e se piú tardi il disaccordo cessa, ciò avviene solo perché i contraddittori non esistono piú. Ma che cosa è dunque, il piú delle volte, questa tanto decantata verità storica? Una favola convenzionale (Sanvitale 1993, 71).

References

Cruciata, Maria Teresa. 1995. Intervista a Francesca Sanvitale. *Inventario* 2: 147–58.

Della Colletta, Cristina. 1994. Historical reconfigurations and the ideology of desire: Giuseppe Tomasi di Lampedusa's *Il Gattopardo*. *The Italianist* 14: 96–110.

Giuffrè, Maria Teresa. 1994. Francesca Sanvitale e il romanzo di idee al femminile. *Tempo presente* 167: 45–51.

Grande, Luigi. 1994. Una relazione-romanzo per la vicenda dell'aiglon. *Il ponte* 50, 10: 142–46.

Hutcheon, Linda. 1987. 'The pastime of past time': Fiction, history, historiographic metafiction. *Genre* 20: 285–305.

———. 1988. *A poetics of postmodernism: History, theory, fiction*. New York: Routledge.

———. 1989. *The politics of postmodernism*. New York: Routledge.

Lazzaro-Weis, Carol. 1993. *From margins to mainstream: Feminism and fictional modes in Italian women's writing, 1968–1990*. Philadelphia: University of Pennsylvania Press.

Mazza, Antonia. 1994. *Il figlio dell'impero* di Francesca Sanvitale. *Letture* 2: 125–26.

Moglen, Helene. 1992. (Un)gendering the subject: Towards a feminist theory of the novel. *Genre* 25: 65–89.

Petrignani, Sandra. 1993. Ritorno al passato. *Panorama*, 17 October, 123–24.

Rigney, Anne. 1989. Adapting history to the novel. *New Comparison* 8: 127–43.

Sanvitale, Francesca. 1993. *Il figlio dell'impero*. Torino: Einaudi.

Seamon, Roger. 1983. Narrative practice and the theoretical distinction between history and fiction. *Genre* 16: 197–218.

Scott, Joan Wallach. 1988. *Gender and the politics of history*. New York: Columbia University Press.

Wesseling, Elisabeth. 1991. *Writing history as a prophet: Postmodernist innovations of the historical novel*. Amsterdam: John Benjamins Publishing Company.

White, Hayden. 1978a. *Tropics of discourse*. Baltimore: Johns Hopkins University Press.

———. 1978b. The historical text as literary artifact. In *The writing of history: Literary form and historical understanding*, edited by Robert H. Canary and Henry Kozicki. Madison: University of Wisconsin Press.

"Si sente la mano femminile?" Feminine Writing and the Concept of History in the Historical Fiction of Silvana La Spina

GABRIELLA BROOKE

"CAN YOU TELL IT WAS WRITTEN BY A WOMAN?" [SI SENTE LA MANO femminile?] Silvana La Spina asked Angiola Codacci-Pisanelli, the journalist of *L'Espresso* who interviewed the Sicilian author shortly after the publication of *Un Inganno dei sensi malizioso*. La Spina was convinced that her narrative is feminine "Because (in writing this book) I have finally let myself be swept away by my feminine imagination, by the pleasure of writing, and even more by that of telling a story" [Perche' finalmente mi sono lasciata andare alla mia fantasia di donna, alla gioia di scrivere, e prima ancora di "cuntare" (1995b)]. This statement immediately brings to mind the concept of "jouissance" that appears so often in the description of "feminine writing" by French feminist critics such as Cixous (1993), Irigaray (1993) and Kristeva (1987) The journalist chose not to elaborate this point and instead compared La Spina's prose to that of several male authors—among whom is Gabriel Garcia Marquez.

Rather than examine all aspects of feminine writing present in La Spina's narrative,[1] this essay intends to focus on a major feminine theme that underlies her historical fiction—her critical outlook on history, which I will define as the official narration of patriarchy-recorded events.

History serves as the basis of patriarchal power by exalting its values and institutions. In the past, the scribes had a vested interest in recording the story that best suited those who paid them. Contemporary historians and women authors of historical novels have begun to challenge their accuracy. La Spina does this in both *Quando Marte è in Capricorno* (1994) and *Un inganno dei sensi malizioso* (1995). In the former novel she shows how easily history is manipulated to further the ends of those in power. In the latter she shows how an alternate realistic account of history can be told, and how this very possibility strips patriarchy-recorded history of its authenticity, thus reducing it to just one version of what happened.

Though they belong to the same genre,[2] La Spina's two historical novels are quite different. In *Quando Marte è in Capricorno*, disillusion and a sense of doom mark the narrative through a language rich with sensory appeal and death imagery. In *Un inganno dei sensi malizioso*, magic and humor combine to evoke lightness in the narrative. In this novel, La Spina uses irony to undermine patriarchal institutions and values. My intent is to trace the common thread that unites these very different novels—their critical approach to official history. I will begin by examining this concept in *Quando Marte è in Capricorno* and show how *Un Inganno dei sensi malizioso* becomes the culmination of the discourse on patriarchy-recorded history initiated by the first novel. More specifically I will show how illusion becomes the authorial device that negates official history.

The negativity that underlies La Spina's narrative is an important characteristic of "feminine writing." In an interview by Françoise van Rossum-Guyon, "Talking about Polylogue" in *French Feminist Thought* (1987) Julia Kristeva maintains that

"female writings, even at their most optimistic, seem underpinned by a lack of belief in any project, goal or meaning. . . . This gives writings by women a content that is always psychological and often dissenting, disillusioned or apocalyptic." (Kristeva 1987, 112)

Certainly La Spina's historical fiction fits this definition. Disillusionment, a pervasive malaise, apocalyptic images of death and suffering aptly describe Iacopo da Lentini's world. Surrounded by treachery, greed, and ruthlessness, the dying Iacopo makes an effort to set things right by offering his view of a major historical event of his time—the alleged plot against Emperor Frederick II's life by Pier delle Vigne. Iacopo's attempt, which clashes with the official stand of the church, is doomed to fail.

There is no redeeming feature in this stark account of how official history is manipulated by those in charge of recording it. According to Julia Kristeva, negativity is characteristic of writing inspired by the semiotic—the area of the psyche that is still in touch with the Mother. Such writing can intrude and disrupt symbolic language. In *Sexual Textual Politics* (1996), Toril Moi translates Kristeva's concept into textual terms: "The poet's negativity is then analysable as a series of ruptures, absences and breaks in the symbolic language, but it can also be traced in his or her thematic preoccupations" (170).

The story of *Quando Marte è in Capricorno* begins at the abbey of Maniace in the year 1249, when Iacopo da Lentini is close to death. Upon hearing of Pier delle Vigne's suicide, Iacopo decides to write a memoir that will exonerate his friend from the accusation of having betrayed the emperor. The plot advances through a series of flashbacks that allow Iacopo to recall his friendship with Pier, plead his innocence, and indict both the papacy and the court of Frederick for Pier's death. Trusting that his adult son, Tommaso, will make his version of the events public, Iacopo wills his finished manuscript to this child.

About a third of the way into the novel, La Spina describes history almost as she would a living organism. "For Iacopo the court is far away and he is at the margins of history. But history has thin webs, veins, canals that make one feel part of their time" (66).[3] This description implies a constant change. The webs that connect people to the events of their time are grounded in their individual experience. Each event is experienced uniquely and each person involved has a unique perspective. This concept of history as a living thing appears also in La Spina's first novel, *Morte a Palermo* (1987). In that novel, one of her characters, Professor Lo Giudice, comments on history as he talks about the death of Professor Costanzo, a renowed scholar and archeologist, "You see, history is a living organism and epochs are born and die just like any organism; to put into discussion again those [epochs] that have already died, as he used to do, is like taking around a decomposed body" (43).[4]

Later in *Quando Marte è in Capricorno*, La Spina shows how "official" history is biased and often propelled by despicable motives. For example, the accusations of high treason that cause the fall of Pier delle Vigne are grounded in gossip, prejudice, and envy.

> But it is so hard to prove the accusations of high treason! And at times they are based on nothing at all: on a web of gossip, on an imprudent act, on a negotiation gone awry—like the one with the

pope in Lyon—on the prejudice that an ambitious man, who has
risen from nothing, is always ready to betray for gain—. (115)[5]

Again in *Morte a Palermo* we find a similar concept of history
when Professor D'Alcontres discusses realism in Manzoni:

It is the realism of ghosts, of the obsessions of the mind; in which
in spite of one's agenda it comes out that providence could care
less about people, that corruption is our daily bread and history
nothing but a heap of violences and prevarication. (61)[6]

But it is not just man's malevolence that causes historical
events; superstition has a part in them too. The title of the
novel, *Quando Marte è in Capricorno*, comes from what Thomas
Aquinas tells Iacopo just prior to Pier delle Vigne's alleged
betrayal of Emperor Frederick. The Dominican monk accuses
Pier of being unreliable, and then he says that the position of
Mars in Capricorn signifies that a plot against a great ruler
will soon take place (138).
Greed and the struggle for power are the main causes of
historical events. Through a narrative that reeks with images
of death and despair, La Spina presents history as shaped and
propelled by patriarchal thought. The patriarchal forces of the
church are locked in a deadly fight with the patriarchal forces
of the empire. Italy is a stage upon which the worst of what is
associated with masculinity—ambition, aggressiveness, cruelty, and violence—dominate and clash to death. Far from being a harbor for wounded souls, the church is depicted as an
organization of men who profit from the terror of mankind
at the idea of being separated from God. God is silent and
unknowable, and the church exploits that silence. Twice this
damning concept appears in the novel. It is first mouthed by
Taddeus, the unscrupulous abbot who will suppress Iacopo's
memorial.

Don't those fanatics know that God is silent? That it is because of
this silence, this chasmlike emptiness that divides us that the
church was born? (31)[7]

Pier delle Vigne is even more explicit in his assessment:

The church is the ruin of the world, Iacopo. The church of the
popes, of the clerics, because the church was born from the silence
of God. From his unfillable distance. Even Christ understood it,

up there on Golgotha. Do you recall? Eli, Eli lama Sabactani.
Where art Thou my God, my Lord? Why do I only hear your silence? (146)[8]

Recorded history is unreliable because the empire and the
church "make" official history not just by masterminding battles, alliances, and conspiracies but by carefully and ruthlessly
controlling what is recorded and preserved. Abbot Taddeus, a
representative of the church, is well aware of this as he wonders about the reliability of the chronicles written by the very
monks of his abbey:

> He had read in the chronicles that the first abbot was of massive
> build, pale complexion, and clever tongue. But had it really been
> that way? Don't some chronicles lie? Aren't monks partial when
> they write? Yet he has no choice but to imagine him the way he
> was described. (112)[9]

At the end of the novel it is again Abbot Taddeus that gives
damning evidence on how history can be manipulated. Before
Tommaso da Lentini can take possession of his father's property shortly after Iacopo's death, Abbot Taddeus hides the no-
tary's completed manuscript, thus destroying Iacopo's
challenge to the church's official version regarding the guilt of
Pier delle Vigne.
    The apocalyptic vision of history that La Spina depicts in
Quando Marte è in Capricorno seems absent from La Spina's
latest work of fiction. But this is only because she chooses to
confront history in a different way. In *Quando Marte è in Capricorno* the two main characters, Iacopo da Lentini and Pier
delle Vigne are among the protagonists of their time. They
have become inscribed in official history in a certain way. Because the author enters into their minds, historical events are
presented in a highly subjective way, thus giving a different
account of what happened and undermining the "official" history. "Official" history has no place at all in *Un inganno dei
sensi malizioso* (1995)—a postmodern "historiographic metafiction" in the words of Linda Hutcheon (1988, 113)—in which
characters, even the main ones, are described from the outside
and are not deeply developed. In this novel, the often chaotic,
fragmented view of history comes from the periphery. To use
Hutcheon's term all of La Spina's main characters are "ex-
centric": a young nun, a religious fanatic who comes from the
gutter, a powerless chaplain. A myriad of minor characters

also interact with them, ranging from historical figures, such as Mohammed III and Rudolph of Hapsburg, to humble ones such as the prostitute Angiolina. Using the pen as a brush, Silvana La Spina creates a beautiful, sweeping portrait of the sixteenth century, structured as three different stories that connect at the end of the novel. The protagonist, Suor Trafitta, is a young nun with high connections in the Vatican. Like a sixteenth-century Cassandra, Suor Trafitta sees catastrophes about to happen but is not believed by her contemporaries. Suor Trafitta's first vision, the assault of her convent near Catania by handsome pirate-prince Abdul and his Turks, earns her a permanent leave to see her family. Once her vision comes true, Suor Trafitta, now definitively *persona non grata*, is hastily sent to the convent of the Clarisse in Naples. Soon after, Suor Trafitta has a vision of the plague sweeping the city. Again no one believes her. Convinced that Trafitta's visions come from the devil, the mother superior of the convent decides to turn her over to the inquisitors of the Santo Uffizio. Terrified, Suor Trafitta flees the convent and takes refuge in Rome in the household of her uncle, a cardinal. After yet another unwelcome prophecy, she is sent to a convent in Prague.

Parallel to Suor Trafitta's odyssey are the stories of don Consalvo, nephew of the viceroy of Sicily, who is asleep until the end of the novel, and of don Crocefisso. The reader learns that don Consalvo is under the spell of a beautiful and wicked Saracen woman. Looking for a cure for his master's slumber, don Jose, chaplain of Consalvo's family, takes the sleeping youth on a journey from Spain to Sicily, and eventually to Prague. The protagonist of the last story, don Crocefisso, is a religious fanatic who roams the country searching for martyrdom to expiate his sins. His quest leads him to Istanbul where he meets Suor Trafitta and don Consalvo who, also unwelcome in Prague, have been sent by Rudolf of Hapsburg to the Sultan Mohammed II. In Istanbul, the stories of these three characters intersect with that of Abdul, the mysterious young pirate who appears in every vision of Suor Trafitta and who is revealed to be a half brother of Mohammed II.

Suor Trafitta has another vision just as Sultan Mohammed (who has already had nineteen of his brothers slaughtered) is about to give the order to kill his newly found half brother. Impressed, the sultan orders her to tell him what she has seen. For the first time in the novel, Suor Trafitta asserts herself by refusing to disclose her vision unless Abdul is freed. The chapter that follows should bring a resolution for all the characters. Instead, the reader finds herself at the same monastery where Suor Trafitta was in the beginning and learns that all that has taken place happened only in the visionary mind of Suor Trafitta—an ending that is designed to jolt the reader into the realization that all she has read and participated in is but an illusion.

The treatment of time in La Spina's novel is interesting. There are no dates, with the exception of the 1600 earthquake of Catania. Readers can orient themselves, however, by checking the historical sequence of events described (the death of Philip II in 1598, the plague in Catania, and the burning of Giordano Bruno in 1600). La Spina's *retelling* of these events, however, is not done in chronological order, and the story jumps from the death of Philip II to the plague in Catania and back to Philip II, following whatever character's story is being told. At the end of the novel (in the year 1600) Suor Trafitta's last vision is one of a major assault on Constantinople by a coalition of Venetians, Spanish, and Genoese forces at the command of Andrea Doria. The mention of the Genoese admiral seems to point to the naval battle of Lepanto in 1571 and not to an actual invasion of the city that never happened in the year 1600. This transposition of historical time accentuates the shift from "official" history to a fictional interpretation of it that leaves readers disoriented.

Elements of "magic realism" present in the novel further disconcert readers by "rocking" their illusion of reading an objective historical account.

In *Ellipse of Uncertainty*, Lance Olsen writes that fantasy can be found at some point on a continuum between the marvelous and the mimetic,

a mode that confounds and confuses the marvelous and the mimetic. It plays one mode off the other, creating a dialectic which refuses synthesis. Often fantasy begins in the realm of the mimetic, then disrupts it by introducing an element of the marvelous, the effect being to jam both marvelous and mimetic assumptions. In other words, fantasy is that stutter between two modes of discourse which generates textual instability, an ellipse of uncertainty. The stutter may last for a phrase, for a sentence, for a chapter, even for a novel, but its result is the banging together of the *here* and *there* so that neither the reader nor the protagonist knows quite where he is. That is, fantasy is a deconstructive mode of narrative. (1987, 19)

The elements of the fantastic present in La Spina's fiction are subtle. For example, the cause of Don Consalvo's slumber—the magic of the Saracen Almudena—is ridiculous by modern standards. Yet the statement makes perfect sense from the mouth of the sixteenth-century priest who utters it, and the reader is left wondering for most of the novel if a natural explanation is forthcoming. The conversations between Don Jose and his terracotta statue of Sant'Antonio are another ambiguous use of the fantastic. The conversations are complete and matter-of-fact, yet the reader might still dismiss them as existing only in Don Jose's overworked mind. However, the reader can have no doubt that the supernatural is at play when Don Crocefisso enters into the dream of the sultan and, later on, into that of Consalvo, with consequences in the "real" world.

The deconstructive nature of La Spina's fiction is apparent in the very title of her novel. In *Neo-Baroque* (1992), Omar Calabrese points out that the "key" to Umberto Eco's *The Name of the Rose* is to be found in the introduction to the novel and that this key consists in "the doubt cast upon the authenticity or falsification of the truth." According to Eco, who is quoted by Calabrese in the same book, the writer should write out of "'pure love of writing,' which leaves *in doubt* any distinction between truth and falsehood." This is exactly what La Spina has done in her latest novel, as she herself disclosed in the interview quoted at the beginning of this essay. However, rather than leading the reader in a labyrinthine search for the key to the interpretation of her fiction, La Spina offers it in the very title of her book. *Un inganno dei sensi malizioso* [A teasing illusion of the senses] is the Italian translation of a verse taken from a sonnet of Sor Juana Inez De la Cruz:

> This colored illusion you see
> which shows off the beauties of Art
> with false syllogism of colors
> is a teasing illusion of the senses.[10]

Art—a portrait in the case of this sonnet—is an illusion for Sor Juana because it presents a beautiful image that does not correspond to the reality of the subject it depicts. By the same token, the art contained between the covers of the book also portrays an illusion because what it tries to represent cannot be represented *as it was*, but only as the artist sees it.

There are other postmodern traits in La Spina's fiction. The most notable is her treatment of myth and fairy tale. In *Strategies of Fantasy* Brian Attebery writes:

> So it seems the Postmodernist prospectus, both an extension of and a corrective to Modernism, involves a return to early narrative forms—the fairy tale movements and mythic structures that never really disappeared from more popular forms of literature—but with an awareness of their artificiality. Postmodernism is a return to storytelling in the belief that we can be sure of nothing but story. (1988, 40)

In my reading, the characters Suor Trafitta and Don Consalvo each represent a patriarchal value embodied respectively in the myth of Cassandra and the fairy tale of the Sleeping Beauty.

In their original versions, myth and fairy tale incorporate and teach patriarchal values and ideals. For example, the myth of Cassandra, the Trojan princess who refused Apollo and was cursed by the god with the gift of making prophecies that would not, however, be believed, contains a warning to women not to defy patriarchy. The fairy tale of the Sleeping Beauty embodies patriarchy's ideal woman: young, beautiful, and passive. Through her choice of characters and their motives, La Spina mocks and deconstructs patriarchal values. For example, in an ironic twist of the original myth and tale, both her characters are obsessed with erotic love, the greatest sin of all in the bigoted patriarchal society in which they live.

In her essay "Cassandra's Daughters: Prophecy in Elsa Morante's *La Storia*," Susan Briziarelli suggests that "to the extent that Cassandra's punishment comes from having refused Apollo's love, her sin is that of the rejection of her sexuality and her destiny as a woman" (1990, 191). In La Spina's novel, Suor Trafitta appears on the surface also to reject her sexuality. It becomes increasingly clear, however, that it is her powerful erotic attraction to the mysterious Abdul that triggers her prophetic ecstasies.

Lust also subverts the fairy tale of the Sleeping Beauty. As Bruno Bettelheim reports in *The Uses of Enchantment* (1989, 227–236) the tale of Sleeping Beauty comes from a story in Basile's *Pentameron*. The heroine, Talia, falls under a spell after a splinter from a spinning wheel lodges under her thumbnail. Talia sleeps until one day a king arrives at her palace, sees her and makes love to her, only to abandon her shortly after. Nine months later, Talia, who is still asleep, gives birth to twins. Not even childbirth awakens her. It is only when one of the babies dislodges the splinter while sucking her thumb that the original Sleeping Beauty wakes up. In Bettelheim's interpretation this is a reflection that in a patriarchal society, woman comes of age only through motherhood. This is of course impossible for La Spina's Sleeping Beauty since he is a boy. But the irony does not stop here. Far from being innocent, Don Consalvo is asleep *because* of his lust for Almudena who, annoyed by his advances, has cast a sleeping spell on him. As in Basile's tale, Don Consalvo is ravished because of his beauty; his seducer, a noblewoman under whose protection Don Consalvo has been placed, also forsakes him in the end.

In "The Laugh of the Medusa" (1993), Hélène Cixous wrote that a truly feminine text cannot fail to be subversive, volcanic in its effect on patriarchal discourse: "There is no room for her if she is not a he. If she's a her-she, it is in order to smash everything, to shatter the framework of institutions, to blow up the law, to break up the 'truth' with laughter" (344).

The concept of laughter as a weapon strong enough to challenge the symbolic order is discussed also by Marina Mizzau (1985). Irony, which Mizzau points outs, occurs when someone says something while making clear the opposite of what is communicated, can be conveyed through tone of voice, emphasis, and also simply through context. Irony can be directed not just toward a person or a thing but also toward a sentence or a discourse attributed to another and from which the person who uses the irony dissociates him- or herself. Excluded from dominant discourse, women are more likely than men to resort to treating language externally, ironically, because it is easier to distance themselves from something that does not belong to them (51–56).

Un inganno dei sensi malizioso also uses parody and intertextuality in the way discussed by Linda Hutcheon (1988, 125–39). The texts of fairy tale (Sleeping Beauty) and ancient myth (Cassandra) are found mixed with historical accounts of events, both verified and unverified, in the lives of the historical figures in the novel. For example, Mohammed III's slaughter of his nineteen half brothers and Rudolph's murder attempt on the life of his brother Matthias are historically true facts. La Spina however embellishes the truculent nature of these leaders with invented facts. Sultan Mohammed, for example, is presented as he wishfully tries to figure out a way to get rid of his mother. Emperor Rudolph's attempt to enlist a Jesuit to kill Matthias is depicted in a fictional scene that presents the emperor as a parodic character. This use of parody and irony has the effect of amusing the reader but at the same time of robbing characters of depth by reducing them to a parodic version of themselves, yet another way of alerting readers to the impossibility of knowing history "as it happened."

In *Un inganno dei sensi malizioso*, parody and irony are present not just in language but in the very structure of the novel, in the choice of characters, and in the ironic subversion of myth and fable. All this is done against a somber background in which emperors conspire with religious leaders to pursue their corrupted ends. An example of the ironic tone that results is found in the dialogue between Emperor Rudolph of Hapsburg and the Jesuit superior Don Juan:

> "So," he [Don Juan] says, "so what is weighing so heavily on your imperial heart?"
> "You must eliminate my brother Matthias."
> "For pity's sake," the Jesuit superior answers, "do not say that. Jesuits are incapable of such dastardly deeds."
> "Ah thieves, ah disgusting breed that you are," the emperor yells, "I know you well, I who have lived at the court of Spain for years." Overtaken by rage, the emperor, who is holding a jug of wine, throws himself against a valet. The wine spills around the room as if it were blood, blood flows and the boy cries. "Listen to me, Don Juan, you son of a bitch." And he begins to recite to the superior a series of injustices, tortures, and persecutions. For in these times it does not take much to find reason to accuse the Jesuits, on the contrary, most rulers try to find reason to eliminate them from the face of the earth. Yet Don Juan looks at him unperturbed. "Go ahead," he says, staring at the emperor from his low position, while by contrast the emperor is tall and majestic, perhaps even fat because of all the wine he drinks and game he eats.[11]

La Spina's sarcasm is apparent in Don Juan's words: "Don't say that. Jesuits are incapable of such dastardly deeds." Several lines later, they are followed by expert advice on how to best get rid of Matthias. Irony is also present in the physical depiction of the characters: the thin and small Jesuit; the emperor who is tall and majestic, *perhaps* even fat. The word *perhaps* points out to the reader how the author's description is pure speculation since she could not possibly know what the emperor looked like. This word is designed to undermine the authority of the narrator and thus show the limitations of fiction.

Another example of irony both in language and in plotting occurs in the scene of the seduction of don Crocefisso by the beautiful donna Matilde, who tries to convince the young man that sleeping with her is his door to salvation.

> To tell the truth don Crocefisso has his doubts about the potential for penance that can arise from sleeping with that prone woman, but, after all, man lives with doubt, forever unable to resolve it. Therefore he makes a hasty sign of the cross and, whispering God save me, he lies on the floor. (103)[12]

In an ironic twist of events, an earthquake shakes Catania at the crucial moment. Convinced that it is a supernatural warning, Crocefisso will spend the rest of his life looking for martyrdom to expiate his sin. The coincidence of the earthquake striking right at the time of Don Crocefisso's transgression, along with other coincidences in the novel—the fact that all three main characters end up in Istanbul at the same time, the fact that the mysterious Abdul is revealed to be a second cousin of Suor Trafitta, the fact that Crocefisso is freed by the sultan just before the execution of Abdul—have the effect of making the reader question the truthfulness of the narrative in spite of the remarkably accurate evocation of the period.

In *A Poetics of Postmodernism*, Linda Hutcheon discusses how the postmodern approach "reinstalls historical contexts as significant and even determining, but in so doing, it problemizes the entire notion of historical knowledge" (1988, 89). History cannot be "known" as it actually happened because its meaning is context-dependent and that context is forever lost *to us.*

In *Un inganno dei sensi malizioso* the reconstruction of the historical context is painstaking; historical referents are in place and are even made more "real" by the use of historical characters. Yet readers are not allowed to forget that they are reading an account that can only give the *appearance* of official history because of the unreliability of the narrator and the use of the fantastic.

La Spina's concept of history evolves as her fiction does. In *Quando Marte è in Capricorno* "official" history is described as a living organism that is controlled by patriarchal forces that have the power to change it at will. In *Un inganno dei sensi malizioso* "official" history is denied, along with the notion that the past can be truthfully re-created today. True to the title she chose, La Spina uses a rich, realistic prose designed to fascinate and draw readers completely in, only to jolt them out of the vivid dream she has created, and through the use of language, irony and the fantastic, to remind them teasingly that it is all an illusion.

True to its title, this fiction draws readers in only to teasingly leave them wondering.

Notes

1. Other characteristics of feminine writing that have been described by Cixous (1993), Irigaray (1993), and Kristeva (1981) such as writing that appeals to the senses, digressions, and simultaneity—are present in La Spina's narrative. For example, in an interview about *Polylogue*, Kristeva said: "As regards the themes to be found in texts written by women, they invite us to see, touch, and smell a body made of organs, whether they are exhibited with satisfaction or horror." (Kristeva, 1987) La Spina's prose uses details and descriptions that appeal strongly to the senses—Codacci-Pisanelli writes in the *Espresso* interview that *Un inganno dei sensi malizioso* is filled with sounds, colors, tastes, and smells. La Spina confirmed, "It is my weakness; I have the sense of smell of a dog. . . . I can't help imagining smells while I write." A detailed analysis of La Spina's language, digressions, and imagery is outside the purpose of this paper. It is enough to say that a careful reading of the text reveals several ruptures in the symbolic language in the form of simultaneous digressions. For a discussion of this, see De Giovanni, 1989.

2. *The Concise Oxford Dictionary of Literary Terms* (1990), edited by Chris Baldick (Oxford University Press), defines a historical novel as one "in which the action takes place during a specific period of time well before the time of writing (often one or two generations before, sometimes several centuries), and in which some attempt is made to depict accurately the customs and mentality of the period. The central character—real or imagined—is usually subject to divided loyalties within a larger historical conflict of which readers know the outcome."

Quando Marte è in Capricorno and *Un inganno dei sensi malizioso* fit within this definition. Both novels are set in a clearly identifiable historical period: the thirteenth century for *Quando Marte è in Capricorno* and the sixteenth for *Un inganno dei sensi malizioso*. The protagonist of *Quando Marte è in Capricorno*, a historical figure named Iacopo Da Lentini, struggles to clear the name of his friend and mentor, Pier Delle Vigne, from the accusation of participating in a plot against Emperor Frederick II. The protagonist of *Un inganno dei sensi malizioso*, Suor Trafitta La Grua, an invented character, becomes entangled in the major events of her time, from incursions by the Turks in Sicily to the plague in Naples to the siege of Istanbul.

3. In the passage I refer to, La Spina writes that after several years away from the court of Emperor Frederick II, Iacopo feels cut off from the events

of his day. That distance, the author says, is only apparent: "Per Iacopo la corte è lontana, e lui solamente ai margini della Storia. Eppure la Storia ha reti sottili, venature, canali, che ci fanno pur sempre sentire partecipi del tempo in cui viviamo" (1994, 66).

4. Vede, la storia è un organismo vivo e le epoche nascono e muoiono come ogni organismo; tirare in ballo come faceva lui quelle già morte è come portare in giro un cadavere putrefatto (La Spina 1987, 43).

5. Ma sono così difficili da provare le accuse di alto tradimento! E talvolta si basano su niente. Su una ragnatela di voci, su un'imprudenza, su una trattativa andata a male come quella col papa a Lione. Sul pregiudizio che un uomo ambizioso, venuto dal niente, è sempre pronto a tradire per lucro (La Spina 1994, 115).

6. È il realismo dei fantasmi, delle ossessioni della mente. In cui, nonostante i propositi, salta fuori che la provvidenza non si cura di niente e di nessuno, che la corruzione è il nostro pane quotidiano e la storia un cumulo di violenze e soprusi (La Spina 1987, 61).

7. Non sanno forse quegli esaltati che Dio tace? che proprio per questo silenzio, per questo vuoto abissale che ci divide che è nata la chiesa? (La Spina 1994, 31).

8. È la chiesa Iacopo la rovina del mondo; la chiesa dei papi, e dei chierici, poiché essa è nata dal silenzio di Dio. Dalla sua inesorabile distanza. Anche Cristo lo capì, lassù sul Golgota. Ricordi? Eli, Eli lama Sabactani. Dove sei , mio Dio mio signore? Perchè odo solo il tuo silenzio? (La Spina 1994, 146).

9. Nelle cronache ha letto che il primo abate era di struttura massiccia, di colorito pallido, acuto nelle risposte. Ma era veramente cosi? non sono menzognere forse certe cronache? o i monaci parziali nello scrivere? ma non gli rimane che immaginarselo in quel modo . . .

10.

> Este que ves, engaño colorido,
> que del arte ostentando los primores,
> con falsos silogismos de colores
> es cauteloso engaño del sentido

(De la Cruz 1943, 46)

11. —E dunque,—dice—e dunque, che mai attanaglia il vostro reale cuore?

—Dovete eliminare mio fratello Mattia.

—Per carità,—risponde il superiore gesuita-manco a parlarne. Noi gesuiti non ci macchiamo di simili delitti.

Ah ladri, ah asquerosos, urla l'imperatore, vi conosco bene io che per anni fui nella Corte di Spagna. E dalla furia si slancia contro un valletto con in mano una caraffa di vino, e quel vino si sparpaglia per la sala come sangue, e il sangue cola e il ragazzo piange.

—Ascoltatemi, don Juan, figlio di un cane.

E subito recita al superiore una serie di nequizie, torture e persecuzioni, chè di questi tempi a trovare motivi d'accusa contro i gesuiti non ci vuole poi molto. E anzi la maggior parte dei regnanti cerca moventi per eliminarli dalla faccia della terra. Ma don Juan non mostra turbamenti.

—Fate pure—dice e guarda l'imperatore in faccia dalla sua bassa posizione, mentre al contrario di lui l'imperatore è alto e maestoso, forse persino grasso a furia di bere vino e mangiare cacciagione (La Spina 1995, 186).

12. Per la verità don Crocefisso ha qualche dubbio sulle possibilità penitenziali di un connubio con quella donna riversa, ma di dubbi l'uomo vive, incapace da sempre di risolverli. Quindi si fa un subitaneo segno della croce e, mormorando Dio mi salvi, si corica sul pavimento (La Spina 1995, 103).

References

Attebery, Brian. 1988. *Strategies of fantasy*. Bloomington: Indiana University Press.

Baldick, Chris. 1990. *The concise Oxford dictionary of literary terms*. Oxford: Oxford University Press.

Bettelheim, Bruno. 1989. *The uses of enchantment*. New York: Vintage Books.

Briziarelli, Susan. 1990. Cassandra's daughters: Prophecy in Elsa Morante's *La storia*. In *RLA*: *Romance Languages Annual*. 2:189–193.

Calabrese, Omar. 1992. *Neo-Baroque*. Princeton: Princeton University Press.

Cixous, Hélène. 1993. The Laugh of the Medusa. In *Feminisms*, edited by Warhol Herndle and Price Herndle. New Brunswick: Rutgers University Press.

De Giovanni, Neria. 1989. La Sfinge cantatrice—realta' come specchio nella narrativa femminile italiana post-neorealism. In *RLA: Romance Languages Annual* 1:105–110.

De la Cruz, Juana. 1943. *Sor Juana Inez de la Crua*. Buenos Aires: Espasa Calpe.

Hutcheon, Linda. 1988. *A poetics of postmodernism: History, theory and fiction*. London: Routledge.

Kristeva, Julia. 1987. Talking about *Polylogue*. Interview by Françoise van Rossum-Guyon, in *French Feminist Thought*, ed. Toril Moi. Oxford: Basil Blackwell ltd.

Irigaray, Luce. 1993. This sex that is not one. *Feminisms*, ed. R. Warhol and D. Herndl. New Brunswick: Rutgers.

La Spina, Silvana. 1994. *Quando Marte è in Capricorno*. Milan: Bompiani.

———. 1987. *Morte a Palermo*. Milan: La Tartaruga Nera.

———. 1995a. *Un inganno dei sensi malizioso*. Milan: Arnoldo Mondadori Editore.

———. 1995. Racconto una Sicilia barocca e al femminile. Interview with Silvana La Spina. *L'Espresso* 18 August.

Mizzau, Marina. 1985. Ironia e parole delle donne. In *Le Donne e i segni*, edited by Patrizia Magli. Ancona: Il Lavoro Editoriale.

Moi, Toril. 1991. *Sexual textual politics*. New York: Routledge.

Olsen, Lance. 1987. *Ellipse of uncertainty*. New York: Greenwood Press.

I dodici abati di Challant: the Metabolized Middle Ages

LAURETTA DE RENZO

ITALIAN LITERATURE OF THE LAST DECADES IS CHARACTERIZED BY A renewed interest in history, as many novels by the major writers of this period clearly indicate. It is enough to mention here Italo Calvino's trilogy *I nostri antenati*, Maria Bellonci's *Rinascimento privato*, Rosetta Loy's *Le strade di polvere*, and Dacia Maraini's *La lunga vita di Marianna Ucría*. Each one of these novels, however, uses history in a daring way by reversing its traditional paths through the invention of what Omar Calabrese calls a "metahistorical syntax," which "eliminates the value of chronology in favor of the unity of knowledge" (1989, 190).[1] The past, therefore, is rewritten and reinterpreted, and this operation implies the awareness that history cannot be understood as an absolute, precise sequence of causes and effects, always univocally decipherable. The infinite number of events and characters that slip away through the loose webbing of historiographic investigations and narrations constitutes an endless, though submerged, polyphony of contrasting voices and of other possible stories.

A "different" possible story is the one Laura Mancinelli tells in her novel *I dodici abati di Challant*, published in 1981. The novel is set in an imaginary medieval time. It is "other" than barbarian or romantic or the Middle Ages of the *philosophia perennis* (Eco 1985, 84) described and desired by each new cultural period. In her novel, Mancinelli systematically carries out a parodic reversal of many topoi that comprise the literary representation of the Middle Ages by assigning, for instance, a nonconventional role to the female protagonist of her narration: a free individual *par excellence* who is perfectly able to control her destiny.

My interest in this book rises not only from its intrinsic qualities, but also from the fact that it was largely ignored by mainstream Italian criticism, even though it appeared in the prestigious series *Gli struzzi* published by Einaudi.[2] The novel, therefore, risks becoming another muted voice within the frame of Italian cultural production in which women's contributions still are largely marginalized. It incurs the risk, once again, of being fatally lost in the black holes of hegemonic discursive practices, those same practices the novel puts at stake.

In the following pages, I will analyze the way in which Laura Mancinelli's book operates the reversal of the themes that are typical of the literary and historiographic tradition surrounding the Middle Ages. Linda Hutcheon has underlined the homogeneity of these themes both in the literary and the historical treatment of the medieval period: "We only know the past (which really did exist) through its textualized remains" (1988, 67), and consequently, "both history and fiction are cultural sign systems, ideological constructions whose ideology includes their appearance of being autonomous and self-contained" (61).

As mentioned before, parody is the narrative strategy that produces the subversion of conventional thematical elements in Mancinelli's novel. As Bakhtin observes about parody,

> the intentions of the representing discourse are at odds with the intentions of the represented discourse; they fight against them, they depict a real world of objects not by using the represented language as a productive point of view, but rather by using it as an exposé to destroy the represented language. (1990, 364)

I dodici abati di Challant is the story of the progressive emancipation of the characters from their own different conditions and different degrees of captivity. The protagonists, Duke Franchino and the beautiful Marquise Bianca, live in the secluded castle of Challant somewhere in the Alps. But unlike conventional damsels in distress in remote castles, Bianca is completely free in her large mansion. The duke, on the other hand, is now a prisoner of the castle he inherited from Bianca's father with the provision, specified in the will, that he live in absolute chastity and under the continual surveillance of twelve hypocritical and bigoted abbots. The irony of this situation is emblematic of the narrative structure of the entire novel: the distorted usage of a conventional theme (i.e., the

patriarchal abuse of power) from which irreverent and contradictory results flow (i.e., the captivity of the duke).

Mancinelli's irony has multiple edges because she is playing
both with the historical version of Bianca di Challant's life
as found in the documents and with the fictionalized account
Matteo Bandello gave of it in his *Novelle*. According to the
documents,[3] Bianca Maria Visconti, wife of Renato di Challant,
left her husband and his gloomy castle and went to Milan
where she lived freely and luxuriously. Her scandalous existence ended on the gallows, where she was executed in 1526.
Bandello's Bianca is not only a scandalous woman, but also
cruel and degenerate, and her execution is depicted as a much-
needed and well-deserved punishment.[4]

The continual allusion to and the mixing and twisting of
historical and fictional facts are already at work in the first
episode of the novel, which, although unrelated to Bianca and
Franchino's story, functions as a *mise en abîme* of the events
that will take place at the castle of Challant. It is the account
of how Isabella of Aquitain "raped" the defenseless abbot Bernardo di Chiaravalle. The narrator tells us that according to
the legend, during his martyrdom, the victim, trapped in a
stone coffin by the woman, "already presaged the open wound,
the surface violated in some points the impudent hand which
would furtively bereave him of virtue and continence" (Mancinelli 1981, 3).[5] The frightful opening on the surface of the
man's immobilized body symbolizes his "femininization," that
is, his inscription within those discursive practices that have
always imprisoned the female body with artificial constructs
such as virginity and purity. The arbitrariness of these conventions and the lack of a scientific or physiological foundation to
legitimize their imposition upon women are represented in the
novel by the controversies between the philosophical schools
of Paris and Salamanca. Both discuss the necessity of considering Bernardo's experience as a form either of martyrdom or
of folly: "The school of Salamanca inclined toward martyrdom, for it reckoned that it would be martyrdom to shirk the
love of a beautiful and noble woman such as Madonna Isabella
of Aquitain. Paris declared that it was not martyrdom as much
as folly" (4).[6]

As it appears from this first episode, love is the catalyst of
all the events of the novel, but the theme of food, its preparation, and the enjoyment it provides is the semantic area that
becomes its preeminent trope through analogic or metaphoric

transformations, metonymic shifts, or symbols. Irony then, becomes more pointed and frequent in the semantic area of food.
A clear example is Duke Franchino's melancholic meditation
"against his fate that had thrown him into that monstrous
nook of the earth" (1981, 42), while the image of his homeland
crystallizes in his mind with the memory of its huge, sugary
figs and ripe grapes.

   In his study *I sapori della modernità*, Gian Paolo Biasin clarifies the nature of the unbreakable link between food, love,
and fiction:

> Since its origins, the novel could not help taking into account this
> alimentary universe as the name of a famous character, Sancho
> Panza, emblematically indicates. The anthropological dimension
> of nutrition and the social dimension of classes, the political di-
> mension of power, and the cultural dimension of values interact
> from the very beginning with the literary dimension.
>   Undoubtedly, at the base of such a system there is the fundamen-
> tal fact that the mouth is the ambivalent site of two kinds of oral-
> ity: the one that articulates voice and language, and the one that
> satisfies a need, the ingestion of food for survival but also for plea-
> sure that overlaps with the value of nutrition. (6)[7]

   Thus, in Mancinelli's novel, tidbits, delicacies, and uncommon drinks inevitably accompany and underscore each event
and often become the motive or the cause of the characters'
actions. The complex love relations between knights and damsels are always mediated by food, and food as a metaphor for
love becomes the most powerful liberating instrument of the
entire novel.

   Since the beginning of the narration, however, food's bene-
ficial, comforting, and reviving effects can be enjoyed only by
those who cherish love and are free to yield to its power. Thus
during the first dinner at the castle, Duke Franchino, who has
taken a fancy to the marquise of Challant but who does not
know how to love, cannot swallow a thing when his desire to
sit next to her is frustrated by the censorious intervention of
Abbot Umidio, who sits between them and stuffs himself without restraint. On this glutton not even food has a positive influence since he dies soon afterward, carried off by the lethal
effects of colchicum juice. In a comment reminiscent of Boccaccio's words at the end of *Decameron*,[8] the narrator explains
that this juice filtered and "taken in very small amounts "preso
in piccolissima dose" ... mixed with the purest honey and

ginger, becomes that prodigious liquor, a few drops of which have the power to heal ailments; at the wrong dosage, it can touch the body with the cold fingers of death" (1981, 20–21).[9] Thus the first act of the liberating process is realized through the physical elimination of the old abbot, whose death is the first breach in the wall that separates the unhappy duke from life's pleasures, and which will be ultimately destroyed by the progressive disappearances of the other abbot-jailers.

Duke Franchino, the man "who did not know how to love" (1981, 11), gains a deeper human dimension as the events of the novel unfold, and his transformation is made possible solely by food. One evening, after the death of the first two abbots, Franchino, exhilarated by the aroma of hot wine and the scent of rose water that emanates from Bianca's body, finally succeeds in touching her. But the true contact between them takes place in a strange and magical moment in which the duke's memory transports him to his native Mantua, its gorgeous pumpkins, and bunches of grapes as sweet as honey. He describes to the mesmerized Bianca the preparation of Mantuan delicacies:

> When all the pork meat is cooked or salted, there remain the hot and bleeding entrails, wrapped in a fatty and rich membrane. It is from this membrane that our peasants obtain their humble treat. They heat it and melt its fat, which is used later throughout the year. What is left is thrown in a sizzling pan, and small bits form, which, roasted and hot, are sprinkled with salt and eaten immediately. It is at this point that people realize that, accompanied by that tart, light wine called Lambrusco, they are so delicious as to satisfy a gentleman's palate and they prepare the stomach for the sumptuous dishes to follow. (1981, 43–44).[10]

These words that Franchino offers to his beloved are full of nostalgic and genuine love for the culinary traditions of Mantua and rise to the plane of a true love declaration. The depiction of the different phases of food preparation, sensual in the richness and "fleshiness" of the details, is the expression of Franchino's desire for Bianca, a transposed confession of his innermost feelings. Her benign and warm response and her proposal to re-create those delicacies at her court to cure Franchino of his homesickness signal her acknowledgment and, in a way, also her appreciation of the duke's sentiments.

This gastronomic dialogue has the same implications as other similar dialogues in Italian literature, in which food becomes in Biasin's words, "the privileged catalyst of need-desire and desire-satisfaction relationships, both in strictly alimentary terms and in terms of eroticism: it is enough to think of Mena and compare Alfio in *I malavoglia* or of Tancredi and Angelica in *Il gattopardo* or of many of Calvino's pages" (1991, 20).[11] But here, differently than elsewhere, the female protagonist is in a position of absolute advantage over her male counterpart, and the power she exerts upon him is liberating rather than oppressive, vivifying rather than destructive. Hence, during the feast that follows the preparation of the Mantuan recipes, a preparation narrated very meticulously and overflowing with smells, color, and sounds (a description that shows the continuity between oral/narrative pleasures and oral/culinary gratification), Bianca presents her guests with an *eau de vie* never tried before, whose wonderful property is "A fire of pleasure that warmed up even the most remote recess of the body with hot sensations and flowed for the happiness of all the guests" [Un fuoco di piacere che fin negli ultimi visceri accese di caldi sensi, scorse per la gioia di tutti i commensali (1981, 48)]. This marvelous, fortifying liqueur, though, kills Abbot Torchiato, (his is the third mysterious death in the castle) precisely because his role at the courts annihilates life and joy.

The links between femininity, life, nutrition, pleasure, and eroticism become emblematic in the central chapters of the novel. Here the narration is set principally in the kitchen of the castle, which appears as a sort of gigantic uterus. In fact, the access to the kitchen is through "a narrow and dark corridor. . . . [A] warmth smelling of milk and smoke" [un corridoio stretto e oscuro . . . un tepore profumato di fumo e di latte (1981, 59)] hangs in the air. When approaching the kitchen, as when putting one's ear to a pregnant woman's belly, "faint noises of liveliness" [deboli rumori di vita] are heard. In the kitchen, the Philosopher who is visiting the castle and the herbalist Venafro meet one morning, both attracted there by the same "impelling craving for hot milk" [prepotente voglia di latte caldo (1981, 59)]. Here the Philosopher sets out for Venafro the foundations of his thoughts. His words have a strong metanarrative meaning because he denies the absolute validity of the principle of causality, thus admitting the possibility that more than one truth may exist and that events may be correctly interpreted in different ways. "Each kind of thinking follows its own logic," he claims, each community of people, each time, each culture has its own type of thinking. The goal

I set for myself is to demonstrate that they are all worthy, even if in contradiction with one another" (1981, 56).[12] This philosophy is also, in a way, the main goal of Laura Mancinelli's book, which intends to pursue the representation of an image of the Middle Ages that is "other" with respect to the tradition. Because of its ironical construction, her "re-creation" of a medieval past questions not only history, but also literary topoi and traditional concepts about that society and its values, and it reveals that both the former and the latter share the same *cultural* background. It is particularly significant, I would argue, that the conversation between Venafro and the Philosopher, two male characters, takes place in the kitchen/uterus of the castle. The kitchen is in fact a metaphor for all that Western culture has traditionally marginalized or hypocritically stigmatized: the female, her sexuality and her right to pleasure. This "womb," warm and full of life, that welcomes and makes possible the new vision of reality proposed by the Philosopher, rejects and ejects Abbot Celorio, the fourth victim, killed when the kitchen's best and heaviest pan slips fatally off its hook. It is the same pan used in the convivial ritual of preparing exquisite chestnut fritters, which Mancinelli depicts with subtle eroticism:

> The guests were presented with a dish of rare exquisiteness. The delicate sweetness of chestnut pulp, heightened by the much sweeter raisins and by the severe taste of the walnuts chopped in rather large pieces, was perfected by being fried in salted lard, which created with the sweetness both a contrast and a refined harmony. The sizzling pancakes were served with large goblets of tart and sparkling white wine chilled in snow, and thus—wine's wonderful power!—instead of chilling the bodies of the guests, it warms and excites them even more. (1981, 63)[13]

The elimination of the abbot by means of the pan responsible for so much pleasure marks, once again, the re-creative trajectory of the novel: The next stage of this trajectory is the episode of the fictitious exorcising of the kitchen operated by the Wise Priestess (*la Saggia Pretessa*)—another visitor to the castle. The absurd ritual she performs with her outlandish paraphernalia is supposed to chase away from the chimney/vagina those demons that, in the collective imagination, infest and contaminate the kitchen, symbol of the female body and of female eroticism, and which surround it with a dark, threatening aura. The blasphemy inherent in the priestess's act—in her superior wisdom she does not believe in the demons of whose destruction she is in charge—reflects the author's ironic use of writing. In the novel, in fact, the totalizing order (for instance, the medieval castle and all the denotations this image possesses) is presented only to be immediately questioned and problemized.

One of the most problematic narrative strategies in the novel is the use of intertextual references. Thus, except for Mistral and Ildebrando, the abbots are all victims of apparently casual accidents dictated by a sort of rule that is obviously a parody of Dante's rule of *Contrapasso*. Hence, obese and lazy Abbot Nevoso, betrayed by his desire for an object that spares him the effort of walking or riding in the snow, dies using a revolutionary sled. The power of his desire makes him forget all precautions and overlook the risks linked to the experimental nature of the sled. In a similar way toward the end of the novel, Abbot Prudenzio, handsome and gallant but coy, dies. During a love skirmish with Ildegonda one of Bianca's guests, he is punctured by the sharp spikes of a gate he had erected around his bed as a defense against the woman's attacks. "This and more happens to him who denies himself to women's amorous desires, and may this be a lesson to all those men who niggardly yield their favors, *for such is the revenge of the Almighty bestowed on them* to suffer cruelly from their own defense" (1981, 120; my italics).[14] These allusions to Dante and the recurring imitations of the lexicon and of syntactical forms characteristic of many medieval genres (see, for instance, the ballads of the troubadour, the exempla and the narrator's moralizing comments, the Philosopher's medical remedies, and the entries in Venafro's herbarium) as well as of Renaissance genres (see the narration of Abbot Leonzio's pursuit of damsel Pilar recalling the vain pursuits of Ariosto's knights) undoubtedly insert this novel into the category of postmodern "historiographic metafiction" as defined by Linda Hutcheon. Intertextuality, she argues,

> is not the attempt to void or avoid history. Instead, it directly confronts the past literature and historiography, for it too derives from other texts (documents). It uses and abuses intertextual echoes, inscribing their powerful allusions and then subverting that power through irony. (1988, 67)

As I have demonstrated through this analysis, the postmodernity of *I dodici abati di Challant* finds its main expedient in food, whose language of flavors and knowledge it combines and conjugates. Through food the novel operates its "metabolization" of the past and its traditions, proposing at the same time a different approach to reality that will recognize the necessity of differences and of "other" possible truths. This disclosure toward a new epistemology is completely achieved in the final scene of the novel when Venafro asks Bianca whether she will reconstruct the castle, burned down by the possessed Abbot Ildebrando. "No, Venafro." she answers. "A castle cannot be reconstructed. I will build a house where all those who come to see us will be allowed to stay" (139).[15]

The dismantled castle epitomizes, I believe, the complex discursive constructs that the narration has revealed and deconstructed. By refusing to rebuild it, Laura Mancinelli, through Bianca's voice, signals her commitment as a woman writer to creating an inclusive rather than an exclusive, a de-totalizing rather than a marginalizing cultural space.

Notes

1. elimina il valore della crono-logia in favore dell'unità delle parti del sapere.

2. Exceptions are Giuseppe Amoroso 1983, 244–46; Stefano Tani 1990, 368–69. The only lengthy analysis of Mancinell's novel, though, is found in Marco Testi 1992, 85–110.

3. See Testi 1992, 93–94.

4. See Bandello 1992. IV; 43–49. Bandello's novellas were published between 1554 and 1573.

5. già presentiva la ferita aperta, la crosta vulnerata in qualche parte, la mano audace che, ladrescamente, gli rapinava virtute e continenza.

6. Salamanca propendeva per il martirio, perchè intendeva che martirio fosse sottrarsi all'amore di una donna nobile e bella quale fu Madonna Isabella d'Aquitania. . . . Parigi sentenziò che non martirio era, sibben follia.

7. Il romanzo, fin dalle sue origini, non ha potuto fare a meno di occuparsi di tale realtà [alimentare *n.d.a*] com'è indicato emblematicamente dal nome di un personaggio famoso, Sancho Panza: la dimensione antropologica del nutrimento, e poi quella sociologica delle classi, quella politica del potere e quella culturale dei valori, interagiscono fin dall'inizio con la dimensione letteraria.

Non v'è dubbio che alla base di un tale sistema di relazioni stia il dato fondamentale che la bocca umana è il luogo ambiguo di due oralità: quella che articola la voce, il linguaggio e quella che soddisfa un bisogno, l'ingestione del cibo per la sopravvivenza innanzitutto, ma anche per un piacere che si sovrappone al valore del nutrimento.

8. See Boccaccio 1966, 673–77.

9. mescolato a miele e zenzero purissimi diviene quel liquore portentoso che può guarire, a gocce, le malattie e può in dosi errate, indurre il gelo della morte nelle membra.

10. Allor che tutta la carne del porco è cotta oppur salata, rimangono I visceri caldi e sanguinanti, avvolti in una membrana grassa e ricca: è da questa membrana che i nostri contadini estraggono la loro umile ghiottoneria. La mettono a fuoco e ne struggono il grasso, che poi s'adopera per tutto l'anno; ciò che rimane viene gettato nella padella ardente e ne escono brevi pezzetti che, rosolati e caldi, si cospargono di sale e si mangiano subito. E allora si accorgono le genti che, accompagnati nello stomaco da quel vinello brusco, che appunto chiamasi lambrusco, son cosa sí buona da soddisfare il palato dei signori e dispongono lo stomaco alle preziose vivande che seguono o seguiranno.

11. catalizzatore privilegiato del rapporto bisogno-desiderio e desiderio-soddisfazione, sia in un senso strettamente alimentare che nell'area dell'erotismo:si pensi a Mena e Compare Alfio nei Malavoglia, o a Tancredi e Angelica nel *Gattopardo* o a molte pagine di Calvino.

12. Ogni tipo di pensiero segue sua logica, ogni comunità di genti, ogni tempo, ogni cultura, ha un suo tipo di pensiero. Il fine che mi propongo è di dimostrare che tutti sono validi, anche se in contraddizione fra di loro.

13. I commensali si trovarono di fronte a una vivanda di rara squisitezza. Il delicato dolce della polpa di castagna, sottolineato da grani di uva passita assai più intensamente dolci e dal severo sapore delle noci rotte in pezzi alquanto grossi, era coronato dall'essere fritto in strutto salato, che creava, col dolce, e contrasto e intesa raffinata. Le frittelle caldissime furono servite con gran boccali di vino bianco frizzante e asprigno, freddo di neve, che meraviglioso potere del vino, invece di raffreddare i corpi dei commensali li riscaldava e eccitava ancor di più.

14. Questo e altro accade [it is the narrator's comment], a chi si rifiuta alli amorosi desider delle donne, e sia di ammaestramento alli uomini tutti che avari son dei lor favori, poi che tal *vendetta contro di essi dispose la divina potestate* che delle loro stesse difese saranno essi le vittime cruente.

15. No, Venafro. Un castello non si può ricostruire. Costruirò una casa perchè possano abitarci tutti quelli che verranno a cercarci.

References

Amoroso, Giuseppe. 1983. *Narrativa italiana 1975–1983*. Milan: Mursia.

Bakhtin, Mikhail. 1990. *The dialogic imagination*. Edited by Michael Holquist. Austin: University of Texas Press.

Bandello, Matteo. [1554–1573] 1992. *La prima parte de le novelle*. A cura di Delmo Maestri. Alessandria: Edizioni dell'Orso.

Biasin, Gian Paolo. 1991. *I sapori della modernità*. Bologna: Il Mulino.

Boccaccio, Giovanni. 1966. *Decameron*. A cura di Cesare Segre. Milan: Mursia.

Calabrese, Omar. 1989. *L'età neobarocca*. Bari: Laterza.

Eco, Umberto. 1985. Dieci modi di sognare il medioevo. In *Sugli specchi e altri saggi*. Milan: Bompiani.

Hutcheon, Linda. 1988. The pastime of past time: Fiction, history, historiographic metafiction. In *Postmodern Genres,* edited by Marjorie Perloff. Norman and London: University of Oklahoma Press.

Mancinelli, Laura. 1981. *I dodici abati di Challant.* Turin: Einaudi.

Tani, Stefano. 1990. *Il romanzo di ritorno.* Milan: Mursia.

Testi, Marco. 1992. *Il romanzo al passato.* Rome: Bulzoni Editore.

Part Three
Representing the Unrepresented

Women Writing History: Female Novels of the Resistance

Bernadette Luciano

Ettore scola's 1977 film, *A SPECIAL DAY*, takes place on the historic date in May 1938 when Hitler went to Rome to sign the alliance treaty between Italy and Germany. While most Italians are in the streets of Rome admiring the spectacle of military strength, two people, a good Fascist mother of six, played by Sophia Loren, and a homosexual dissident, portrayed by Marcello Mastroianni, remain inside their neighboring apartments and by chance meet. In the course of their exchanges, Mastroianni asks Loren why she agrees with the Fascist statement that genius is strictly male. Her response: "It is always men who fill history books, isn't it?" Mastroianni's retort: "Yes, too much perhaps—in that way there isn't room for anyone else, much less women."

As Joan Scott observes, "Historians of women have long been conscious of the need to articulate their relationship to History. They have challenged the notion that women were non-actors by making visible those 'hidden from history,' and they have exposed the biases of a political history that omitted significant contributions by women" (1987, 22). In their novels of the Resistance, Renata Viganò and Lalla Romano attempt to correct the omission of women from recorded history during a unique period in which women actively participated in their nation's civil war. *L'Agnese va a morire* and *Tetto murato* are two Resistance novels that highlight in different ways the roles women played in history and present a revisionist view of history.

Novels of the Italian Resistance focus on resistance to empowered forces. For women, this struggle assumes a gendered dimension. Like their male counterparts they were resisting a tyrannical political ideology. As women they were also resisting the Fascist oppression targeting them, for while the

151

women's movement began in Italy at the end of the nineteenth century, its progress was severely hindered by Fascist laws. Women's participation in the public realm was legally limited to a few professions. Under Fascism women were encouraged to stay home and produce and raise children, preferably male ones who could grow up to serve the state.

The partisan struggle seemed to provide an alternative to women, a means of protesting on both a political and personal level. As De Grazia astutely points out in her study of women under Fascism, the decision for women to join the Resistance required making a more active and risky choice than it did for men (1992, 283). As the nation's warriors, young men were expected to choose sides—not choosing meant risking one's life and being assumed to belong to the other side. By contrast, women were more advantaged materially by not participating. At home they were assured supplies and additional rationing cards (284). Furthermore, they were adhering to the traditional role of keeping the home fires burning by providing protection and stability for the family. By participating, women endangered the social fabric. They abandoned home and children and exposed their own bodies to the risks of rape and/or death that often accompanied the torture of women. However, many women saw their participation in the partisan cause as a means of fulfilling the traditional roles as mothers and wives. By fighting against the forces of Fascism, they provided more for their families and worked to secure a better future for their children (284). Most partisan men, on the other hand, justified their actions not in domestic or personal terms but in political ones. They perceived the struggle as a battle to eradicate Fascism and to create a new and better nation.

In their interviews of women who had participated in the Resistance, Anna Maria Bruzzone and Rachele Farina found that the women themselves proposed the importance of so-called female values: "spontaneity, a refusal to be calculating, a sense of justice, the passionate ability to love and suffer, the antirhetorical respect for the truth of facts and of silences; communicative generosity, modesty, mercy" [spontaneità, rifiuto del calcolo, senso di giustizia, capacità appassionata di amare e di soffrire, rispetto antiretorico della verità dei fatti e dei silenzi, generosità comunicativa, modestia, pietà (quoted in Passerini 1991, 23)]. When considering women's participation in an armed struggle, the question is how to position the violence of war among these traditional values. As Jean Bethke Elshtain observes in her work *Women and War,*

> We in the West are the heirs of a tradition that assumes an affinity between women and peace, between men and war, a tradition that consists of culturally constructed and transmitted myths and memories. Man construed as violent; woman as non-violent, offering succor and compassion. (1987, 4)

In Viganò's *L'Agnese va a morire* we see how a woman's choice to participate in war requires, in fact, that she achieve a new level of consciousness. In order to become a participant in war, she must accept and participate in violence, violence that in accordance to the Resistance myth is totally justified because it is utilized in the struggle against an ultimate evil, Fascism. According to Elshtain, "Women warriors, like their male counterparts, see their violent actions as a form of defence preservation, life saving" (1987, 179). Marisa Masù, an Italian Resistance fighter, claims that "It was clear that each Nazi I killed, each bomb I helped to explode shortened the length of the war and saved the lives of all women and children." (quoted in Elshtain 1987, 179). According to both Elshtain and Masù, the instinct that dominates is one in which a personal moral code must give way to the cause.

In *L'Agnese va a morire,* however, the personal is never forgotten, and in fact is what finally motivates the protagonist to commit her first act of violence. Agnese is a middle-aged, uneducated peasant who undergoes a political awakening, beginning at the end of the first part of the novel when she confesses to having committed an act of violence. She explains to the head of her brigade that she had wanted to kill the Germans when they had come to take her husband away, but that at the time, she had been paralyzed by fear. Her eventual killing of a German soldier signifies the conquest of her fear, of her passivity—the passage from inaction to action. Within the structure of the novel, this moment of articulation and subjectivity is a moment of epiphany—it is dawn, the beginning of a new day and a new phase in Agnese's life. The companions, having heard her brief description, stare in silence at her large hands, in awe of her heretofore unrecognized strength. Because of her commission of this violent act, she is apparently admitted into their ranks.

Nonetheless, the larger-than-life androgynous portrayal that ends the first part of the book is followed by an anecdote that codifies Agnese's traditionally female representation in the novel. While crossing a canal with her companions, Agnese finds that the *comandante* reminds her of an old acquaintance, a doctor who had mistaken her for her husband's mother rather than his wife. In fact, "mamma" is how the partisans address her and is the role she assumes for herself later in the novel when the Germans question her relationship to the comrades she is sheltering. In essence, it is in her role as surrogate mother and wife that Agnese still seems most at ease. Her involvement in the Resistance movement is born out of wifely obligation, out of a desire to continue the work of her dead husband. Agnese draws her strength from visions she summons, dreams in which her husband appears before her, reminding her that she had been a good wife and encouraging her to carry on his cause. Her strength arises from a continual desire to fulfill the traditional duty of pleasing the husband, and her rewards are her male companions' often patronizing compliments. Back from her arduous solitary missions, she regularly falls back into a traditional female role, usually of a mother figure preparing meals, washing clothes, and securing the men's comfort. In exchange, she receives from her male companions the respect exhibited not to an equal but to a mother. Their concern sanctifies the assistance and comfort she provides them. This symbiotic relationship provides security to both Agnese and her companions, and provides the illusion of normalcy to a lifestyle that is everything but normal. The Resistance was in effect a movement that, while relying on female participation, did not espouse a subversion of gender roles but rather reinforced them. As Passerini reminds us, many of the functions undertaken by partisan women were "typically" female: preparing food and clothing, preparing bodies for burial, and sometimes assuming stereotypical roles such as posing as prostitutes to deceive the enemy (1991, 24).

Women's subordinate position is mirrored by Agnese's physical isolation from the men. Even when she is in the company of her comrades, she is segregated from them, occupying her own corner where she sits, knitting in hand. At these times, she is more their servant than their equal, often eating alone after having prepared meals for them. The fact that she remains an outsider among her male companions is reinforced by her silence. She listens but does not participate in discussions. When she finally does speak, the company, having forgotten her presence, is surprised and in fact disturbed. As De Grazia suggests, the Resistance

> did not encourage critiques of male supremacy nor contemplate situations in which to confront complex issues of self-identity and gender reconstruction. Partisan combatants were uneasy in the company of women, though they relied on them in order to conduct their operations. Women's presence at campsites far from being a consolation, signaled the messiness of partisan warfare (1992, 285).

In fact, Agnese's companions seem uneasy with her independent thinking, especially when such thinking exhibits "female qualities." For example, on one occasion she is reprimanded for what can only be recognized as human mercy: the sheltering of six soldiers who had nowhere to turn. The *comandante* only sees the political risk involved in her action and punishes her by patronizingly making her prepare a meal—a traditional female task—and orders her to do nothing "of your own device" [di tua testa]. He cannot recognize the value of her contribution to the party through actions motivated and governed by an uncalculated instinct—human sentiment, female nurturing, maternal solicitude. In this world of men, she is the only one who understands and verbalizes human suffering and tries to put an end to it: "I don't understand anything, but what needs to be done gets done" [io non capisco niente; ma quello che c'è da fare, si fa (Viganò 1974, 162)]. Viganò applies an individual moral code to wartime decisions, a code not common to military strategy and one that is not acceptable to the empowered. Women in war are sometimes called upon to execute the same duties as men, but this neither empowers women nor encourages their subjectivity because their behavior is meant to correspond to a predetermined code. Paradoxically, civil war, which forces a nation to reconceive its political structures, only reluctantly accepts the temporary subversion of gender roles. As Margaret Higonnet suggests, "The radical changes for women precipitated by war are understood to be mere interruptions of 'normal' gender relations. The nation calls upon women to change their roles only 'for the duration'" (1987, 31).

Viganò intended to create a character who represented the thousands of disempowered Italians who, prior to the Resistance, had little hope of playing a decisive role in the forging of a post-Fascist Italy. Their struggle and sacrifice is Agnese's sacrifice, the necessary precondition for the redemption of the working class. The standard Marxist doctrine resonating in Viganò's novel reflects the pro-Communist feeling that prevailed in Italy in the post-war period. Symbolically, Agnese dies a mythic heroine, sacrificed for a cause, alone, outside of history, her physical largeness ultimately reduced to an uncharacteristically small mass—a pile of rags. In the final pages of *L'Agnese va a morire*, the dying figure of Agnese, the proverbial earth mother who has featured less and less prominently in the third part of the book, finally disappears from the text. The stage turns to quasi-documentary accounts of the struggle of male partisans. The *comandante* declares that after the Liberation he personally will spread the word of Agnese's important contribution to the company and to the Communist Party. However, the assumption that history will remember and record her, and by extension other female achievements, is inaccurate. The contribution of the 70,000 partisan women has been largely forgotten—many textual accounts of their participation are missing. In the numerous history books of the period, women are referred to only peripherally. At a 1978 congress on women's role in the Resistance, Giuliana Gadola Beltrami attributed this absence from history to the fact that our society remains male, and while the participation of women in a war or in a struggle may be requested when necessary, it is easily and readily deleted from recorded memory (quoted in Franceschi 1978, 16). Agnese's role in the novel is representative of woman's situation vis-à-vis a traditional definition of "history." After all, according to "history" it is the young partisan men, and not a middle-aged woman, who carved out the Communist future for which the myth of the Resistance had provided the rationalization.

Hence, women writing about the period were, by their very act of writing, resisting the representation or misrepresentation of their cultural experience. *L'Agnese va a morire*, both in its narrative structure and in its development of character, highlights the achievements of a Resistance fighter but accepts the inevitable outcome propagated by the male myth of the Resistance. The novel is told in the style of a quasi-documentary neorealist novel with the female protagonist eventually disappearing from the text and leaving the new history of Italy to be forged by its young male hero.

Lalla Romano's novel, *Tetto Murato*, published in 1957, provides, instead, a truly alternative vision of the Resistance and of history. Rather than starting from a political myth, as Viganò's novel does, and going on to highlight the personal achievements that exalt the partisan cause, Romano unveils an intimate personal narrative. Through the personal, a political reality is deduced. Romano explores the possibility of intimacy and human solidarity afforded us by rare historical moments.

Tetto Murato questions the neorealist contention that historical reality possesses a narratable order that may be represented without distortion or transfiguration and suggests rather that the fundamental basis of historical narration must be reconsidered. As Romano herself writes in "Scrittura e l'inconscio" (1991),

> Novels are historical if they are not novels. Because there should not be a substrata of history that has been learned and studies from books and fictionalized characters that are no less imaginary. History is born from authenticity and the writer can only be authentic when talking about him/herself.[1]

Hence in narrating history, the personal overrides but does not exclude the political. A writer represents his or her experience consisting of historical events filtered through memory and even dreams, the combination of which make up the reality of an individual experience. In other words, in the historical novel the individual dominates the foreground and the historical event makes up the background. The two do not run parallel courses, but the pretext is that the link between the event and the individual is inextricable.

While Romano claims that her books do not present external conflicts or historical events, the historical circumstance in *Tetto Murato* is by no means irrelevant. In fact, the war and the Resistance are necessary preconditions for the novel. This alternative approach to representing history as a personal event steeped in individual psychology approaches Carla Lonzi's feminist theory of history, which suggests that it is human error "to find the causes of anxiety in the outside world, in the form of a hostile structure against which he must struggle" (quoted in Bono and Kemp 1991, 57). Rather, as interpreters of history we must consider that problems of humanity lie not exterior to but "in the rigidity of psychological structure" (57). Such a theory discredits the long prevailing myth that the problems of wartime and post-war Italy lie solely in the evils of Fascism and Nazism and that the Liberation and a new political machine could solve the country's ills. Through its examination of personal relationships, *Tetto Murato* brings us closer to an understanding of the hope inspired by the Resistance as well as of the danger of too much faith in the Liberation.

Tetto Murato begins in a small town in Piedmont where the narrator, Giulia, has sought refuge in the home of two elderly cousins. Giulia is immediately intrigued by a young couple she meets who has recently moved to this same town—namely, Paolo, a mysteriously ill partisan intellectual, and his wife, Ada. After the armistice, Paolo and Ada are forced to seek refuge in the protected *tetto murato*, a type of construction typically found in Piedmont consisting of a group of houses, courtyards, and orchards enclosed by four walls. Giulia visits the couple on an ever more frequent basis, providing them with company and assistance, and the relationship between the three intensifies. It is a relationship based on solidarity and mandated by the censorship and oppression of Fascism and Nazism. This restriction encouraged a mute symbolic order marked by nonverbal communication. Honest and clear, that shared silence accounts for the solidarity suggested by the Pavese citation with which Romano prefaces the novel: "There is no real silence unless it is shared" [Non c'è vero silenzio se non condiviso (1957)]. Lalla Romano presents this kind of alternate lifestyle as something that could only exist under extraordinary circumstances, and while it may seem magical and dreamlike, in the unfolding of the novel it comes to represent a new notion of reality.

The novel seems suspended in time, immobile. The passage of days and months is expressed in terms of a natural calendar—the turning of the seasons—rather than a historical one. There are minimal references to dates, and these are marked by absence rather than engagement. The narrator remembers the important dates (25 July and 8 September) in the recounting and reconstruction of the collective historical narrative as dates in which she was away from the city, from the political, and as one removed and disempowered by history, existing in a marginal reality.

However, it is this very marginalization that allows for the breakdown of social conventions and for the emergence of non-traditional relationships that would not otherwise form. The two most important relationships that develop (and then dissolve with the Liberation) are the crossover relationships between the two married couples: between Giulia and Ada's husband, and between Ada and Giulia's husband. These are relationships based on "elective affinities" (a term Romano borrows from Goethe): Ada and Stefano are attracted to each other's shared faith and optimism about life; Giulia and Paolo, to their mutual silence and suspicion. The new "couples" understand each other because they are similar and because there is a natural attraction between them. However, there is a symbiotic and cultural order that matches the weak with the strong, and it is that order that is ultimately restored.

Words and the traditional symbolic order are the currency of the corrupt power structure. Fascism imposes silence, which in turn subverts language, and words are relegated to the level of rhetoric and superficiality. The relationships that develop in the alternative world of *tetto murato* are nurtured by less conventional forms of communication. The truth resonates in that which is unsaid. Communication involves a form of decoding. For example, in order to unveil the mystery of Paolo, Giulia must learn to interpret signs: his silence, his books, and his smile. Ada and Paolo communicate through gestures that are either visual or tactile. These alternate forms of communication create a deeper and more honest level of understanding and of solidarity among the friends.

However, despite the intensity of these sentiments, the bonds formed at *tetto murato* dissolve after the Liberation. Giulia and Stefano return to the city and occasionally speculate on the well-being of their friends. When Giulia finally goes to visit Ada, she finds the period of their closeness is past; the spell has been broken; the two couples are not only physically separated but have lost the intimacy allotted them during the war, when societal norms could be ignored. As traditional life resumes, so do the publicly acknowledged relationships. Giulia attempts to redeem herself with her cousins by apologizing for her behavior, and their response reflects their support of a status quo that they do not want to question: no need, they claim, to ask for forgiveness among loved ones; they seek only to forget the period that disrupted the social order. Just as the reconciliation of Giulia and her family suggests a reestablishment of traditional class roles, the reestablishment of gender roles is seen as the owner of *tetto murato* tells Ada he does not want her to remember him as she had seen him, "reduced" to wear-

ing an apron and engaged in daily chores. While the reversal
of gender roles was reluctantly accepted during the period of
upheaval, it is unacceptable now. Ironically, the end of war
disrupts an order that was fundamentally more honest and yet
which must also be denied. As Romano explains, the historical
circumstance provided for a lifestyle that would not otherwise
have emerged and that would not normally survive:

> The historical circumstance was not irrelevant to the novel: in
> fact, the possibility of intimacy was due precisely to that living
> on the edge, in a forced suspension that involves concentration,
> receptiveness to contemplation, to the discovery of pure and poor
> beauty; and above all it favored the birth of feelings which were
> intense but tacit, secret.[2]

The conclusion is dismal, for how can the Liberation provide
hope for a new and better future if there is desire only to rein-
state the norm and to come to terms with the age-old hypocri-
sies that underlie society? In this sense, *Tetto Murato* looks back
and questions the positive historical outcome suggested at the
end of *L'Agnese va a morire* and by the official party line.

Romano's descriptions of the world beyond the walls add to
this negative presentiment. It is only by looking at the real
world from the protection and the idealized perspective of *tetto
murato* that the violence between a Nazi spy and a partisan
cannot be blindly justified in political terms, as many violent
acts committed by partisans were considered. Instead, this
violence appears as yet another act of human cruelty and
senseless violence. Upon first witnessing the scene, Ada does
not understand her lack of sympathy for the partisan who slaps
the face of a Nazi sympathizer. She attributes it initially to a
maternal instinct. She feels she is protecting the young boy in
the company. Finally she concludes: "violence, even when it
was just violence was frightening, and justice, therefore, was
so much more virtuous" [la violenza, anche quando era giusta
era spaventosa e forse la giustizia, perciò, era tanto piú meri-
toria (Romano 1957, 134)]. This is perhaps Romano's most
politically risky statement in the novel, as she dares to paint
a less than glorious picture of the Resistance and of some of
its questionable tactics. She does not participate in or justify
violence from an ideological perspective as Viganò and Masù
do.

Ultimately this novel departs from other fictionalized accounts of the Resistance because it does not make a myth of

the partisan experience but rather boldly questions the justi-
fication of violence and the blind belief in the facility with
which political change occurs. Romano's novel marks a clear
divergence from Viganò's *L'Agnese va a morire*, in which the
heroine is sacrificed for the partisan cause that paved the road
for an idealistic new male dominated order and post-war future for Italy. *Tetto Murato* lacks such traditional closure, offering instead a vision of history that could include women
among its players. While important relationships dissolve at
the end of *Tetto Murato*, the women do not disappear from the
text (as Agnese does) but are exclusively featured in the final
chapter. The men are absent or silent. Giulia and Ada, united
throughout the novel by their shared nurturing of a physically
weak man, exchange a parting embrace, a symbol of female
solidarity that suggests the promise and uncertainty of the
future and of history. What *Tetto Murato* finally proposes is a
feminist historical discourse that celebrates the possibility of
intimacy and human solidarity and writes history as the personal event inextricably linked to the historical moment.
While Viganò's novel features a sole female protagonist
fighting for equality and recognition in official history, Romano examines history through shared female experience. Finally, *Tetto Murato* is not about the ultimate effect of official
history on women but of women on official history. While Viganò's novel seems to be a closed chapter, Romano's suggests
that there is a continuity to women's history based, among
other things, on a tradition of female solidarity.

Notes

Translations are my own.
1. I romanzi sono storici se non sono romanzi storici. Perché non ci deve
essere un substrato di storia imparata e studiata sui libri e poi i personaggi
fittizi più o meno immaginari. La storia nasce dall'autenticità e lo scrittore
non può essere autentico se non quando parla di se stesso. . . . (1550).
2. Non era indifferente, nel romanzo la circostanza storica: anzi, la possibilità dell'intimismo era offerta proprio da quel vivere al margine, in una
sospensione forzata che comporta concentrazione, disponibilità alla contemplazione, alla scoperta della bellezza pura, povera; e soprattutto favorisa
il nascere di sentimenti intensi però taciuti, segreti (1068).

References

Bono, Paola, and Sandra Kemp, eds. 1991. *Italian feminist thought: A reader.*
  Oxford: Basil Blackwell.

De Grazia, Victoria. 1992. *How fascism ruled women.* Berkeley: University of California Press.

Elshtain, Jean Bethke. 1987. *Women and war.* New York: Basic Books.

Franceschi, Lidia, ed. 1978. *L'altra metà della Resistenza.* Milan: Mazzotta.

Higonnet, Margaret R., and Patrice L. R. 1987. The double helix. In *Behind the lines: Gender and the two world wars,* edited by Margaret Randolph Higonnet, Jane Jenson, Sonya Michel and Margaret Collins Weitz. New Haven: Yale University Press.

Lonzi, Carla. 1991. *Let's spit on Hegel,* excerpted, translated, and reprinted in Bono and Kemp, eds.

Passerini, Luisa. 1991. *Storie di donne e femministe.* Turin: Rosenberg & Sellier.

Romano, Lalla. 1991. Nota to *Tetto Murato.* In *Opere,* edited by Cesare Segre. Milan: Mondadori.

———. 1991. Scrittura e l'inconsio. In *Opere,* edited by Cesare Segre. Milan: Mondadori.

———. 1957. *Tetto Murato.* Turin: Einaudi.

Scola, Ettore. 1977. *A special day.* [a film]

Scott, Joan Wallach, 1987. Rewriting history. In Higonnet et al. eds.

Viganò, Renata. 1974. *L'Agnese va a morire.* Torino: Einaudi.

Brushing Benjamin against the Grain: Elsa Morante and the *Jetztzeit* of Marginal History

MAURIZIA BOSCAGLI

IN A LETTER OF MARCH 1937 TO WALTER BENJAMIN, MAX HORKHEIMER comments upon a passage from "Edward Fuchs, Collector and Historian," which Benjamin had written for the *Zeitschrift für Sozialforschung:*

> I have long been thinking about the question whether the work of history is complete. Your formulation can certainly stand as it is. I have but one personal reservation: that I think this is a relationship only to be perceived dialectically. The pronouncement of incompleteness is idealistic if it does not incorporate completeness as well. Past injustice is done and finished. Those who have been beaten to death are truly dead. Ultimately you are making a theological statement. If one takes incompleteness absolutely seriously, then one must believe in the Last Judgement. My thinking is too contaminated with materialism for that. (Quoted in Tiedemann 1988, 181)

The question of the "incompleteness of the past" is further elaborated by Benjamin in the "Theses on The Philosophy of History," a text of 1940. In the "Theses," by opposing the work of historical materialism to that of historicism, Benjamin presents a theory of the real course of history, as well as a theory of materialist historiography. This new historiographical practice inaugurated by Benjamin is at work in Elsa Morante's novel *History* (1984) published in Italy in 1974,[1] where the "incompleteness of the past" is foregrounded (and compensated for) by confronting the "objective" narration of the history book (realism) with the rich language of fiction, this time in a tone that could be defined as magic realism or, perhaps, "hyperhistoricism." Both Benjamin's and Morante's writings are critiques (and in the case of the latter a real *j'accuse*) of the

163

supposedly scientific and disinterested character of history in Western culture. History, in their thinking, is a form of representation. With a move that anticipates the perspective of Michel Foucault and of Hayden White,[2] both Benjamin and Morante show that history is first of all narration, a cultural practice that takes shape in the always already-colonized territory of language: that is, history is a form of knowledge produced and governed by power. In turn, power proceeds through the logic of the same: the victor, he who survives and has the means of formulating and managing the *representation* of the "facts," will pose himself at the center of history, and will delete any memory of his victims. Both Benjamin and Morante establish their reconstructive notion of historiography by questioning the privileged discourse of rationalism with "irrationality": through Jewish messianism Benjamin exposes the fallacy of Western philosophy (both idealism and marxism), while Morante deploys *and* debunks realism as a bourgeois narrative mode through an unorthodox religious discourse.

The "Theses" constitute a critique of historicism, the dominant, teleological vision of history in both its hegelian and orthodox marxist interpretation. Benjamin rejects the historicist view of the past as an uninterrupted flow of events and linear development, together with the notion of history as progress, which is founded on the belief in the perfectibility of man and of the social formation. While the historicist critic believes that "the truth will never run away from us," the historical materialist (as Benjamin himself) knows that history is a history of loss:

> The true picture of history flits by. The past can be seized only as an image which flashes up at an instant when it can be recognized and is never seen again. . . . Every image of the past that is not recognized by the present as one of its concerns threatens to disappear irretrievably. If the past is not completed, if history is not retrieved from the representation provided by the victor, "even the dead will not be safe." (255)

It must be made clear that for Benjamin the historical flow of facts, what is remembered of the past, is the history of the victor. This particular version of history—"And all the rulers are the heirs of those who conquered before them" (256)—makes invisible the history of the oppressed, in Benjamin's instance, the working class. While "historicism sympathizes with the victor," reproducing the lie of history as the all-encompassing flow of a "completed" past, the task of the historical materialist is to redeem what is, or could become, irretrievably lost: the "anonymous toil" of those who guarantee power its course. In particular, the task of the historian is to make visible the barbarism inscribed in any document of civilization, to use Benjamin's own words.

The lost past flashes up, intermittently, at moments of danger, of emergency. Fascism, the historical conjuncture that Benjamin experienced personally, constitutes such a moment of danger, a danger that the historicist does not recognize as such, and rather poses as the norm: "One reason why fascism has a chance is that in the name of progress its opponents treat it as historical norm" (275). To fight fascism, therefore, "it is our task to bring about a real state of emergency." Yet revolution, "the real state of emergency," is not posed by Benjamin as inevitable. It is exactly on the question of history and the revolution that Benjamin's theory takes distance from the assumptions of orthodox marxism. In Marx's vision, the conflict between the forces of production inevitably leads to the blowing-apart of the property relations, and then produces a new social formation. Instead, Benjamin sees the proletariat of his own times as the blinded subject of history, reduced to conformism and complicity with capitalist power, and no longer the promoter of an inexorable historical development. If the revolution is no longer the necessary telos of history, how can historical movement itself be theorized? What can inject a new revolutionary stimulus into the calcified theory of historical materialism is not philosophy but theology. The "leap into the open air of history," what will interrupt and change the course of history, takes place not through an act of will, but through an act of faith.

In order to do away with the notion of historical progress purported by the historicist, Benjamin needs a new notion of time: "The concept of the historical progress of mankind cannot be sundered from the concept of its progression through a homogeneous, empty time" (261). This homogeneous, empty time (*das Immergleiche*, the always-the-same) is what produces the illusion of the completeness of the past. It is by focusing on rupture, intermittence, interruption that the "other history," the history of the oppressed, can be made visible: "History is subject of a structure whose site is not homogeneous, empty time, but filled with the presence of the now *Jetztzeit*"

(261). In order to grasp the movement of history, its flow must be brought to a halt. The *Jetztzeit* is exactly the moment that cuts through history, the "now" that blasts its continuum open, thus disrupting and contradicting history's claimed completeness: "In this structure [the historical materialist] recognizes the sign of a messianic cessation of happening—or, put differently, a revolutionary chance in the fight for the oppressed past" (263). Here there are two Benjamins speaking: one is the younger man who begins his reflection on the incompleteness of history through the images and the concepts of Jewish mysticism; the other is Benjamin the unorthodox marxist, enlisting his theology in the service of historical materialism in order to denounce its insidious participation in the logic of oppression, ultimately in fascism. In the "Theses," the "politicians" that have reduced the proletarian to passivity and conformity with the capitalist norm, are not only the German social democrats, but, even more, Stalin. The "Theses" were written during and in the immediate aftermath of the Hitler-Stalin Pact, in the summer of 1939, and represent Benjamin's attempt to dissociate himself from a "thinking," and a political practice (orthodox marxism), that at that moment was compromising with fascism: more precisely, from Marxism as a science that legitimized the politics of Stalin.

This is the historical state of emergency that prompts Benjamin to revise historical materialism's faith in progress through theology, and particularly through the discourse of Jewish mysticism. The messianic idea of redemption, central in the "Theses," the suspension of the continuum of history through the *Jetztzeit*, relies upon the antithetical distinction (and the possibility of a clash) between historical and messianic time. In the Kabbalah, the access to the realm of redemption is depicted as a violent and dangerous process: the transformation of historical time into the messianic era takes place through a series of future natural disasters and catastrophes. However painful and costly this process may be, the historical materialist must exercise his "weak messianic power"; that is, he must enact, even provoke the same catastrophe and ruptures, in order to redeem the past. Only a disrupted and disruptive historiography can properly signify the catastrophic character of history: the *Jetztzeit* becomes then the focal point of historiography, as the moment that reveals and reintegrates what has been canceled from the records.

This same moment of disruption, denunciation and, finally, reintegration of the "other history" from the "space off,"[3] the realm of invisibility to which the history of the oppressed has been reduced, is at the core of Elsa Morante's narrative in *History*. In this essay I read her novel as an enactment of Benjamin's theory of history and historiographical praxis, and at the same time as a revision and a manipulation of the literary conventions of sentimentality and of realism from a materialist and, more problematically, feminist point of view.

Benjamin's and Morante's intentions and methods of analysis overlap more than once: both are concerned with the same historical period, a period whose "historicity" they experienced in person; both consider fascism as a historically specific embodiment of power, of the logic of the victors (the bourgeoisie); both write under a desperate pressure, precisely with the intent of "reawakening" the dead, as well as the conformist subject of history. In her *L'Unità* article, "Censorship in Spain" (15 May 1976), Morante affirms:

> Now, almost an old woman, I felt that I couldn't depart from this life without leaving the others a testimonial memory of the crucial epoch in which I was born. Besides being a work of poetry (which, thank God, it is!) my novel *History* wants to be an accusation of all the fascisms of the world. And at the same time, it represents an urgent and desperate demand—addressed to everybody—for a possible, communal awakening. (My translation)

Morante shares with Benjamin the awareness that marginal history is a flash that might never be seen again, depending on who constructs and manages the circulation of this memory. Like Benjamin, she starts by deploying a materialist analysis of the past, and at the same time—thus showing the shortcomings of the orthodox marxist interpretation of history—she too moves into the realm of theology, this time that of the Gospel. These points of juxtaposition between Morante's and Benjamin's texts are what make the exploration of their writing interesting to me. By no means, however, do the similarities imply identity. As an analysis of Morante's novel in the light of Benjamin's theory, this essay illustrates the particular strategies through which *History* enacts, and simultaneously modifies, Benjamin's concept of history. At the same time, I show how Morante makes Benjamin's theory of oppression more specific in terms of gender and race, and, last but not least, how her writing questions Benjamin's theory. Although both writers deploy the same method of inquiry (a marxist view "theologically" revised), each comes to a different conclusion about history and its redemptive possibilities.

Morante's novel is constituted by a series of intermittent *Jetztzeiten*, moments of historical rupture when the Other of history is made visible. Benjamin's imperative of interrupting, the "messianic" cessation of happening he describes in the "Theses," is visible at the level of the narrative, precisely in the way the plot is constantly articulated and disarticulated. The book, and later each chapter, begins with a sequence of dates, each listing a number of political, "public," national, and international events: "1918. World War I ends with the victory of the Entente . . . ten million dead." A long period of Italian, as well as world, history, from 1900 to 1967, is remembered year by year and "fact by fact": the death of Lenin, the march of Mao, the Spanish civil war, Mussolini's ratification of racial laws, the rise of Nazism, and then the German occupation of Italy in 1941. At this point we have the first Benjaminic rupture: the flow of history is interrupted and the novel begins. Later, the narrative action will be interrupted over and over again in order to introduce other sets of "dates and facts," now reaching to our times.

Through her weaving in and out of history, through this movement across macro-and microtemporal structures, Morante shows us that the private and the public are not opposites: history directly shapes the lives of its individual subjects, and conversely, the apparently meaningless individual is really part of history. The continual exchange between the general and the particular, the official and the banal, is signified and anticipated by the title: *History: A Novel* (in Italian, *La storia*, a semiotically ambiguous term, meaning both "story, narrative" and "history"). History, as Morante implies, is a piece of fiction, artificial because narrated. Already at the opening of the book, the author posits the nature of history as "interested" narrative, structured by power and deploying specific rhetorical strategies to persuade the audience of the "truth" about a certain event. Yet the traffic between historiography and fiction writing suggested by the title points to a further interpretation of Morante's intentions: the history of the excluded, of the marginal, is necessarily made of stories. Since no documentation, no records have been kept, how can the historian fix the traces, register the presence of those who have been silenced and deleted from history except through an act of imagination? The existence of those who did not, who could not speak, who could not bear witness to their own existence on earth, can only be reconstructed through an act of fiction. Their history needs to be a novel.

Morante's narrative opens with an act of violence that symbolically refers to the logic of oppression informing historical "progress": in 1941, during the German occupation of Rome, Ida Ramundo is raped in her own house by a young German soldier. Ida is an elementary school teacher, half-Jewish by birth, and the widowed mother of a child, Nino. She is a subjected figure, bowing down and bearing the yoke of any form of constituted authority: men, the family, her superiors at school, the state and its racism. As a consequence of the rape, she becomes pregnant, and gives birth to Useppe, who will die of epilepsy in his sixth year. Ida is a survivor, and not only of rape: she literally survives the hunger, the homelessness, and the deprivations of war. Although she could be considered the heroine of the novel, Morante inserts her story in a larger narrative frame, thus inextricably mixing it with the stories of other marginal characters with whom Ida comes in contact: her petit bourgeois family, the Jews in the ghetto of Rome, the refugees of Pietralata, the partisans whom Nino, her eldest son joins, and Davide Levi, another key figure in the novel. The stories Morante tells and the detailed account of the lives of the figures she introduces invariably end with their irretrievable eclipse, their death. Ultimately, Ida's own family will be destroyed: Nino dies in a car accident, Useppe dies of a violent epileptic crisis; Ida will survive him only for nine years, dying alone in a mental hospital.

Gender is the crucial element through which Morante complicates Benjamin's historiographical method. The subject of history is defined as genderless by Benjamin: the proletariat have only a class determination in his writing. Although Morante does not exclusively privilege women as the depositories of historical knowledge, she shows interest in the way in which women's oppression and deletion from history is produced: the "struggling, oppressed class" of which Benjamin writes in the "Theses," (1987, 260), is individualized and gendered in Morante's text.[4] Women in *History* are exploited and oppressed *as women*, through sexuality and the body, and in the name of "femininity"; that is, by a specifically patriarchal construction of femininity. Mariulina and her mother are raped; Santina, the prostitute, is exploited and then murdered by Nello, her pimp; Ida herself (without ever complaining) is literally a servant to men. She is the Althusserian subject, working "all by herself," successfully interpellated by a sexist ideology of femininity: as a daughter, bride, mother, widow, and unaware propagator of fascist knowledge for her students, she blindly respects authority, thus reproducing the internalized LAW (of capital, of racism, of gender, of the state), without recognizing its effects on herself.

At the same time, gender is not the only (not even the main) category that defines oppression in *History*. Although Morante recognizes the specificity of female oppression, she does not fetishize women as the only subject of history; rather, she closely looks at the ways in which their victimization intersects with the victimization of other marginalized groups: the ill, the old, the insane, the poor, for instance.[5] By focusing on the historical juxtaposition of different oppressions, Morante avoids an easy, Manichaean division between good and bad, a superficial reading of who the victors and who the victims are. In this perspective the German soldier Gunther is recognizable both as Ida's rapist and as a childlike being "caught in the war" and actually looking for maternal shelter. He is sentimental; before leaving Ida, he gives her his penknife, and while taking a flower as a souvenir and "gravely placing it among some papers of his wallet he said, "Mein ganzes Leben lang!" [for all my life!] (Morante 1984, 62). This contradictory representation of Gunther as defenseless oppressor shows that even characters who seem to occupy a position of power are actually only power's subjects. In this sense, through Morante's endless work of revealing what history and historical progress leave unsaid, the tables are continually turned in the novel.

The detailed inquiry into the individual life of each of her characters is perhaps the most effective strategy the author deploys to open up the continuum of history. Through what could be defined as a technique of "refamiliarization," Morante "identifies" both the victim and the enemy one by one, thus giving each one a face, a voice, a story. In other words, she tries to unmake what history does: depersonalizing human beings, equating difference, reducing everybody to numbers, flattening individuality and differences to a common denominator. While history says "fifty thousand dead," Morante tells the story of one of those fifty thousand in detail, thus taking a leap from the general, impersonal macrostructure of history into the particular, the everyday.

By giving these "numbers" a face, she turns them into recognizable individuals. By telescoping from the public (impersonal) to the private (the personal) with what could be called a photographic zoom technique, she is able to show what the reader could never detect and recognize with the naked eye. Through her novelistic close-ups, Morante pushes to the limit the conventions of realism to produce an effect of closeness and familiarity. Nothing is left out of her text: both the lives and the deaths of her characters are told, and not even the most atrocious details of their suffering are passed by in silence. One of the most unforgettable and painful passages of the book describes the tortured body of the partisan and ex-refugee Moscow, left on the streets of Marino by the Germans for days, and kicked by the passersby. The unbearable horror is almost unreadable. And yet, what this passage represents is exactly what we don't want to see, what goes untold in history books. This is a moment when pain is made material on the page, the moment when we are reminded that our blindness, our choice of not seeing is impossible, only a false choice.

This moment of strident contradiction between "brute reality" and the particular rhetorical strategies through which history discursifies events (the strategies through which we are constructed as an anesthetized audience) is repeated throughout the novel by Morante, with the aim of defamiliarizing our commonsensical view of history. This time, we are asked to see and experience the horror of murder through the eyes of a child: Useppe at the kiosk, looking at the photographs of hung and tortured partisans in an illustrated magazine; Useppe at the Tiburtina station, zooming in on the cattle cars in which the Jews have been imprisoned, while Ida tries to spare him the view by covering his eyes. Another example of the contradictory relationship between "raw reality" and ways of explaining it is Davide's speech on power: "Power ... is degrading for those who submit to it, for those who administer it and for those who control it. Power is the leprosy of the world" (306). This speech is delivered to Santina the prostitute, whose injured and exploited female body is subjected to the inevitability of the power that Davide deprecates and, at the same time, embodies as her client. This contradiction is again perceptible in Giovannino's letters from Russia. The tragic irony of the letters lies in their clashing discourses: Giovannino's ungrammatical writing, full of pain and fear, appears under the word "CONQUER," heading the official stationary of the Italian army. The linguistic and discursive clash, as in the case of Gunther, reveals the duplicity of Giovannino as "conquered conqueror," sharing both in the arrogance of fascism and in the submission of the wretched.

Morante's narrative is centered upon the contradictory relationship of History to "stories": her aim is to make visible and audible what otherwise could not be seen and heard. In its work of interrupting, denouncing, and reintegrating, the novel addresses three major concerns: the inadequacy of language (the impossibility of translating human suffering into language; the automatic exclusion of those whose language is not understandable to the rationality of history); the question of visibility and of "vision" (here Morante is concerned not with sensory vision, but with the visionary capability of the marginal); and the question of self-recognition, that is, the consciousness of one's position in history as the necessary, or perhaps not so necessary, condition for self-redemption. While the first two concerns are dealt with through the logic of Benjamin's theory, the question of self-recognition is another crucial point in which Morante's writing distances itself from Benjamin's.

According to Benjamin, redemption is not transcendental: "It's our own task," he says. "Our coming was expected on earth. Like every generation that preceded us, we have been endowed with a weak messianic power, a power to which the past has a claim" (1987, 254). Endowed with such "weak messianic power," the oppressed themselves are capable of interrupting the continuum of history. As thesis 15 reads, "The awareness that they are about to make the continuum of history explode is characteristic of the revolutionary classes at the moment of their action" (255). For Benjamin the *Jetztzeit* is a moment of revelation that produces consciousness *and* praxis: it becomes, on Benjamin's page, both the necessary condition to operate the revolution *and* the beginning of a messianic era inaugurated through a violent interruption of history through praxis (revolution in this case). In other words, in order to change the course of history, Benjamin's system implies the presence of a self-aware subject, a subject capable of *seeing* his oppression. Perhaps, we could add, the realization of this oppression is corroborated by vision, "theology enlisted in the service of historical materialism." Yet for Benjamin, the oppressed, through their awareness of their real conditions of existence, can become active agents of history. The irruption of messianic time historical time will at least question and jeopardize bourgeois history and bring a yet unknown, new temporality that will see the proletariat as its subject.

Morante finds herself in a quite different position, because her subject is not so automatically capable of self-awareness and of self-recognition. In fact, the novel presents a series of characters "invested" by history, figures at the margins upon whose anonymous toil the edifice of power is erected. But these figures understand neither the logic of power nor their own part in making the machine of history function. Ida herself is totally blind to her own complicity with the social and political structures that oppress her: "she knew how to do nothing except transmit to her elementary pupils those ordinary notions that to her, as an elementary pupil, had been passed on by her teachers, who in turn had received them from their teachers. On occasion, obeying the dictates of the Authorities, she introduced into their themes and dictations the king, Duce, Fatherland, glory, battles that History imposed; however she did it in all mental innocence, unsuspecting, because History, no more than God, had never been an object of her thoughts" (402). Morante often underlines the innocence of these figures by sympathetically comparing them to animals. It is their lack of self-awareness that redeems them, and not their class consciousness. In *History* the working class is not the depository of a higher historical knowledge: the workers to whom Davide tries to get close in the factory in Mantua are completely blind to their own oppression, and forgetfully spend Sundays listening to the radio and talking of "women, music and sport."

Morante's choice of an omniscient narrator speaks exactly of the characters' incapability to know and to see. Nonetheless, at a certain point in the narration, the omniscient narrator shares the power of vision with Davide, both counterfigures of Morante the historian. While the narrator can see through a stroke of narrative artifice, Davide is made aware of oppression exactly because he simultaneously lives in two worlds: he belongs to the class that administers power and at the same time subjects himself to that very power. Because he is at once a bourgeois, a Jew, and an anarchist intellectual, his subjectivity is constructed through a series of contradictions, of ideological and material clashes that make him acutely aware of other people's oppression. His passionate denunciation of the "pornography of history" in the speech he delivers in the bar, represents the culmination of his process of self-awareness as historical subject. Yet, notwithstanding his "enlightened" condition, Davide is helpless and totally unable to change things (in the end, he will commit suicide). In this instance, he seems to play the role of Benjamin's *Angelus Novus*, the Angel of History, whose clarity of vision—"where we perceive a chain of events, he sees a single catastrophe, which keeps piling wreckage upon wreckage and hurls it in front of its feet" (243)—cannot prevent the storm and the disaster. All he can do, like Davide, is to express despair at the obscenity of history.

Nonetheless, in Morante's tale, the angel's desperation grows in stages into a visionary hope. In another part of his speech Davide counterposes to the irredeemable historical time the "oneness" of a catastrophic time outside the progression of history: "existence is one, the same, in all living human things. And the day consciousness knows this, what is left to death? In the 'all-one' death is nothing. Does the light suffer, if you or I close our eyelids? Death is nothing. Unity of consciousness: this is the victory of the revolution over death, the end of History, and the birth of God" (1984, 484). Morante proposes here her own version of materialist theology; the end of history for Benjamin brings the birth of the oppressed; for Morante it brings instead the birth of God as a *Jetztzeit*, a moment of historical suspension. The past is "completed" not through the revolution, but through the recourse to an eternal time, a cyclical time in which life and death unceasingly partake of each other and are no longer opposites. It is Morante's faith in this space of a historical present that redeems the horror of history in her novel. As we have seen, even its narrative structure, made of ruptures and separations, reproduces this horror. The novel respects the formal conventions of the realist novel only apparently: neither the narrator's omniscience nor the deployment of the fictional plot can guarantee final reconciliation, solution, or happy ending.

In fact, the narrative proceeds through a series of frustrating disconnections and losses that divide the characters, instead of bringing them together. The characters Morante introduces are not a function of the plot, they are both created so that the plot can come to completion and any conflict can be resolved. Human beings are not partaking in the progress of history; rather, they are wiped off its scene. Things as well as people disappear silently: in the first chapter, the soldier Gunther, Ida's parents and husband. Objects that are affectively associated with people are lost as well: for instance, Gunther's penknife, and the African mask that Alfio gives Nino. The story develops through a series of painful separations, made even more painful by the familiarity Morante is able to establish between reader and fictional character. All of the characters, in fact, exit like the characters in a play, until the stage—at the moment of Ida's death—is totally empty. This emptiness can be redeemed, but only outside history and outside the realm of rational, censorial experience. In this sense, a key moment of the narration is Ida's visit to the Jewish ghetto after the Jews have been deported. The scene is totally silent and deserted: "They are all dead," Ida says to herself. The silence of the ghetto is filled only within Ida's mind, through a state of "auditory hallucination" that re-creates the quotidian prattle of female voices, the everyday life she once had witnessed: "I'm on the roof collecting the laundry . . . If you are not finishing your homework you are not leaving the house. . . . Put the light out, electricity costs money" (290). In this same mnemonic and semi-oneiric dimension, opposites lose their contradictory nature, so that even the laments and the desperate cries of the Jewish people in the cattle cars, in the scene witnessed by Ida at the Tiburtina train station, sound to her like familiar voices, "a place of repose that drew her down into the promiscuous den of a single, endless family" (209). Here the materiality of history is transfigured into a different order of existence, and historical materialism as a method of inquiry, on which Morante's social and individual analysis was founded, is ultimately abandoned.

Orthodox historical materialism is rejected also by Benjamin, but not abandoned. He deploys theology to revise and correct the marxist interpretation of history and to give "a new stimulus to revolution" Even though for some of his critics the "Theses" are nothing more than "a handbook of urban guerrilla" (Tiedemann 1988, 202), bearing witness to the less materialist and most anarchist and mystical moments of Benjamin's critical activity—even though the new historical realm opened by the irruption of messianic time into the linearity of events is an unknown, apocalyptic time—for Benjamin the revolution is possible, and the oppressed will be redeemed in *history*.

For Morante, history must be completed, and the *Jetztzeit* constitutes the moment of premonition and revelation that precedes its completion. Yet, for the writer the injustice, the "pornography" of history can be exposed, but not redeemed, at least within the time of human experience. No revolution is possible, nor perhaps even desirable; not even in Benjamin's unorthodox formulation ("a leap in the open air of history"). The course of history does not, cannot change, as the conclusion of the novel indicates: after Ida's death, the sequence of dates that had opened the novel reappears, "and History continues" (1984, 555). Redemption for Morante is possible at a different level, on another plane of existence, signified exactly by what history does not have the tools to deal with, the many other marginal textualities, voices, and language that Morante includes in her writing.

For the historical materialist this is utopia: he cannot accept that humanity can be redeemed in the absence of history. Yet the spheres of messianic and historical time are for Morante unreconcilable; her redeemed subject is an Oedipus whose power of vision is acquired only through historical blindness. In *History* as readers and subjects of history ourselves, we are asked to take a very wide jump: from Benjamin's "leap into the open air of history," to a leap into a necessary blindness, a leap into what is, to date, unspeakable and unknowable ("the unity of consciousness"). Morante's leap can be taken only through an act of faith, and it is this very moment of faith that closes the book. The real conclusion, the only conclusion that for Morante can allow the words "the end" to be written, is a further rupture in the frustrating and unredeemed continuity of history, a moment of unstable hope that replaces the optimism of the historical materialist. The real conclusion is another marginal text, another marginal and transitory inscription, this time written on the walls of a prison:

> All the seeds failed except one. I don't know what it is but it is probably a flower and not a weed. (Prisoner 7047 in the penitentiary of Turi)

Notes

1. Elsa Morante, (1984). Future references to the novel quote the page number of this edition.

2. Michel Foucault (1972) elaborates the theoretical grounding of his critique of history in *The Archaeology of Knowledge;* see also Hayden White's seminal work (1973b) on the rhetorical value of the language of history, *Metahistory.*

3. In film theory the space off is that part of the screen, of the image, that is not made visible to the viewer, but that can only be inferred and desired

by the audience. Teresa de Lauretis (1987) uses the phrase in *Technologies of Gender* to hypothesize not-yet articulated formulations of gender.

4. The words—"No man or men but the struggling oppressed class itself is the depository of historical knowledge" Walter Benjamin, *Theses on the Philosophy of History*, thesis 12, 260.

5. Ettore Scola's film A *Special Day (Una giornata particolare)* offers another interesting dramatization of Morante's operation, this time presenting and debating the analogy and the impossible solidarity between a woman and a gay man under fascism.

References

Benjamin, Walter. 1987. Theses on the philosophy of history. In *Illuminations*, edited and with an introduction by Hannah Arendt and translated by Harry Zohn. New York: Schocken.

De Lauretis, Teresa. 1987. *Technologies of gender: Essays on theory, film, and fiction.* Bloomington: University of Indiana Press.

Foucault, Michel. 1972. *The archaeology of knowledge.* Translated by A. M. Sheridan Smith. New York: Pantheon.

Morante, Elsa. 1984. *History: A novel.* New York: Vintage. Translated by William Weaver. (Originally published: La Storia, 1974).

Smith, Gary, ed. 1988. *Walter Benjamin: Philosophy, aesthetics, history.* Chicago: University of Chicago Press.

Tiedemann, Rolf. 1988. Historical materialism or political messianism? An interpretation of the theses "On the concept of history." In Smith.

White, Hayden. 1973a. *The content of the form: Narrative discourse and historical representation.* Baltimore: Johns Hopkins University Press.

———. 1973b. *Metahistory: The historical imagination in nineteenth-century Europe.* Baltimore: Johns Hopkins University Press.

Feminist Historiography and Dacia Maraini's *Isolina: Una donna tagliata a pezzi*

RODICA DIACONESCU BLUMENFELD

IN FEMINIST HISTORIOGRAPHY WE FIND TWO IMPORTANT ISSUES: THE recuperation of lost history and the deconstruction of the ideal of absolute objectivity.

Reclaiming the past is a project feminist historiography shares with the school of social history, the post-structuralist cultural history and new historicism. Challenging traditional historiography's universalizing focus on the public sphere, through the documentation of ordinary lives, these approaches study the role of particular marginal groups in the formation of cultural practices.[1] This trend in the works of male historians has, for the most part, ignored the concept of gender or used it as a descriptive rather than analytic tool.[2] When practiced, however, by feminist historians writing on the history of silenced women, this trend takes on greater theoretical significance. The feminist historian, reconstituting the texture of life lost in the male accounts of history, writes what some call her-story.[3]

The second major issue, the deconstruction of the ideal of absolute objectivity, posits an awareness that questions and politicizes the subject-object relation. The historian becomes interactive with her material. In the past, the removal of the historian's subjectivity from the writing of history has created false objectivities. The enterprise of historiography cannot be straightforward, for in it subject-object must be problematized. Further, since the fiction of scientific objectivity has always served to claim for the "objective" metapercipient the subject status, uncritical repetition of a classic subject/object relation is antithetical to a history that attempts to recover the subjectivity of lost women's lost lives. This subjectivity cannot be treated as a kind of object.[4]

178

Both of these concerns are present in Dacia Maraini's *Isolina* (1992): the recovery of a lost life, and the subjectivity of narrator that problematizes the subject-object relation.

On the 16th of January 1900, two women washing clothes on the bank of Verona's river Adige come upon a sack containing six parts of a human body wrapped in remnants of clothing. The dragging of the river recovers many other parts. The head remains missing for another year. The official investigation reconstitutes the body of a nineteen-year old woman who had a slightly deformed spine and was three-months pregnant. Forensic examination establishes a failed abortion and the expert dismembering of the body. The police list of missing persons supplies the name of Isolina Canuti.

The reconstruction of the facts is undertaken by prominent local and national newspapers (which will ultimately remain the only surviving documents).

In Verona, an army town, Isolina Canuti's family is making ends meet by renting rooms to army officers. In September of 1899, Lieutenant Carlo Trivulzio of the Italian Alpini Corps comes to the house, and during a week of house arrest, sleeps with Isolina. When Isolina discovers that she is pregnant, Trivulzio pays for medicinal powders to provoke an abortion since he does not want a son "from a rickety humpback like her" [da una gibbosa rachitica come lei (Maraini 1992, 14)].[5] Isolina does not take them and also refuses Trivulzio's attempt to arrange for an abortion, saying to her friends, "I'm warming up a little soldier" [sto scaldando un alpinello (29)]. On the 14th of January 1900, at the Trattoria del Chiodo where one of the many military circles passed its free time, friends of Trivulzio invite Isolina for a party where eventually all get drunk. As a joke, a medical lieutenant proposes to Isolina to climb on the table for an abortion. He sticks a fork into her, making her bleed and scream so loudly that they gag her with a table napkin, later found with the body parts. To cover up, the officers proceed to cut her in pieces and get Trivulzio's orderly to throw the different packages in the river, at the Villa Canossa.

After the discovery of the body, Trivulzio is arrested, but remains under investigation for less than two weeks. He denies everything, with the exception of sleeping with Isolina, having had "nothing better to do" than read D'Annunzio in bed. He denies that the child is his, for she, he says, had many lovers.

He denies trying to procure an abortion for her, and finally he denies being at the Trattoria del Chiodo.

As the political newspapers have gotten involved, Trivulzio cleverly interprets the accusations against him as a socialist attempt to smear the good name of the army. Under pressure from the *Ministero degli Interni*, the Chief of Police releases Trivulzio who takes a leave, disappearing from public life for more than a year.

During this time, the socialist Parliament representative Todeschini continues to offer provocatory investigative reporting in the socialist newspaper *Verona del Popolo*, in the attempt to put on trial the establishment of the army. Todeschini wants to force Trivulzio into suing him and thus unmasking himself. In response, the lieutenant and the army, with typical solidarity of caste, will cover up for one another, destroying at last Isolina's name as well.

Trivulzio will live another half century, still pursuing his military career but withdrawn from public life, if not with a clear conscience, at least with the knowledge that his silence has saved the honor of the army. He dies of stomach cancer, having refused medical attention.

Maraini's text witnesses preeminently to the disappearance of Isolina, self and name.

The structure of the text itself conveys what will become most important about Isolina—her absence. The book is divided in four chapters, of which only the first two, "The Facts" [I fatti] and "On the Traces of Isolina" [Sulle tracce di Isolina], explore the murder. The last two chapters, "The Todeschini Trial" [Il processo Todeschin] and "The Sentence" [La sentenza] deal with the political clash between the socialists and the army, while Isolina's death recedes into insignificance. Todeschini will be found guilty of libel and sentenced to two years in prison, Trivulzio and the army will be legally and morally exonerated. Looking at the table of contents, the reader might have expected the tracing of Isolina to be placed either at the beginning or at the end of the book, establishing a trajectory or functioning as a closure. But although there is a closure, as we shall see, it does not come as suggested in the word "sentence"—a righting of the wrong. Maraini does indict the ideology that produced this outcome, but the *sentenza* with which she concludes is not a restitution either of or to Isolina, the sort of quasi metaphysical restitution common in certain feminist historiography. An enterprise of restitution is futile.

The silencing of Isolina was progressive: from the failed attempt to expunge the proof of the illicit affair (the child), to the achieved annihilation of Isolina's life, to the disposal of her body, to the wrecking of her name and the subsequent erasure of her memory. So is Maraini's endeavor of rediscovery. She employs various forms of search and inscription that correspond to the forms of Isolina's obliteration. To articulate that range of occlusions that now constitute the absent body and being of Isolina, Maraini draws upon a spectrum of rhetorical and narrative techniques, from deductive and inductive reasonings, assertions and refutations, empirical and extrapolated testimonials.

Since there are no letters, no official documents relating to the investigation of the murder, and no memories left in the discourse of the Canuti descendants, Maraini concentrates on the actual and possible spaces inhabited by Isolina and her butchers.

There are no portraits of Isolina. Except, perhaps, a bas-relief on the corner of Via del Chiodo:

> Stone on stone. The hair pulled back in a thick braid, the heavy lips, the thick nose. Popular rumor has it that this small sculpture of a woman is the portrait of Isolina Canuti. It is suspended halfway on the wall, a wise and perplexed air, the eyes of gray stone empty, the cheeks eaten by time. (49)[6]

Of the physical and symbolic settings of the story, what is gone or not there is significant. Isolina's house is gone.

Gone also is the place where her body was first discovered. Gone is the class of the *lavandaie*. What can still be seen are "Along the brick wall ... the traces of the stairs the washer women descended toward the river" [Lungo la parete mattonata ... le tracce delle scalette da cui scendevano le lavandaie al fiume (7)]. Gone are the traces of the female existence. There is no tomb for Isolina.

What is left, on the other hand, are the monuments of a military city, the splendid forts, the Villa Canossa and Castel Vecchio, still housing the *Officers' Club*, the monumental beauty of a male social order. Maraini reflects:

> Autocratic societies, playing boldly with air and light even when their aim was military defense and aggression, have always known how to create the greatest delights for the eyes: magnificent monu-

ments that leave one breathless, symmetries inspired by stellar perfection, and massive bodies both delicate and ethereal.

A mystery to solve: the most perfect architectures are the daughters of tyrants and butchers: pyramids, temples, obelisks, churches, towers, castles, palaces, monuments. Beauty is married to arrogance and despotism. It would be interesting to know what the architectural daughters of humility and play might be like. But the future gives us no answers. (70)[7]

A similar move is traceable in terms of character. For Isolina it is the destruction of her name; for Trivulzio, a buildup. She was from an impoverished family; he was from a noble one. She was "rickety, not very pleasing" [rachitica, poco piacente (14)], "a scrofulous anemic" [anemica scrofolosa (28)], "hunchbacked, short, homely" [gobba, bassa, bruttina (28)]; he was "tall in stature, jovial" [alto di statura, gioviale (14)], "always smiling" [sempre sorridente (15)]. She was "just a girl, a prostitute" [una ragazzina, una prostituta (18)]; he was "an honest man, courageous, discreet" [un uomo onesto, coraggioso, discreto (77)], "a man who believed in certain values" [un uomo che credeva in certi valori (77)]. Through her "impudence and immodest lifestyle" [inverecondia ed immodesto sistema di vita (181)], if Isolina suffered violence, "it means that she has asked for it" [vuol dire che se l'è voluta (18)], while Trivulzio suffered unjustly for a slight indiscretion (188).

In her *leggerezza*, the "light-loose" woman Isolina has vanished into defamation. Thanks to his weighty *valori*, Trivulzio is left with his good name.

Finally, to the socialists, who kept the issue open until Trivulzio sued for libel, Isolina became an abstraction, the pretext for an antimilitaristic campaign that raised the fight to an institutional level, thus erasing entirely her lived being.

* * *

In Dacia Maraini's text, we also find the narrative of her own involvement in the enterprise an affirmation of her own activity.[8]

To the movement of the erasure of Isolina in history, Maraini counterposes a movement of deductions and imaginings about her protagonist that is at the same time her own reflection on her reconstruction of the case.

From the same damaging data put together by the defenders of Trivulzio and of the army's honor, Maraini gives us another image of the young woman: she was a generous and enchanting friend, she was "cheerful, affectionate, vivacious, intolerant of any form of control, curious, intelligent" [allegra, affettuosa, vivace, insofferente di ogni disciplina, curiosa, intelligente (29)]. She loved dancing, going out at night; she loved life: "we can imagine her, with her long purple skirts, her light step" [possiamo immaginarla, con le sue gonne lunghe scarlatte, il passo leggero (29)]. In the courtyard of the *Collegio delle Perico-lanti* where Isolina spent four years, Maraini cannot help but "imagine her":

> I cannot but imagine Isolina as a child, closed up in her gray school uniform, playing ball with her friends. I see her run unbridled inside the square of the courtyard. I see her suddenly tired, with white anemic cheeks, leaning on the magnolia tree with the ball in hand, panting. The hunched spine adheres badly to the rough tree trunk. But she does not care. She has such a desire to play that even that undersized courtyard seems to her a park, and that tree seems a sequoia boldly holding united the sky and the land of Verona. (60)[9]

And in the beautiful city full of military men, all intent on seduction, "for the girls that were freer—because poorer—the temptations were many" [per le ragazze più libere perché più povere le tentazioni erano tante (72)]. Maraini asks: "How could one say no to all the amusements? . . . How to resist the desire to throw oneself into parties, to play, to fall in love, to let oneself go?" [Come dire di no a tutti i divertimenti? . . . Come resistere alla voglia di buttarsi nelle feste, giocare, inna-morarsi, lasciarsi andare? (72)]

Maraini talks, all the while, of her own movements in this city that seems "to have put all its energies into erasing every trace of its wretched daughter" [che abbia messo tutte le sue energie nel cancellare ogni traccia di questa sua figlia disgrazi-ata (59)]. Her research seems a profanation: "These fingers, alive in 1983, . . . chase, rummage through dead and distant papers" [Queste dita vive del 1983 . . . inseguono, frugano den-tro carte morte e lontane (54)]. Her exhaustion seems related not so much to the indifference of the present, or to the resist-ance of the past, as to an exigency that comes from the process of immersion itself:

> Digging through time is difficult and gives me a slight sense of nausea. How to enter a world of the dead who unexpectedly be-

come intransigent, chatting and greedy. They want you to remember them according to their own ideas (of themselves). They pull you in all directions with their assailing demands and do not let you be. (75)[10]

Maraini's act of attentive imagination seeks the absent living trace, but cannot evade the emphatic horror of "the thud that the sack made falling into the water in the silence of the night" [il tonfo che fece il sacco cadendo in acqua nel silenzio della notte (67–68)]. The silence resonates not with Isolina alive, but with proof of her death.

An old abandoned ammunition depot where Trivulzio was supposed to have been on duty on the night of the murder becomes the site of Maraini's attempt to bring together Isolina and Trivulzio in a fantasy of the sleeping beauty. Going back to find Isolina, Maraini finds instead Trivulzio, a prince, moving along through the dusty, empty corridors:

> And there, in the back of a dark and motionless hall, a light blue flicker: the body of Sleeping Beauty with blond hair in which spiders are playing.
>
> Moved, the prince stops and looks at the Beauty with glassy cheeks and bloodless lips in the moth-eaten dress. He leans over with a light, delicate movement and touches his blood-red lips to her dead ones.
>
> There, Lieutenant Trivulzio has kissed his beloved and has brought her back to life for us. But in that moment when he woke her, he took fright. And now, with true terror, he looks at her waking up. Where will the Sleeping Beauty go? To the courthouse, to church, to the newspapers? What will she say about him? How tranquil and reassuring is beauty when it is dead! (74)[11]

This is a strange reconstruction, a fantasy absolutely opposed to history, a fairy tale. A textual moment of great complexity, Maraini's fantasy tale must signify at once both the transcendence and failure of historiography. Continuous with her imaginative efforts to restore Isolina, to make her into living time, Maraini's narrative abandons the historical ground where she has sought her traces and moves into a realm of fantasy, and hence of subjective satisfaction. Yet even here, it is not Isolina she finds, but Trivulzio. The prince dominates the tale.

Finally, Maraini, visits the cemetery from which Isolina's tomb is missing. There she looks at the common grave:

> In the middle of the half-circle of columns, there, on the ground, is a round and gray stone. It is the common grave. Above, is a

rusty tin can with a little bunch of fresh flowers. Here, by now reduced to crumbs, the broken bones of Isolina have probably been thrown: a fragment of tibia, a splinter of dorsal spine, a phalanx, a piece of cranium.

There's something senseless in this obstinate rage against the body of a pregnant girl. Erasing a life from life is not easy. Something always stays behind, something irreducible, indestructible, which refuses to be annihilated. . . . [T]he bones remain, even though broken to pieces, the testimony of a body that once was alive against every attempt to annul it, continuing to give a sign of itself, in silence but decisively, as if to say: nine months were necessary to give me a form, years and years were necessary to make of me an adult, years of labor, of love, of sleep, of food, and you cannot, you simply cannot eliminate me. (52)[12]

The imagined incarnation of Isolina becomes a voice, but a voice in silence, "as if speaking."

The nature of incarnation as temporality is powerfully part of Maraini's reconstruction, marking the continuity of this book with her other work in which sensuality evokes incarnation as time.[13] Dacia Maraini has been able to express the incarnation of Isolina through various devices of trace. So also is this embodiment evoked in negation: the bas-relief that may or may not be Isolina and is not percipient (the eyes are empty, the face is stone on stone). Isolina is not in time, has no temporality, her time is gone. Her incarnation was rejected, hacked to pieces; she is not alive.

Maraini indicates incarnation also by reflection on Trivulzio's embodiment in time. Looking at his photographs, she affirms his progression in life. She reconstitutes him as a living body. She sees his pictures, taken through half a century, which show him at first young and beardless, and then older, with a beard. As he ages, his beard goes from dark to white, his hair from short to very short. She sees him in different kinds of uniform, in the studio, on the street. She sees him a lieutenant, then a colonel, then a general. His body is subject to the passing of time, precisely what Isolina's cannot be.

Ultimately, Trivulzio dies of stomach cancer, and the reader finds in Maraini's account of this a dream of closure in the body:

This death recalls symbolically the one suffered by Isolina. The belly of a nineteen-year-old girl that hosted a child was desecrated and destroyed. So he, the officer, responsible even if only indirectly for that death, has kept the illness that was undoing him there, precisely in the belly, the symbolic place of procreation and nourishment. (84)[14]

Death becomes life and life becomes death. Perhaps at this moment Maraini found it unbearable not to feel a closure, a symbolic justice. Isolina's death becomes something alive in the living body of the person who killed her. This closure, however, can only be imagined. It marks only the intolerable nature of Maraini's seeking out of the fragments of a body, a seeking that can have no closure. It is a literary closure, needed by a literary, not a historical, imagination.

But it is not the end of the book. Maraini does not permit this need for closure to dominate her text. She goes on, committed to an art of representation that will not falsify itself in the dream of redemption of an irremediable flesh. There is no theory of contemporaneity in Maraini.

It is a powerful thing—to represent a silence, to give a voice to a voice that is silence. It is Isolina's *absence* that is made real in this text. This is the difference made by this reading: now we know that Isolina is dead.

Notes

1. Such approaches are represented by a range of works, from Marc Bloc's 1931 text on the French peasant classes to those of the proliferating fields of popular culture history and history of consciousness.

2. On the use of gender in historiography, see Scott 1988, 31–33.

3. On the various types of "her-story," see Scott 1988 (18–22), which also provides a vast bibliography of feminist historiography (206–11).

4. Breaking down the subject-object relation in favor of a double subjectivity is also the concern of the new historiographic fields of oral history Borland (1991) Benmayor (1991) and personal narrative (Personal Narratives Group 1989). Experiments with subjectivity in the writing of history in such literary texts as those of Toni Morrison 1987 and Marise Condé 1992 remain problematic for the analytical feminist historians. These may call for the exploration and utilization of literary paradigms, but do not sufficiently theorize the import of "novelistic" historiography (Rendall 1991).

5. Unless otherwise indicated, the translations are mine.

6. Pietra su pietra. I capelli ravviati all'indietro che finiscono in una treccia folta, le labbra pesanti, il naso grassoccio. La voce popolare ha voluto vedere in questa piccola scultura di donna il ritratto di Isolina Canuti. Se ne sta sospesa a mezza parete, un'aria savia e perplessa, gli occhi vuoti di pietra grigia, le guance mangiate dal tempo.

7. Le società autocratiche hanno sempre saputo creare le più grandi delizie per gli occhi: monumenti magnifici da lasciare col fiato sospeso, simme-

trie che si ispirano alle perfezioni stellari, corpi massici ma nello stesso tempo delicati e aerei che giocano arditamente con l'aria e la luce anche quando lo scopo era la difesa e l'aggressione militare. Un mistero da risolvere: le architetture più perfette sono figlie di tiranni e massacratori: piramidi, templi, obelischi, chiese, forti, torri, castelli, palazzi, monumenti. La bellezza si sposa con l'arroganza e il dispotismo. Sarebbe curioso conoscere le figlie architettoniche dell'umiltà e del gioco. Ma il futuro non ci dà risposte.

8. My reading of Maraini's *Isolina* is in tension with Foucault's and other post-structuralists' concept of power, which undermines that of agency. This does not mean that an analysis cannot be made of Maraini's own intervention in the life/death of Isolina. Indeed, it would be the subject of another study. But I suggest that Maraini herself is aware of the issue and tries to resolve it textually, when she makes reference to her own subjectivity. For the relation of feminism to Foucault, see Schor (1987), and Diamond and Quinby (1988).

9. Non posso fare a meno di immaginare Isolina bambina, chiusa nel suo vestito grigio da collegiale che gioca a palla con le amiche. La vedo correre sfrenata dentro il quadrato del cortile. La vedo di colpo stanca, le guance sbiancate da anemica, che si appoggia alla magnolia con la palla in mano, ansimante. La schiena gobba aderisce malamente al tronco ruvido. Ma lei non se ne cura. Ha una tale voglia di giocare che perfino quel cortile striminzito le sembra un parco e quell'albero una sequoia che tiene baldanzosamente uniti il cielo e la terra di Verona.

10. Scavar nel tempo è difficile e dà un leggero senso di nausea. Come entrare in un mondo di morti che improvvisamente si fanno intransigenti, pettegoli e golosi. Vogliono che tu li ricordi secondo l'idea che loro hanno di sé. Ti tirano da tutte le parti e non ti danno tregua con le loro richieste assillanti.

11. Ed ecco, nel fondo di una sala buia e immota, un lucore cilestrino: il corpo della Bella addormentata dai capelli biondi su cui giocano i ragni.

Il principe si ferma emozionato a guardare la Bella dal vestito tarlato, le guance vetrose, le labbra esangui. Si china con un movimento leggero, delicato e appoggia le labbra sanguigne su quelle morte di lei.

Ecco il tenente Trivulzio ha baciato la sua innamorata e l'ha riportata alla vita per noi. Ma nel momento che l'ha risvegliata se ne è spaventato. E ora la guarda alzarsi con un vero terrore. Dove andrà la Bella addormentata? In Tribunale, in chiesa, ai giornali? Cosa dirà di lui? Come è quieta e rassicurante la bellezza quando è morta!

12. In mezzo al semicerchio di colonne ecco per terra una pietra tonda e grigia. È la fossa comune. Sopra, una lattina arruginita con un mazzetto di fiori freschi. Qui, ormai ridotte a briciole, sono state buttate probabilmente le ossa spezzate di Isolina; un frammento di tibia, una scheggia di spina dorsale, una falange, uno spezzone di cranio.

C'é qualcosa di insensato in questo accanirsi sul corpo di una giovane ragazza incinta. Cancellare dalla vita una vita non é facile. Qualcosa rimane sempre, di irriducibile, di indistruttibile che si rifiuta di essere annientato. . . . [L]e ossa rimangono, anche ridotte a pezzetti, a testimoniaza di un corpo che una volta é stato vivo contro ogni volontà di annullamento continuando a dare segno di sé in silenzio ma con decisione come a dire: ci sono voluti nove mesi per darmi una forma, ci sono voluti anni e anni per fare di me una persona adulta, anni di lavoro, di amore, di sonno, di cibo, e non puoi, semplicemente non puoi eliminarmi.

13. The sensual detail of Maraini's narratives is perhaps their most distinctive feature. This sensuality marks a relation between corporeality and temporality that has multiple manifestations in all her novels. The "età" of *L'età del malessere* [Age of malaise] is synonymous with Enrica, her erotic hungers and forming self-awareness as she is swept in a current of other wills. Or, in *Donna in guerra* [Woman at war], its diary structure iterating the significance of temporality both as brutal quotidian and as trajectory of bodied consciousness, Vanna's visits to the laundry world and her submergence in an *other* time of pornographic invention serve as a deep resource for rebirth at the close of the novel. The framing of these episodes through contrast to her life of drudgery, emphasizes their importance as an *alter* temporality. In *Voci* [Voices], dreams and ghostly presences, the time of memory, inflect the living flesh of the characters. Haunting is the multitemporality of desire and motive. My essay on temporality/corporeality in Maraini will appear in a collection of critical essays on Maraini under preparation by Ada Testaferri and myself.

14. Una morte che ricorda simbolicamente quella patita da Isolina. La pancia di una ragazza di diciannove anni che ospitava un bambino è stata profanata e distrutta. Così lui, l'ufficiale, responsabile anche se indirettamente di quella morte, si è tenuto la malattia che lo disfaceva proprio lì nel ventre, luogo simbolico della procrezione e del nutrimento.

References

Benmayor, Rina. 1991. Testimony, action research and empowerment: Puerto Rican women and popular education. In *Women's words: The feminist practice of oral history*, edited by Sherna Berger Gluck and Daphne Patai. New York and London: Routledge.

Bloch, Marc. 1966. *French rural history: An essay on its basic characteristics*. Translated by Janet Sondheimer. Berkeley: University of California Press.

Borland, Katherine. 1991. "'That's not what I said': Interpretive conflict in oral narrative research. In *Women's words: The feminist practice of oral history*, edited by Sherna Berger Gluck and Daphne Patai. New York and London: Routledge.

Condé, Marise. 1992. *I, Tituba, black witch of Salem*. Translated by Richard Philcox. Charlottesville: Virginia University Press.

Diamond, Irene, and Lee Quinby, eds. 1988. *Feminism and Foucault: Reflections on resistance*. Boston: Northeastern University Press.

Foucault, Michel. 1978–86. *The history of sexuality*. 3 vols. Translated by Robert Hurley. New York: Pantheon.

Maraini, Dacia. 1992. *Isolina: una donna tagliata a pezzi*. Milan: Rizzoli, 1992.

Morrison, Toni. 1987. *Beloved*. New York: Knopf.

Personal Narratives Group. 1989a. "Origins." In *Interpreting women's lives: Feminist theory and personal narratives*, edited by Personal Narratives Group. Bloomington and Indianapolis: Indiana University Press.

———. 1989b. Condition Not of Her Own Making. In *Interpreting women's lives: Feminist theory and personal narratives*, edited by Personal Narratives Group. Bloomington and Indianapolis: Indiana University Press.

———. 1989c. Whose voice?. In *Interpreting women's lives: feminist theory and personal narratives*, edited by Personal Narratives Group. Bloomington and Indianapolis: Indiana University Press.

Rendall, Jane. 1991. "Uneven narratives": Women's history, feminist history and gender history in Great Britain. In *Writing women's history: International perspectives*, edited by Karen Offen, Ruth Roach Pierson, and Jane Rendall. Bloomington and Indianapolis: Indiana University Press.

Schor, Naomi. 1987. Dreaming dyssymetry: Barthes, Foucault, and Sexual Difference. In *Men in feminism*, edited by Alice Jardine and Paul Smith. New York: Methuen.

Scott, Joan Wallach. 1988. *Gender and the politics of history*. New York: Columbia University Press.

Sicilian Philomelas: Marianna Ucrìa and the Muted Women of Her Time

Gabriella Brooke

In *la lunga vita di marianna ucrìa* (1992a), dacia maraini uses an interesting reinterpretation of the myth of Philomela to make a powerful statement about the condition of aristocratic women in eighteenth-century Sicily. This essay intends to explore the implications of this myth as it relates to the silencing of Marianna Ucrìa and her contemporaries, and in a wider context to the silencing of all women. It will also discuss the connection between Philomela's weaving and Marianna's writing as forms of liberation and resistance to violence.

In the *Concise Oxford Dictionary of Literary Terms*, myth is defined as

> a kind of story or rudimentary narrative sequence, normally traditional and anonymous, through which a given culture ratifies social customs or accounts for the origin of human and natural phenomena, usually in supernatural or boldly imaginative terms. (Baldick 1994, 143–44)

Greek myths have been said to originate from ritual. They have been explored for kernels of actual history and have been compared to Indo-European and Near Eastern myths. They have been analyzed according to different literary theories, such as structuralism, semiotics, and psychoanalysis.[1] Theorists, however, have hardly been of one mind. The one thing that male theorists and critics have tacitly agreed upon is that *man* determines the standard for what is considered universal. Because of this, in examining myth, they have not taken into account the notion of gender and the reality that myths have been created and transmitted by men.[2] Feminist critics have given different interpretations to archetypes found in literature. Annis Pratt's study (1981) of several hundred women's novels has revealed archetypes underlying their fiction that

190

are quite different from, and in some cases diametrically opposed, to those that underlie the fiction of male authors. Although outside of the scope of this article, Maraini's *La lunga vita di Marianna Ucrìa* could be reread in view of Pratt's "rape-trauma" archetype.

In "Archetype and Structure: On Feminist Myth Criticism," Cynthia Davis (1990) writes that rather than accepting blindly the meaning of myth passed along by patriarchal culture, feminist critics have preferred "to treat myth in literature (as in culture) as *tradition*" (116; italics in text). The realization that myth has been influenced by culture, history, and literature allows the critic to extract different meanings for the "same" story or figure. This is what Adriana Cavarero (1990) has done in *Nonostante Platone* [In spite of Plato]. In her critical rereading of mythical female figures in Plato, the Italian philosopher has shown how to extract mythical female figures from a patriarchal context and return them to a feminine symbolic order. For example, in her analysis, Penelope is shown as rooted in the here and now of her time and thus engaged in "weaving" together body and soul, a task opposite to that of Plato and other Greek philosophers.

In *La lunga vita di Marianna Ucrìa*, Dacia Maraini has chosen to reinterpret another mythical weaver, Philomela. While Cavarero "tears off" her mythic figure directly from the fabric of an ancient text, Maraini uses the myth of Philomela indirectly, by weaving the myth into the life of her heroine, Marianna. This indirect use of myth, through substitution and appropriation, is discussed at some length by Neria De Giovanni "La sfinge cantatrice-realtà come specchio nella narrativa femminile italiana post-neorealismo" (1989, 105).

Prior to writing *La lunga vita di marianna Ucrìa*, Dacia Maraini spoke of the difference between history and mythology. In an interview with Grazia Weinberg, Maraini said that while formal history is a male concern that ignores women, mythology "deals with women's life and thus offers many insights into what happened in the past. Today we can make use of mythology symbolically, meaningfully" (Weinberg 1989).

In the case of *Marianna Ucrìa*, Maraini's symbolic use of myth involves the reinterpreting of an ancient archetype in the feminist way mentioned above. This process enables the novelist to place her female character in an ahistorical time even if historical referents appear in her novel. If the ancient myth of Philomela can be traced in the life of an eighteenth-

century duchess, it can also be found in the lives of other
women who have endured violence and have learned to resist.
In this sense, Maraini makes a statement about women and
violence in general.[3]

The myth of Philomela has been the subject of two important
essays that help enlighten and make even more relevant Maraini's choice of this myth for her novel. In "Disarticulated
Voices: Feminism and Philomela," Elissa Marder (1992) discusses the double rape of Philomela—the physical violation
that deprived her of her virginity and the cutting of the tongue
which deprived her of speech. In "The Voice of the Shuttle is
Ours" Patricia Joplin (1984) concentrates instead on the act of
weaving as a form of resistance to violence.

In creating Marianna Ucrìa as an eighteenth-century Philomela, Dacia Maraini used myth in the symbolic way she advocated in her interview with Grazia Weinberg (1989). The
ancient myth of the violated and mutilated virgin who found
a way to tell her story through her art underlies Maraini's
novel and gives meaning to the experience of her character,
Marianna, and that of the women of her class and time. In the
version used by Ovid, the myth of Philomela has three parts:
the rape-mutilation of the Greek princess by her brother-in-
law Tereus, her message to her sister Procne in the form of a
peplos on which her story was recorded, and the revenge of
the two sisters (Ovid 1964, 143–51).

In her reading of the myth of Philomela, Elissa Marder discusses the relationship between the rape and the mutilation of
Philomela. The *rape of the speech*—the cutting off the tongue—
repeats metaphorically the physical act of sexual dominance
that had just occurred (Marder 1992, 159). Marder's interpretation, that the cutting of the tongue, the silencing of Philomela, was a reenactment of the rape finds confirmation in the
story of Marianna. In *La lunga vita di Marianna Ucrìa*, Marianna is raped by her uncle at age five. The *mutilation* of her
senses, however, does not come from this initial rape. Rather,
it comes from her father's injunction to forget what was done
to her. This metaphorical rape, rather than the actual, physical
violence, is the one that deprives Marianna of speech. In language that is reminiscent of the myth, Marianna refers to her
condition as mutilation. In the initial passage that describes
the noises that Marianna imagines while riding to Palermo
next to her sleeping father, for example, she uses the word
"mutilated" to refer to her lost senses; "even if she can only

imagine all these sounds, for him they are real. And yet it is she who is disturbed and not him. What tricks intelligence can play on *crippled* senses!" (11; my italics) and again, "The child is just seven years old. In her *disabled* body the silence is like dead water." (12; my italics).[4]

The English translator of *The Silent Duchess* (Maraini 1992b) chose the words "crippled" and "disabled" to translate *mutilati* and *mutilato* in the original Italian. The verb *mutilare* literally means to cut off (Zingarelli 1963), "crippled" and "disabled" do not. The result is that the close parallel between the language of the myth and the language used by Maraini is not as clear in the English translation.

Later in the novel, an even stronger reference to the myth of Philomela can be found in words that Marianna uses when she realizes why she can't speak or hear. Before she remembers the rape she endured at age five, Marianna understands suddenly that it was the denial of her pain and her feelings by her father that had caused her condition.

> At that moment a revelation transfixes her from head to foot, like an arrow: for the first time in her life she comprehends with a diamond clarity that it was him, her father, who was the one responsible for her disablement. From love or from carelessness she can't say. But it is he who *cut* her tongue and it is he who has filled her up her ears with molten lead so that she can hear no sound and circles perpetually in the kingdoms of silence and fear.[5] (172; my italics)

The metaphor used by Marianna when she says that her father cut her tongue refers to the psychological coercion by her father to forget the rape and thus deny her feelings of pain and betrayal. The consequences of this symbolic rape to the psyche of the little girl were as destructive as Philomela's physical mutilation. In "Rewriting the Female Destiny: Dacia Maraini's *La lunga vita di Marianna Ucrìa,*" JoAnn Cannon cleverly elaborates on the betrayal of Marianna's father and discusses the defense mechanism that enabled Marianna to survive the rape (1995).

Philomela's and Marianna's double rapes (physical and metaphoric) find a parallel in the symbolic rape and silencing to which eighteen-century women were regularly subjected by society.

Webster's dictionary (1980) defines rape as "something taken or seized and carried away by force." By "seizing" women's freedom, patriarchal society symbolically raped Marianna's contemporaries. The absence of freedom in a woman's life means that somebody other than herself defines who she is—her desires, aspirations, and hopes are subordinate to somebody else's. It means that somebody else decides what she should or shouldn't do, say, *and* feel. Silencing their victims, depriving them of a language "to speak rape" (Marder 1992, 160)—the second metaphoric rape—was accomplished through subtle, though not less effective forms of coercion: by convincing Marianna's contemporaries that their proper role was that of breeders of children—or nuns—and by denying them education. A woman who is subjected to this kind of brainwashing from birth may never have a chance to develop a "language to speak rape" because she may never realize what is taken from her.

Despite the Enlightenment, aristocratic women in eighteenth-century Sicily were in fact denied education and exposure to the new ideas. Women were valued for the dowries they could fetch and the children they could breed. They had the appearance of freedom but no control over their lives or those of their children. Marriage in the eighteenth century was based on economic considerations, not women's wishes. Women could decide what the family would eat for dinner, but not at what age their daughters would marry. They could organize a grand ball, but not choose their husbands.[6] Because they were forced into marriage with men they did not choose or love, women often became alienated from their bodies and feelings. They often reacted to their reduced lives by becoming sick or dependent, or by taking drugs.

To facilitate the smooth working of the patriarchal system, women were socialized to imprison other women. This explains why it was often women who enforced the code of behavior for their class on their sisters and daughters. These realities of eighteenth-century life are reflected in Maraini's novel.

When the family decides that thirteen-year-old Marianna must marry her uncle, Duke Pietro, it is Marianna's mother who insists on the marriage. At Marianna's vehement written protest, the mother takes the quill from her and writes the true reason for this decision: her brother's offer to "buy" Marianna: "In ready money that is a saving of fifteen thousand escudos" (29) [In contanti e subito quindicimila scudi (30)].

Duchess Maria is not cruel; she is merely trying to do the best for her family and her daughter according to the custom of her class. Constrained by patriarchal thinking, she does not see the imposition of marriage on Marianna as evil. When Marianna runs back to her father's house after being raped by her husband, she is bitterly reproached by her women relatives, her mother, her aunt Teresa and even old aunt Agata who "had taken her by the hand, ripped off her wedding ring and stuffed it forcibly between her teeth" (31) [l'aveva presa per una mano, le aveva strappato la fede e gliela aveva fatta mettere fra i denti con la forza (33)].

The women tell her to close her eyes and think of something else when her husband violates her. Socialized to perpetuate the rules of their class, not one of her women relatives could see the cruelty of Marianna's situation.

An "accomplice" of the system, Marianna's mother herself is deeply alienated from her life. Marianna suspects that her mother chose "to become lifeless so that she would never have to die" (27) [di farsi morta per non dover morire (28)]. A woman who was *immaginosa*, or full of imagination, curiosity, and joy of life, was not allowed to retain these qualities past adolescence in eighteenth-century Sicily. The solution for Marianna's mother has been a retreat from life to the nirvana brought on by laudanum and tobacco. The duchess Maria is not the only woman who has found life too painful to be endured. Other women retreat into illness: Marianna's grandmother Giuseppa, for example, who disappeared into her room for days, refusing to see anyone.

Like the historical women of her time, Marianna has no control over her life. When she has children, she is excluded from decisions regarding their future, as in the case of the marriage of her twelve-year-old daughter Manina. Marianna's powerlessness frustrates and prematurely ages her. In this she is not alone. Her sister Agata, for example, has child after child and views motherhood as martyrdom. Splendid as a teenager, Agata soon becomes old before her time until, at twenty-three, she looks like "a wizened Madonna" (64) [una madonna incartapecorita (69)].

The pattern of dominance and submission continues from one generation to the next when Marianna's daughter, Manina, is married at age twelve and chooses her aunt's destiny. This is described by the narrator with a telling metaphor:

Two miscarriages and a baby stillborn. But she has survived it all without too much damage. "My body is a waiting room, there is

always an infant coming in or going out," she wrote about herself
to her mother, and these entrances and exits do not in any way
disconcert her, indeed she has thrived on them. (127)[7]

That Manina can see herself as a waiting room where children
are always coming or going shows how deeply she has accepted her role as a breeder of children. Marianna, too, has
internalized this view, but eventually, as she educates herself,
she comes to question it.

The denial of education has kept the women of Marianna's
class imprisoned in a patriarchal system that slowly deadens
the women's spirit and intelligence. As part of her inner development, Marianna comes to understand the reduced lives of
the women of her time. She describes her contemporaries as
hands. The use of the synecdoche is particularly effective in
the context of the novel because it not only highlights the idle-
ness that noble women endured, but also echoes the feeling of
alienation toward the body that they experienced:

Hands that have never held a book for longer than two minutes,
hands that have had to learn the art of embroidery or how to play
the spinet, but even then have never been permitted to dedicate
themselves with any real seriousness: the hands of noblewomen,
fated to be idle. (213)[8]

It is through vivid figures of speech, such as the one just mentioned, that the narrator weaves her tale. The reader does not
know who the narrator is; although she is not Marianna, yet
she does become Marianna's voice. Like her character, she
knows intimately the violence done to women. It is tempting
to believe the narrator is a Philomela herself who has endured
violence and has learned to speak out by using her art.

According to the original myth, once freed, Philomela and
her sister, Procne, took their revenge by killing Tereus and
Procne's son, Iti, and serving his flesh to Tereus for dinner. By
portraying Philomela as capable of outdoing in ferocity her
violator, the myth obscures the violence done to her. One must
remember, however, that the myth was told and recorded by
the Greeks and the Romans, men who embraced patriarchal
rule. In "The Voice of the Shuttle is Ours," Patricia Joplin
(1984) maintains that Philomela's resistance (through her
weaving) and return to society were unacceptable to the ancient Greeks. Therefore the Greeks fabricated an ending that
portrayed the resisting woman as even more violent than her

violator and, in a sense, made the violence done to her more comprehensible. But in doing so, Joplin writes, they eliminated the story that the loom tells. For Joplin, Philomela's weaving represents a moment of choice, the refusal to return violence for violence. Weaving, Joplin points out, takes time:

> Revenge, or dismembering, is quick. Art, or the resistance to violence and disorder, inherent in the very process of weaving, is slow. . . . In celebrating the voice of the shuttle as ours, we celebrate. . . . Philomela weaving, the woman artist who in recovering her own voice uncovers not only its power, but its potential to transform revenge (violence) into resistance (peace). (51)

JoAnn Cannon (1995) argues that Joplin's view of Philomela as active, empowered, and resistant cannot apply to Marianna because "Maraini does not portray Marianna's position as particularly empowering." In fact, Marianna does not use the pen the way Philomela uses the shuttle—Marianna does not tell the story of the violence done to her. But Marianna, like Philomela, does learn to resist through the knowledge she acquires by writing.

In "La lunga vita di Marianna Ucrìa: tessere la memoria sotto lo sguardo delle chimere" Giuseppina Sant'Agostino (1996) identifies several mythic figures that underlie Maraini's text. In her discussion of the parallel between Philomela and Marianna, Sant'Agostino identifies their manual dexterity (the ability to write for Marianna and the ability to weave for Philomela) as central to their ability to communicate, learn, and ultimately survive (414–15).

Awareness and the ability to communicate—abilities that both Philomela and Marianna achieve through their hands—are the keys to overcoming the isolation of the senses and of the intelligence that perpetuates women's imprisonment.

Surviving for Marianna means escaping the patriarchal rules that have suffocated her. Leaving her golden cage to continue to learn is an act of defiance that changes Marianna from passive victim to active resistant.

To free herself, Marianna leaves behind children and grandchildren, duties and rules that would constrict her again were she to return to Sicily. In his review of La lunga vita, Bruce Merry (1992) points out that

> A duchess in 1740 did not have the option of moving into a "Granny flat," like the retired widows of 1990. Yet Maraini shows that

> mourning, staying at home and looking after the grandchildren
> may all be forms of imprisonment. (31)

If this interpretation of the text is correct, the forces that conspire to keep women enslaved are insidious. For some women,
true freedom may mean a conscious choice to be alone.

Philomela's art freed her. The long hours at the loom taught
her to endure and resist. In Joplin's interpretation, her choice
to resist was also a choice to refuse revenge. In the case of
Marianna, the innumerable hours of study, which translated
into the ability to write and thus express herself, also taught
her to resist. A resistance that also excluded revenge.

According to Marder (1992), by raping Philomela, Tereus
broke the rules of patriarchal Greece—which were based on
the orderly exchange of women. Up to that point Philomela
had meekly accepted the patriarchal order in which she was
raised. By cutting off her tongue, Tereus prevented Philomela
from appealing to the law of the father that should have protected her. Philomela reacted by rebelling against both Tereus
and the paternal order that had let her down. In Marder's
words,

> Philomela has been doubly silenced, first by the rapist who trans-
> gresses the father's law and then by the paternal law itself. Philo-
> mela's tongue speaks only the language of the law; the name of
> the father. While the horror of the rape violates the paternal order,
> the effects of the rape disclose the implicit violation *by* the pater-
> nal order. (160; italics in the original)

Marianna too accepts the law of the father and is not a rebel.
She does all that is required of her. She submits to the will of
the men in her life, fulfills her duty as a breeder of noble children, and conforms to the rules of her society. Like Philomela,
Marianna rebels after she understands the extent of the wrong
done to her not just by her uncle—who according to patriarchal law had married her and therefore set things right—but
by the patriarchal system itself.

Ironically it is Marianna's mutilation that provides her with
the key to freedom. Her father allows her to learn to read and
write to communicate with her family. No one supervises her
reading and Marianna reads voraciously. Through a sympa-
thetic visitor, she encounters the philosophy of David Hume.
It is the English philosopher who first brings Marianna to
question the philosophy of life imposed upon her.

It is a slow, inner change. Marianna does not attempt overt rebellion, but she begins to make some changes in her behavior. It is symbolic that Marianna begins her journey to independence by opening her eyes. Marianna finds the courage to refuse the sexual advances of her husband by refusing to close her eyes as he approaches her.

> How many times has she yielded to this wolfish embrace, shutting her eyelids and gritting her teeth! . . . Now for the first time, looking uncle husband in the face, she manages to shake her head in denial. And he is paralysed, with his member erect and stiff and his mouth open, so astounded by her refusal that he lies stock still, at a loss what to do. (83)[9]

La lunga vita di marianna Ucrìa is important for the transcendence of the message it conveys about the muted position of women. Though the novel is set in the eighteenth century, Maraini's book has deep implications for modern women. Myths, as feminist critics have chosen to interpret them, are timeless. Today, many women are still victimized physically and emotionally, and their tongues are symbolically cut. The myth of Philomela is alive. One can find it in the lives of women living in Los Angeles as well as New Delhi.

In writing Marianna's story, Dacia Maraini suggests that the key to resistance is education. Only the slow, inner change brought about by knowledge and learning can eventually lead to freedom. In the case of Marianna this process takes most of her youth. The bittersweet ending of the novel leaves the reader wondering about the blighted lives of all the other Mariannas, the ones who are physically whole but not allowed to cultivate their minds.

Notes

A shorter version of this article, which was based on a paper read at the April 1994 American Association for Italian Studies conference in Madison, Wisconsin, was published in volume 13 of *Italian Culture*.

All English quotes are taken from Maraini's 1992b. All Italian quotes are taken from Maraini 1992a.

1. See Brenner 1986, 121–52; also Edmunds 1990, 93–238. For a "traditional" interpretation of the role of women in Greek myth, see Lefkowitz (1986, 133–35).

2. For an interesting discussion on these issues, see Davis 1990. Also for a discussion of Frye and Barthes, see Godard 1991. For a discussion of Jung's archetypes as they relate to women see Pratt 1981.

3. In the interview with Dr. Daniela Cavallaro (1994) on 7 June 1993, Dacia Maraini confirmed that the myth of Philomela underlies her novel. (My translation)

> DC—In Marianna's story one can trace the myth of Philomele and Procne.
>
> DM-Without any doubt: it is a myth I know and love well.
>
> DC—In writing, Marianna finds what Philomele found in weaving. She had had her tongue "cut off" too.

4. Anche se per lei sono solo rumori immaginati, per lui sono veri. Eppure lei ne è disturbata e lui no. Che scherzi fa l'intelligenza ai sensi *mutilati*. . . . (9) Il silenzio è un'acqua morta nel corpo *mutilato* della bambina che ha da poco compiuto i sette anni (10).

5. In quel momento un'idea la attraversa da capo a piedi come una saetta: per la prima volta nella sua vita capisce con limpidezza adamantina che è lui, suo padre, il responsabile della sua mutilazione. Per amore o per distrazione non lo saprebbe dire; ma è lui che le *ha tagliato la lingua* ed è lui che le ha riempito le orecchie di piombo fuso perchè non sentisse nessun suono e girasse perpetuamente su se stessa nei regni del silenzio e dell'apprensione (193).

6. For a telling discussion on the conditions of women in the eighteenth century in the West, see Duby and Perrot 1993. For a discussion on marriage customs in Sicily during this century, see the section on "Matrimonio e classi sociali" in Romeo 1978, 81–82. For another interesting account of the condition of supposedly "free" Parisian women in this century, see Edmond and Jules de Goncourt, 1927 (140–59).

7. Due aborti e un figlio nato morto. Ma ne era uscita senza troppi danni. "Il mio corpo e' una sala d'aspetto: c'e' sempre qualche infante che entra e che esce" scriveva di se' alla madre. E di quelle entrate e uscite non si adontava per niente anzi se ne beava (140).

8. Mani che non hanno mai sorretto un libro per piu' di due minuti, mani che dovrebbero conoscere l'arte del ricamo e della spinetta ma nemmeno a quelle hanno avuto il permesso di dedicarsi con pignola assiduità. Le mani di una nobildonna sono oziose per elezione (242).

9. Quante volte ha ceduto a quell'abbraccio da lupo chiudendo le palpebre e stringendo i denti! . . . ora per la prima volta, guardando in faccia il signor marito zio, riesce a fare un segno di diniego con la testa. E lui si paralizza, con il membro rigido, la bocca aperta, talmente sorpreso del suo rifiuto da rimanere lì impalato senza sapere che fare (89–90).

References

Baldick, Chris. 1994. *The concise Oxford dictionary of literary terms*. Oxford: Oxford University Press.

Barthes, Roland. 1973. *Mythologies*. Translated by Annette Laver. London: Paladin.

Brenner, Jan. 1986. *Interpretations of Greek mythology*. Totowa: Barnes and Noble.

Brooke, Gabriella. 1995. Sicilian Philomele: Marianna Ucrìa and the muted women of her time. *Italian Culture*. 13 : 201–11.

Cannon, JoAnn. 1995. Rewriting the female destiny: Dacia Maraini's *La lunga vita di Marianna Ucrìa*. In *Symposium*. 49, no. 2 (1995): 136–47.

Cavallaro, Daniela. 1994. Conversazione con Dacia Maraini. Roma, 7 giugno, 1993. In Clytemnestra, Phaedra and Medea in contemporary theatre in

Italy and Spain: Greek characters in search of female authors. PH.d. diss., Northwestern University.

Cavarero, Adriana. 1990. *Nonostante Platone*. Rome: Editori Riuniti.

Davis, Cynthia. 1990. Archetype and structure: On feminist myth criticism. In *Courage and tools: The Florence Howe award for feminist scholarship 1974–1989*, edited by Glaslow and Ingram. New York: MLA Association of America.

De Giovanni, Neria. 1989. La sfinge cantatrice-realtà come specchio nella narrativa femminile italiana post-neorealismo. *Romance Languages Annual* 1:105–10.

Della Corte, Francesco. 1971. *Le metamorfosi di Ovidio*. Genoa: Fratelli Bozzi.

Godard, Barbara. 1991. Feminism and/as myth: Feminist literary theory between Frye and Barthes. *Atlantis* 16, no. 2:3–21.

Goncourt, Edmond and Jules de. 1927. *The woman of the eighteenth century*. New York: Minton, Balch & Company.

Duby, Georges, and Michelle Perrot. 1993. *A history of women*. Vol. 3. Cambridge: Harvard University Press.

Edmunds, Lowell. 1990. *Approaches to Greek myth*. Baltimore: Johns Hopkins University Press.

Frye, Northrop. 1957. *The anatomy of criticism*. Princeton: Princeton University Press.

Joplin, Patricia. 1984. The voice of the shuttle is ours. *Stanford Literature Review* 1, no. 1:25–53.

Lefkowitz, Mary. 1986. *Women in Greek myth*. Baltimore: Johns Hopkins University Press.

Leone, Salvatore. 1978. "Matrimonio e classi sociali" in *Storia della Sicilia*, ed. by Rosario Romeo. Palermo Società editrice Storia di Napoli e della Sicilia. VII:80–81.

Maraini, Dacia. 1992a. *La lunga vita di Marianna Ucrìa*. Milan: Rizzoli.

———. 1992b. *The silent duchess*. Translated by Dick Kitto and Elspeth Spottiswood. London: Peter Owen.

Marder, Elissa. 1992. Disarticulated voices: Feminism and Philomela. *Hypatia* 7, no. 2:148–66.

Merry, Bruce. 1992. Review of *La lunga vita di Marianna Ucrìa*, by Dacia Maraini. *International P.E.N. Bulletin of Selected Books*. 42 n. 1 (1992): 33–35.

Ovid. 1964. *Metamorphoses*. Translated by Rolfe Humphries. Bloomington: Indiana University Press.

Pratt, Annis. 1981. *Archetypal patterns in women's fiction*. Bloomington: Indiana University Press.

Rabinowitz, Nancy, and Amy Richlin. 1993. *Feminist theory and the classics*. New York: Routledge.

Sant'Agostino, Giuseppina. 1996. *La lunga vita di Marianna Ucrìa:* tessere la memoria sotto lo sguardo delle chimere. *Italica* 73, no. 3:412–28

Webster, Noah. 1980. *Webster's new twentieth century dictionary*. 2nd edition. Williams Collins Publishers.

Weinberg, Grazia. 1989. An interview with Dacia Maraini. *Tydskrif Vir Letterkunde* 27: 64–72.

Zingarelli, Nicola. 1963. *Vocabolario della lingua italiana*. Milan: Zanichelli.

Rethinking History: Women's Transgression in Maria Rosa Cutrufelli's *La briganta*

MONICA ROSSI

IN ORDER TO RECAPTURE THE LIVES OF WOMEN IN THE PAST, ONE must research and collect data. One must also reinvent a subjectivity that is not found at the "center" of history but rather at its "margins." In *La briganta* (1990), Cutrufelli writes of acts of transgression such as cross-dressing, homosexuality, murder, and violence as vehicles for her female protagonist's discovery of self and discovery of the boundaries existing outside her person. In the past, women's subjectivity was filtered through the practice of objectifying the female body. The accepted, principal male ownership of the female body coincided with women having no power to act, to write, and to speak. In *La briganta*, Margherita transcends these imposed limitations by transforming herself into a brigand. As such, she wears male clothing and learns how to kill. In Cutrufelli's novel, transgressive behavior of the central protagonist Margherita is a tool in the process of her growth into self-awareness and emancipation from the patriarchal symbolic order. Maria Rosa Cutrufelli thereby imbues Margherita with "male" characteristics in an attempt to transform her from an object of history into a subject of history. This essay explores and analyzes the reasons for and the mechanisms followed by Cutrufelli in rewriting history in her historical novel.

The second part of this article is an interview with Maria Rosa Cutrufelli that took place in July 1995. Cutrufelli talks extensively about her reasons for writing a historical novel, her difficulties in finding historical sources, her willingness to vindicate those women who did not have any voice in the past, and ultimately her profound emotional involvement in the process of writing this novel. She also talks about the relationship between women and literature, and women and history.

Cutrufelli states that the "power of the word" gives women their freedom and pushes them to talk more about themselves as subjects. The author also analyzes her use of transgressive and extreme behaviors to explore the possibility of a new and improved relationship between women and their bodies. Transgressive behavior reveals our most hidden desires. It exists at the margins of accepted human behavior; in the same way, the history of women has always been a marginalized, undocumented history.

Body Language and Cross-Dressing in *La briganta*

La briganta recounts the fictional memoirs of Margherita, a noblewoman from the south, who, during the spring and summer of 1863, joins one of the peasant brigand bands of south Italy that fought the new order of Garibaldi and King Vittorio Emanuele II in favor of restoring the monarchy of Ferdinand II of Borbone.[1] In contrast to the then generally accepted rule that women were not to be taught how to read and write, Margherita receives an education from her mother. Upon her mother's death, Margherita is forced into an arranged marriage with a much older man. When her husband confiscates her books to relegate her to a more subservient female role, she murders him in his sleep. Following her brother's example, she joins him and his group of bandits, which operates in the bush. To play an active role within the group, Margherita disguises herself as a man and is accepted as such by the other group members who accept her androgynous status. After a series of victories, the band is defeated by the National Guard. To avoid being shot, Margherita bares her chest to the attacking soldiers and is spared. Ultimately, she is placed on trial and then sentenced to life imprisonment.

The story is multilayered and complex, therefore allowing several levels of analysis. In fact, the text can be analyzed from many vantage points. It may be approached literally as a study of the class and gender struggle faced by Margherita, a woman of noble origin living in the south at the time of Italy's unification. It may also be approached more generally as a treatise by Cutrufelli on the effects of war on society and the changing roles assumed or foisted upon women living in such societies. This paper will take the latter approach and will examine more specifically the effects such historic upheaval has on the traditional definition of female and male identity as portrayed in *La briganta*.

The structure of the novel, a collection of memories from a prison cell, frames the plot within the boundaries of the real historical events that took place in the South (*Meridione*) of Italy between the spring and summer of 1883. The historical period described in *La briganta* is one of great turmoil and anarchy; in placing her novel at that particular time, Cutrufelli is free to develop Margherita's character beyond social and gender restrictions which have been subverted by the everyday drama of living through a civil war.

At the beginning of the novel, Margherita kills her husband in their bed. By taking this action, she violently opposes and renounces the role that the southern Italian nobility of that time had carved for her. Having taken her destiny into her own hands, Margherita no longer has a place in the social milieu in which she was born and raised. By her own choice, she then becomes an outlaw by joining the band of the peasant Carmine Spaziante.

At this point, the problem of cross-dressing arises because Margherita needs to belong to a new societal form constructed by men and modeled exclusively on men's needs. The resulting changes in her exterior appearance and body language deeply affect her psyche and her sexual desires. Margherita increasingly becomes androgynous, sharing both feminine and masculine traits. This, in turn, allows the author to explore several issues of gender identity that are not solely connected to the particular historical period.

Several theories have been presented on the nature and the limitations of historical fiction. Most critics agree that the true historical novel is one that transcends history, that it fills in history's unfortunate gaps and that it inspires readers to think about personal fate and society.[2]

Following a similar analysis, Cutrufelli has the narrator immediately reveal her intent in writing her memoirs: she is "buried alive," and despite the "emptiness in her mind and the numbness of her body," the fact that she can write and express herself through words has a powerful redeeming effect on her imprisoned psyche (1990, 5). She is addressing her future readers when she says, "Maybe tomorrow someone will understand how this [writing] is much more intoxicating than escaping from prison; how enormously liberating it is being able to 'talk'" (1990, 5–6). This last sentence reveals a great deal about

Cutrufelli's use of memorial writing and her particular interest in the historiographic metafiction as a tool for the transmission of memory.

Cutrufelli participates, like other contemporary Italian women writers, in a new form of feminist historicism that has been developing in the past decade in Italy. The new literary trend focuses on restoring the forgotten history of women by reinventing their lives based on the experience of women living in the present. This approach is directly connected with the political agenda of the early years of the feminist movement in Italy. During those times, as Cutrufelli states in the interview included in this article, "the issue of 'retrieving history' went hand in hand with that of 'retrieving the female body . . . [T]he 'negation of the female body' coincided with an absence of women from history." This explains Cutrufelli's decision in *La briganta* to rewrite the history of women through cross-dressing, androgyny, and the transformation of the female body into a male body. Margherita's transgressive behavior is an example of early female emancipation. At the time described in *La briganta*, it was only by becoming outlaws, by becoming androgynous and abandoning any connotation of traditional femininity, that women had a chance to be remembered as active protagonists of great historical events. Only in this way could women participate in the making of history instead of being erased in the process.

Cutrufelli also states that in writing *La briganta*, her intentions were to "vindicate" those women whose lives had been forgotten by official history. By reinventing their lives, the author gives them back their lost voices, their lost "word." By bringing forth these "lost words," the author is, in effect, allowing for the reinterpretation of history.

Cutrufelli's struggle to re-create a historical identity for women is evident in another of her works, *Mama Africa* (1993), an autobiographical narration of the time the author spent working as a correspondent for an Italian newspaper in Angola and Zaire from January 1975 through October 1976. In this memoir, she states, "Without memories one cannot construct a historical identity, and solidarity is not possible without the transmission of experience. . . . The transmission of knowledge is the real moment [in which one takes] responsibility . . . [That is] the task that I set up for myself" (1993, 122; 160).

In *La briganta*, the historical events of the time function as a backdrop for the protagonist's personal journey of discovery.

Neither Margherita, in the act of recounting her memoirs, nor
Cutrufelli, in creating the fictional life of her character, is exclusively concerned with the political and social change
caused by the unification of Italy. Margherita informs the
reader that she wants her confessions to "reveal a higher truth
than that of history itself." In talking about herself, she mentions how the strong impulses that guided her made her forget
how to be a woman (1990, 8). This brings us to the problem of
cross-dressing and body language. Margherita already per-
ceives herself as different as an adolescent because she receives
an education at a time when "generally, girls are not taught
how to write out of fear that they might exchange letters with
possible lovers" (10). She grows up isolated from other women
and from the contemporary common female experience. The
death of her mother and her ensuing arranged marriage de-
prive her of her own identity. The destruction of all of her
books represents her loss of intellectual freedom and of her
capacity to dream about other countries and other cultures.
She is now relegated to the traditional role of women prevalent
at that time, which calls for women to be submissive, ignorant,
silent, and passive. Symbolically, the sexual relationship with
her husband, which she experiences as rape, augments her profound sense of loneliness and triggers a dangerous split in her
personality.

The murder of her husband is a step into the unknown, the
ultimate act of freedom. However, as her brother Cosimo
points out, by committing this act, she has betrayed an unspo-
ken, sacred rule: killing is a male activity. At the time, a crime
that can be forgiven if performed by a man but not if performed by a woman. Cosimo, in fact, reminds her that "If he
[her husband] had offended you in any way, it was not up to
you to kill him. You did not have to pay for this. Why did you
humiliate me like this?" (68).

Margherita, by abandoning the familiar, safe realm of the
feminine world and of her social, privileged status, becomes
an active participant in "male history," and therefore she will
be judged as a man and not as a woman. Traditionally, women
are exonerated from the responsibilities of history, which men
carry by themselves. Therefore, she must be punished even
more severely not only because of her crime, but above all as
an example to other women.

Margherita is, at this point, "homeless." She has no home to
go back to, her brother does not recognize her for who she is,

and she has no gender identity that satisfies her. She becomes a seeker. Cross-dressing and the change in her body language are an exploration of other forms of identity.[3]

According to Carol Lazzaro-Weis, "Cutrufelli, like many feminists, believed that a series of superficial changes (here Margherita's shedding of women's clothes) would facilitate her participation in social change" (1993, 149) In this instance, however, Margherita's psychological development and her progression of "subjective states" are crucially related to her cross-dressing choice, which is anything but superficial.

Despite the fact that becoming a *briganta* is, initially, purely casual—a liberating act, and the beginning of a new adventure—wearing male clothes is also a necessity. Margherita is not the only cross-dresser in the band; another woman named Bizzarra—which in Italian means out of the ordinary, weird—also wears male clothes so she can actively participate in armed incursions with the men. Bizzarra, though, never gives up her femininity; her long, black hair makes her look like "a legendary animal" and, unlike Margherita, she is insistently courted by men whom she manages to keep at a safe distance (51). Moreover, Bizzarra, an expert in herbs and potions, nurses and cures various sicknesses and wounds. Her role of caretaker, her closeness to the secrets of nature are, in her own words, a prerogative of women. She fights like a man and acts tough wearing two guns in her belt at all times, but the reader never doubts her intense femininity and her awareness of it.

In contrast with Lazzaro-Weis' analysis, it may be seen that cross-dressing, in Margherita's case, involves a more complex transformation. She is not only wearing a new outfit but she is taking on a new life. She deliberately chooses to renounce even the last semblance of femininity, and she claims that her mask is merely helping her to deceive her fate. This points to the fundamental contradiction in Margherita's feelings. The "mask" becomes the catalyst leading to the clash between Margherita's feminine and masculine traits. Thus, when wearing male clothes, her latent masculinity, represented by her attitude toward violence and her hidden sexual curiosities and desires, emerges for the first time. At first, the "mask" gives Margherita power, a sense of freedom never known before that exhilarates her. This aspect is more in touch with the characteristics of a male identity. Nevertheless, these feelings soon become overwhelming, and the initial excitement is replaced by sadness and horror at the atrocities Margherita witnesses

as a bandit, thereby revealing the "more" feminine side of
her nature.

Several times during the narration, Cutrufelli underlines
Margherita's androgyny through this dual reaction to moments of crisis. Margherita's maleness makes her feel like a
wild animal, all instinct and alertness; her femaleness transforms her into a rational, sensitive human being that can recognize danger and tremble in front of atrocities (37–38).
Cutrufelli's description of the protagonist's contrasting reactions makes it clear that there is no solution to her duality; it
only paralyzes and frustrates Margherita since she is never
able to take a stand. The author seems to communicate to the
reader that androgyny does not represent a solution to the
quest for an alternative gender identity. On the other side,
Bizzarra always seems to be in control of the situation by keeping her female and male identities separated. In so doing, she
is capable of being more of a woman and, at the same time,
more of a man.

The contrast of opposing gender traits and the problematic
issue this represents is also described in Margherita's relationship with the leader of the band. Carmine and his woman
Antonia. Antonia possesses the stereotyped, feminine characteristics of that time. As Michela De Giorgio points out in *Le
italiane dall'unità ad oggi:* "In eighteen hundred, young women
had to be delicate-looking, physically and emotionally vulnerable, and easily impressionable" (1993, 216). This perfectly describes Antonia's character: talkative, gentle, childlike, tender,
and giving, with a strong need for security. Carmine's masculinity is also much stereotyped and exaggerated: he is aggres-
sive, self-confident, ambitious, forceful, willing to take a stand,
and sexually active and demanding.

Margherita becomes sexually attracted to both of them with
the same intensity. This attraction becomes stronger during
and after the band's armed incursions against the National
Guard. It is then that Margherita finds herself caught between
Carmine's and Antonia's prompt reactions to the crisis versus
her own sense of inadequacy and incapacity. At one point, the
band's safety is at stake, and Carmine makes the decision to
hide in a different location. In the confusion of the sudden
departure, Carmine is "confident, capable of efficiently orga-
nizing the time available and taking charge of everything, even
the unexpected, according to his own coherent and well designed plan." At the same time, "[in] the kitchen, Antonia was

gathering food ... with precise and agile movements made quick by a long practice." Each one of them has a specific role, which they perform rapidly and skillfully, essential to the functioning of the entire community (42–43). On the contrary, Margherita is almost paralyzed and incapable of taking any kind of action: "I was perspiring profusely and ... I could not move ... wearing those awfully tight pants, suddenly not adequate anymore for my female body" (43). Once again, the experience of cross-dressing, at crucial moments, is one of confusion, frustration, loneliness, and unhappiness. Margherita's sexual desires toward both Antonia and Carmine could never become reality; Antonia only sees her as a "woman" and is oblivious to Magherita's attraction to her; Carmine treats her like a man and challenges her feminine side by ignoring it.

The problem of gender identity as demonstrated by Bizzarra's attitude is not in the exterior appearance, but in a comfortable relationship with one's own self and one's own body. Cross-dressing had been described by Margherita as a mask that helped her deceive her destiny. In reality, it is Margherita herself that will ultimately be betrayed by her new "mask." Toward the end of the novel, her body has lost any sexual connotation and sexual appeal, both feminine and masculine. She describes it as colorless, drained, with no more tears left, no more blood. After participating in several incursions with the men, the excitement of wearing male clothing, which at first made her feel free and wild, which allowed her to take active part in a world forbidden to other women, vanishes. She is left with a sense of purposeless void; she is tired of fighting and of seeing violence.

Immediately before the final surrender, Carmine's band is led to believe that it is safe to establish headquarters in the city. Leaving the bush brings Margherita back to the society that she had left. In so doing, she falls victim to a process of "normalization": life goes back to the same traditional values system that existed prior to the beginning of the revolution. For the first time, Margherita has to wear a skirt on top of her pants to attend church. Also, since there are no more incursions, she shares the daily chores of Antonia and the other women. Furthermore, she is no longer allowed to have meals with the men. She now describes her short hair as a mutilation, while the sophisticated city women laugh at her funny appearance. Bizzarra, instead, refuses to comply with the same mandate. One morning Bizzarra disappears without a trace and leaves Margherita to ponder over her last words uttered the night before her vanishing: "I am a brigand, not a brigand's woman" (105).

When Carmine and his men decide to take to the bush again in a last attempt to save themselves, Margherita does not follow them because she knows that they too, like herself, will be the victims of an inevitable fate. She remains behind with Antonia, and when the two of them try to escape from the city, Antonia is killed. At that point, Margherita reveals herself as a woman by baring her chest to the soldiers, and she consequently avoids being shot. She has had several choices before coming to this final decision: she could have followed Bizzarra or Carmine back to the bush or she could have escaped on her own and started a new life somewhere else. At the end, she could have chosen death and let the soldiers kill her. Instead, the author decides that Margherita must voluntarily allow society and history to judge and condemn her. By denying a positive conclusion to the protagonist's quest, Cutrufelli shows the reader that Margherita's androgyny could not have survived the privileged and sheltered existence of the hidden bush, where everything was possible. The narration takes the form of a circle when the final events come to be connected with the initial ones as if they were their logical continuation and nothing had come between them. History has to resume its natural course, which, at the time, could not have been modified by the revolt of a single individual.

Interview with Maria Rosa Cutrufelli

This interview was conducted in Italian. It is published here for the first time. The translation is mine.

What did it mean for you to rewrite history, in La briganta, *from a female point of view?*

Cutrufelli: It was initially very difficult to find the historical sources, difficult to know where they were located. I wanted my main character to be a woman; I do not know why. Maybe because of my personal history, I am more inclined to choose female characters. There are some women writers, also in the past, who would rather write stories about male characters. I know myself as a woman; I have understood my "sexual difference" for many years. When writing a historical novel, choosing a female protagonist represents a problem because few official documents pertain to the life of women in the past. During my research, I happened to read diaries written or dictated by brigands, but none of them was narrated by women. For example, the *capo brigante* Carmine Crocco Donatelli, who inspired one of the main characters of the novel, existed in real life. While in prison, he dictated his memoirs to a historian who collected them and published them as if they were an autobiography, which is what happens with my female protagonist. *La briganta* recounts her fictional memoirs. There were no women who told, wrote, or narrated their own brigand stories, so I decided to vindicate them by inventing their lives. The most valuable historical sources were the trial documents collected in the state archives where there is a whole section dedicated to the activities of the brigands in 1800. There I found documents on the trials against women brigands, which I read diligently for months. It was an excruciating process because these documents are handwritten in the handwriting style of the time, and it was very hard for me to read them. Then I had to order all of the information into a coherent structure and give it plausible shape, and that was also very demanding. Nevertheless, it was worth it. For example, there is a female character in the novel who says "I am a brigand, not a brigand's woman." The critics said that this statement revealed an attempt, on my part, to make the text a feminist text. That is not true. I actually found this statement as made by a peasant woman from Calabria who had been tried for being a brigand in 1864. It was I, with my female eyes, who read it and took it out of its context. No male historian had ever noticed it before. I chose to use it for my book. What the critics said reveals their biased way to read history, their prejudices against women.

Why did you decide to create a protagonist of noble origin?

Cutrufelli: At the beginning I thought my character Margherita had to be a peasant. During those times, almost all brigands were peasants, as the phenomenon of *brigantaggio* after the unification of Italy in 1861 was the first example of an organized peasant revolt. In reality, I was incapable of relating to a nineteenth-century peasant woman. Reading through the documents of the trials, I found a note about a woman of knowledge, very educated, who also participated in the *brigantaggio*, and that was the key to the construction of my novel. In that way I was able to identify with my protagonist and to narrate her story in the first person. There are peasant women characters in the novel, but for the "main voice" of my story, I needed someone closer to me.

Why did you choose this particular historical background, the unification of Italy, for La briganta?

Cutrufelli: Ten years before I wrote the novel, I wrote a critical essay on the unification. Upon reflection, I felt that essay's tone too aseptic, too cold, and I wanted to tell history in a more fluid, passionate way. That is when I chose to write the novel. When writing the essay, I was moved and emotionally involved with the material I was researching: for example, the photographs of the murdered female brigands whose bodies were left naked. I was shocked by the inhumanity with which they would deal with those who had been taken prisoner. The enemy, especially if it were a woman, was dehumanized. At a time when it was scandalous to expose a naked ankle, they would take pictures of the naked bodies of peasant women who had been brutally murdered. Men were treated in the same way. Some pictures show the triumphant soldiers of the Italian Army holding the heads of the defeated, murdered peasants as if they were trophies. To me, that was a painful moment of our history and is still hard to deal with today. I became very emotional about the whole thing. That is why I decided to transform my historical knowledge into a novel.

This is what interests me the most: the mechanism used by a woman writer to re-create historical female characters. What were the historical data you privileged and those you chose not to include in the creation of your character? Where does reality stop and invention begin and why?

Cutrufelli: For the protagonist, Margherita, I included only some of the information gathered. In general, I always kept in mind, and used as a model, the novel written by Enrichetta Caracciolo, *Misteri del chiostro napoletano* (Mysteries of a Neapolitan convent). That novel tells the story of a noblewoman living at the time of the unification of Italy who was forced by her mother to became a nun. Later she adheres to the cause of Garibaldi and is able to leave the convent and become her own person. It is a very modern novel, even though it was written in 1864. That is the ideal model on which I based my *briganta,* even if it is a completely different story. Other than that, I was concerned with maintaining a certain historical coherence. I decided not to set the story in a specific region or city of the south of Italy but, instead, in an imaginary, almost magical southern land where everything that happens is real. The events that I describe in the book actually took place in the past, but one was in Apulia, one in Sicily, and another in Calabria. I put them all together because I wanted to describe a historical process that involved all of the *meridione* and not tell the story of a particular geographical place.

The structure of the novel is that of a diary, an autobiographical narration. As Margherita says in the first pages of the novel while addressing the reader, writing a diary represents the last chance she has to redeem herself as she is now in prison for life. Margherita tells us that the written word has the extraordinary power to liberate (6). Do you think that literature is the best way women have of expressing themselves?

Cutrufelli: I think that the use of the "word" (*la parola*) is, in literature and in other forms of expression. To have conquered the "word"—the "word" that allows us to communicate—in politics, in literature, and in science is the sign that reveals that we, as women, have finally conquered ourselves. This is the way to ultimate freedom. In *La briganta,* I wanted to underline the importance of Margherita's conquest of the written word when she says: "To start talking (as Margherita is being allowed to write her memoirs) is more of a scandal than having been a murderess brigand" (8). Action is a form of freedom, but if it is not accompanied by the "word" that explains the meaning of the action, then it is never an accomplished form of total freedom. I give much importance to the process of thinking about the meaning of the "word," which exists not only in literature but in any form through which knowledge and power express themselves.

In my reading of your novel, I identified three main topics through which the story can be analyzed: the relationship of women with official "history," the relationship of women with war/violence, and the relationship of women with their own bod-

ies. All three of these symbolic aspects of the narration can be read through the all-inclusive issue of women versus power. History is a product of the struggle for power: it tells the story of a few men subjugating others through violence and injustice. The violence of wars is imposed on most of mankind; above all, it is forced upon women who do not usually take an active part in it. Finally, history recounts the story of how men, during the passing of centuries, have imposed their own power and ownership over the bodies of women without women's consent. In your novel, you deal with these issues in a transgressive fashion by making Margherita a woman who transgresses the accepted norms of the time. Her behavior becomes your key to interpreting the madness to which women fell victim. According to you, are history, violence, and the problematic relationship of women with their own bodies the ways in which the symbolic order of the father manifested itself in the past, to the present? Are there other manifestations of patriarchal dominance?

Cutrufelli: The absence of women from mainstream history was a fundamental issue addressed early on by feminist activists who were in search of their lost female identity. During the early years of the feminist movement in Italy, the issue of "retrieving history" went hand in hand with that of "retrieving the female body." Everything that had to do with the "female body," and official history was at the center of any feminist discussion. It is not by chance that later, the issue of the "negation of the female body" coincided with an absence of women from history. Power and violence run through history and through the history of "the body." They function as connectors between historical events and manifest themselves through the history of our bodies. History and the "body" are those spaces that contain our questions on power and violence.

Let's talk then about the many transgressions of Margherita in the novel: she is a murderer, a brigand, a cross-dresser, and is about to discover her own homosexuality. Does rewriting history mean looking for examples of female transgression in the past?

Cutrufelli: That is what I am interested in. Margherita's transgressions take different forms and are extreme examples. I am fond of extreme forms of transgression. I am attracted to them as narrative material; in fact, all of my novels talk about extreme transgression, such as violent death. All my novels push the reader to wonder about the origin of desire and where desire leads. In *La briganta* there is transgressive sexual behavior, because during those times there weren't words to describe any form of sexual desire. Homosexuality could not be verbalized; therefore it was not conscious of its own existence. That is why in my novel it becomes transgressive behavior. Margherita's will to exist in her world, to establish her own identity is so strong that it brings to the surface everything that had been hidden in her subconscious. When she breaks with all conventional social rules, all of her sexual hunger explodes outward, and she directs it in the only way possible for the time in which she lived.

The historical background you chose for this novel is also extreme: it is the moment of the biggest change in the history of Italy; Italy becomes a unified country for the first time and, consequently, a clash of different cultures and dialects causes a crisis that is still unresolved. Every day the history of the country was in the making, in continuous transformation. The social web was mutating, the differences between social classes were blurred. It was not clear who the enemy was. Did that situation allow for Margherita to engage in transgressive behavior?

Cutrufelli: Of course. Breaking points are those moments in which it is easier to act in a transgressive way. Everything seems possible; daily habits do not exist anymore; paradoxically, periods of war have allowed women to emancipate themselves. It is at those times when the social order is destroyed that the family order is also changed forever. Because of wars, women could leave their homes and find working opportunities outside.

It appears to me that La briganta *takes place in a "bubble" outside of mainstream history, a kind of ahistorical period of time. Official history stops at the moment Margherita kills her husband and it starts again when she is taken prisoner, Garibaldi wins, and the band of brigands is dispersed. At that moment, the old, conservative social order is reestablished. Margherita, in order to be transgressive, walks out of history and out of the rules imposed on her by society. She loses or, more precisely, abandons herself to the chaotic ambient and the disorganized lifestyle of the brigands. Through transgression, she finds her own order, she looks for a new identity. Nevertheless, she is forced to reenter mainstream history when the bubble is destroyed by the events. At that moment, she loses all that she had painfully achieved in her quest through her sexual desires and the discovery of her own body. Is her transgression her ultimate moment of redemption? As society does not allow for Margherita to exist as she wants to, has she experienced her last, brief moment of truth?*

Cutrufelli: Redemption comes through the possibility of writing her memoirs. It is an invention of my imagination: I am the one who offers my protagonist her redemption. Unfortunately, in real history such a redemption does not exist. Women who became brigands were not allowed the chance that I gave my protagonist. As I said before, it is my personal historical vindication. I wanted one of these women to have the right to write, to narrate their side of the story.

It seems to me that most women authors who write historical novels end up deconstructing mainstream history into little moments: they would rather rewrite women's history from a marginalized point of view than look for an all inclusive, global past. In so doing, they give preference to times of revolutionary changes. Do you agree that marginalizing history means to break the compact uniformity of mainstream history and find there, in these breaking points, the true history of women?

Cutrufelli: This is exactly what I had to struggle with when I was putting together the information that I had gathered through my research. All I had found were bits and pieces of the life of several women brigands, all at the margins of the numerous autobiographies narrated by male brigands. I had to painstakingly pull out, one by one, the feeble traces left in mainstream history by these women who were not stereotypical heroines but who were real, true human beings. I could only track the real true story of the women brigands in the documentation pertaining to the trials against them, not in official historical documents. It is only during the trials that these women's bodies and true existence came to life again. It was I, a woman who read the past of other women who came before, who could see things in those documents that a male historian probably would have disregarded.

Someone said that the history of women can be found inside their homes. In Margherita's case, it is everywhere else but home.

Cutrufelli: That is not entirely true. Margherita writes her autobiography in prison, so we can say that hers is an inside-outside story. Her "brief life of freedom" is contained within the prison's walls. *La briganta* has a circular narration: it opens in prison and it ends in prison. Usually, the opposite phenomenon takes place: the outside world tries to force itself into the inside one. This time, it is Margherita's world inside the confinement of her cell that tries to escape outside and reach those who are out there. Freedom is outside. Freedom had been outside when she was living in total transgression for a while. But now she has returned to the great prison where all women are held captive.

Is it a historical necessity that the protagonist ends up being punished for her transgression? We couldn't have had a happy ending?

Cutrufelli: Absolutely, it is a historical necessity; it could not have been otherwise.

Is it your position that Margherita exists in mainstream history only with a female body, and not as a cross-dresser or a homosexual?

Cutrufelli: Margherita belongs to history only if she reenters the feminine norm, which is to dress like a woman again. She had come to possess her own body and herself during her time of transgression, and now she has to hide her body within the time's concept of femininity.

Why does Margherita, at the beginning of the novel, say that courage and violence are "dangerous weapons in the hands of women"?

Cutrufelli: I was inspired by Lombroso's theory which stated that women are not cruel by nature, but if it happens that they become cruel, then they are much crueler than men.[4] In the nineteenth century, people thought that the concept of ownership was a male concept. Women were never supposed to oppose the idea of male ownership. Margherita, by joining the band of brigands, turns against the unchallenged right of men to own or disown women. By being a brigand, she takes part in the destruction of property and she enters, so to speak, the

territory of the enemy, the male territory. Moreover, she refuses to accept typical feminine characteristics such as a sense
of purity, of measure, of decorum, and of knowing her own
place. According to Lombroso's theory, she is twice as guilty
for having trespassed into a male world to which she does not
belong and for unnaturally opposing her own innate wom-
anly nature.

Is it because she goes "against nature" (contro natura) *that she
is faced with a dramatic chain of events that starts with the
killing of her husband and unfolds more and more tragically,
leading to her life imprisonment?*

Cutrufelli: We can say that it is the fusion of a private drama
with a collective drama. Margherita runs away from home and
disappears into the bushes not because of her patriotic sense
of duty but because she has just murdered her husband. Her
brother is a brigand himself, but in his case he is so for political
reasons. He facilitates her involvement with his band of brigands. Margherita's private drama is a collective drama, that
of all the women who, like her, have been forced into marriages
of interest.

*I would like to talk about cross-dressing. Margherita trades in her
female clothes and wears only male clothes during her months of*
brigantaggio. *In time of war, the transgression of cross-dressing
is, in a way, allowed. War is fought by men; therefore, in order to
be able to fight, one has to wear male clothes. But cross-dressing
for Margherita becomes more than just a disguise. It changes her
body, her sexuality, her mind and, more importantly, it permanently modifies her way of relating to others and her relationship
with power.*

Cutrufelli: Margherita, by cross-dressing, wears a "new life"
on her old body, which soon becomes a new body. She acquires
a new identity because cross-dressing, in her case, is not hiding
under a mask but, on the contrary, is a way to reveal her true
nature. Cross-dressing allows her deepest desires to surface. It
is not role-playing: it is the freedom to become whatever or
whomever you have never been able to be before. Italian literature, from Tasso or Ariosto to today, is full of female characters
who cross-dress, of women warriors, women soldiers. History
has many examples of women who dress in male clothes in

time of war, like the women partisans in the Resistance during the Second World War. For all of them, cross-dressing represents not only freedom of movement but freedom of feelings, of emotions.

I found Margherita to be a rather passive character. You allow cross-dressing to create such a strong change in her that her sense of self and of her own feminine body is permanently altered by it. Isn't it a way to give in to the patriarchal system of values? After all, Margherita ends up being unhappy and out of place in a female as well as in a male body. By the end, she has lost her sense of self; she feels that something is missing in both her male and female identities which she is struggling hopelessly to blend together. Are you, Maria Rosa Cutrufelli, surrendering to the idea that only men can be happy and fulfilled individuals in this society?

Cutrufelli: Mine is only a problem of historical coherence. It is a historical correctness issue: Margherita belongs to the noble class; she is a rich, privileged, well educated woman. Like most women of that time belonging to her same social milieu, she has no political understanding of her sexual difference. Moreover, our body has its own habits; it is only by breaking those habits that one can acquire a certain freedom. For historical reasons, Margherita cannot possibly be aware at a conscious level of what is happening to her, whereas the character of a novel that takes place in the present time might be.

Then is it for the same reason that Margherita does not choose between one sexual identity or the other, does not know who she is anymore, cannot remain an androgynous and bisexual individual but has to be punished and imprisoned? I am asking this because every other main character in the novel has a specific identity that leads to a precise destiny: Bizzarra, another female cross-dresser, has definitely become a hybrid, and is happy and fulfilled as such. At the end of the novel, she will disappear during the night to avoid being captured by the Italian army. Carmine, the capobanda, *is made prisoner and will continue to support his political cause while Antonia, the epitome of the real feminine woman, will die in the arms of Margherita. Each one of them has chosen a path to follow and has a clear knowledge of who they are. Margherita, on the other side, after taking a stand and killing her husband, seems to have lost any willpower and is swept away by the events of history and of her personal life.*

Cutrufelli: Margherita is a "creature of the frontier." She lives on the wave crest of history in the making, and for this reason she is the only character who questions herself on her own identity, who doubts herself, and who does not have a clear-cut personality. Hers is an identity in progress. Through her, history develops; she provides the link between the old and the new. She is a creature of doubt.

Margherita ultimately pays the price for all of us; she is a sort of sacrificial victim. To tell you the truth, I expected her to run away with Bizzarra and disappear, happy and free. But there could not be a happy ending.

Cutrufelli: This business of the happy ending is bothering a lot of people, not only you. Apparently every woman wanted a happy ending to this story.

I was hoping for a great moment of redemption at the end. The history of women is so full of sorrow that we want to envision a more positive one. But then there is the issue of reality and historical coherence. Some female authors prefer to respect that coherence even if it is at the expense of their own creative process.

Cutrufelli: As you know, Margherita is a murderer even before becoming a brigand; therefore she cannot be redeemed.

Is it her fate to be remembered in mainstream history as an assassin?

Cutrufelli: Well, she is a peculiar murderer: her hate toward her husband grows along with the progressive loss of freedom imposed upon her by her marriage. Above all, her husband took away the privileges she had as an educated woman, which included her right to keep her books after the wedding. She can only free herself from this "cage" through murder and then, later on, must return to a different "cage," a real prison. This time, however, her return is a willful act. It is true that in doing so she renounces the right to live, but this is her own choice. She did not choose to get married but she chooses to be put in prison. Moreover, there has to be a certain narrative coherence. Margherita could not have survived in that society as an androgyne or a homosexual. Nevertheless, she refuses to return to the norm imposed by said society. I think there are some similarities between my character and the women terrorists of our contemporary society.

My last question is: what do you think is missing from women's collective memory?

Cutrufelli: I believe that there is a lack of connection among different generations of women. My generation had to struggle greatly to gain a sense of memory. I do not think that we struggled as much to transfer this sense of memory to future generations. I am strongly aware of this gap, and I am definitely going to work to change that.

Notes

1. Cutrufelli, 1990.
2. I refer to historical theory by Feuchtwanger (1963), White (1973), Lukacs (1973), and Manzoni (1984).
3. The idea of the protagonist/subject of a novel being a "homeless" seeker for the "truth" is taken from Georg Lukacs (1971, 40).
4. For Cesare Lombroso's anthropological and social study of the nature of crime, see Lombroso 1893, and Lombroso and Loschi 1890.

References

Caracciolo, Enrichetta. 1986. *Misteri del chiostro napoletano.* Florence: Giunti.

Cutrufelli, Maria Rosa. 1990. *La briganta.* Palermo: La luna.

———. 1993. *Mama Africa.* Milan: Feltrinelli Editore.

De Giorgio, Michela. 1993. *Le italiane dall'unità ad oggi.* Bazi: Editori Laterza

Feuchtwanger, Leon. 1963. *The house of Desdemona or the laurels and limitations of historical fiction.* Detroit: Wayne State University Press.

Manzoni, Alessandro. 1984. *On the historical novel.* Translated by Hannah Mitchell and Stanley Mitchell. Lincoln: University of Nebraska Press.

Lazzaro-Weis, Carol. 1993. *From margins to mainstream: Feminism and fictional modes in Italian women's writing.* Philadelphia: University of Pennsylvania Press.

Lombroso, Cesare. 1893. *Uomo delinquente.* Turin: Bocca.

————. 1890. *Il delitto politico e la rivoluzione.* Turin: Bocca.

Lukács, György. 1971. *Theory of the novel.* Cambridge: MIT Press.

————. 1973. *The historical novel.* London: Merlin Press.

White, Hayden. 1973. *Metahistory: The historical imagination in nineteenth-century Europe.* Baltimore: Johns Hopkins University Press.

Trascolorare: Metamorphoses in Rosetta Loy's *Le strade di polvere*

Stefania E. Nedderman

ALICE OSTRIKER OBSERVES THAT AMONG WOMEN AUTHORS, "H.D.'s concept of 'the palimpsest' seems to be the norm, along with the treatment of time that effectively flattens it so that the past is not then but now" (1982, 87). In this essay I propose to explore Loy's variant of the palimpsest strategy, the process of "changing color," or *trascolorare,* a technique she obviously borrows from cinema. *Trascolorare* actually corresponds to a dissolve, a form of cinematic transition where one image is gradually replaced by another that superimposed upon it for a brief time, produces a feeling of continuity, although time and often space have changed. Loy composes space and time as with a camera. In a tangle of flashbacks and flashforwards, she uses the zoom and slow motion, the wide and the narrow-angle techniques to overcome the constraints of time and space.[1] She revisits and rewrites the past. Changing color, *trascolorare,* becomes the act of re-vision that Adrienne Rich urges women to undertake, "the act of looking back, of seeing with fresh eyes, of entering an old text from a new critical direction . . . [the] refusal of the self-destructiveness of male-dominated society" (1979, 35). Loy's narrative strategies dissolve the dominant concealing picture to reveal the latent picture underneath. People, events, and objects, even a house can change color, *trascolorare,* and reveal hidden stories.

Le strade di polvere is a novel in which everything changes, transforms, permutes: bodies undergo a metamorphosis, emotions ankylose and wear out, memories disappear, generations reproduce variations of themselves, and images fade in and fade out and dissolve. We see the day fade, *trascolorare,* into night and the night into day (Loy 1990, 245; 1987, 235). Emotions fade one into the other, *trascolorano* (1990, 75; 1987, 70). Memories ebb one into another, *si scolorano* (1990, 108; 1987,

102). And finally, life also fades, *trascolora*. Commenting on future events the narrator exhorts:

> But now we must not think of what will be, who can know destiny, who knows how and where events will be superimposed on preconceived images; life *fades* and allows what was hidden to appear. (133; Italics mine)[2]

Life—that is, time—appears as a process of stratification and erosion that paradoxically covers and uncovers. Life's events superimpose themselves upon our intentions, deposit sediment on top of our desires and dreams while time gradually erodes them. The verb *trascolorare* captures the essence of Loy's writing—all the processes of permutations that permeate her novel—and synthesizes her vision of life, history, and fiction. It is a word pregnant with meanings, full of suggestive possibilities that the English "to fade" fails to convey. *Trascolorare* means to fade, but also to grow pale, and to change color; it indicates the process by which something becomes less opaque, more transparent, thus making it possible to see through it, or for another image to transpire, to bleed through, to leak out as in a palimpsest. Webster's New World Dictionary defines a palimpsest as "a parchment, tablet, etc., that has been written upon or inscribed two or three times, the previous text or texts having been imperfectly erased and remaining, therefore, still visible." In Loy's text, lives unroll, pass, fade, change color, are eroded, dissolve, and duplicate the lives of previous generations. The future appears as already written, a past waiting to be repeated; as a consequence, the present emerges also as a palimpsest of the past.[3]

Le strade di polvere opens and closes with the image of a house. The first paragraph of the novel describes the exterior of the house and relates the story of its hasty construction by the Gran Masten; the epilogue of the novel shows us the interior of the house, now decrepit like its two old inhabitants Gavriel and Luìs, the Gran Masten's grandchildren. A century has passed between these two pictures; in that span of time a peasant dynasty has been born, has prospered and declined, and a nation has come into being. But from these two enclosing frames, women are absent. The house, a woman's traditional domain, reveals itself as a male territory, and the chapters' titles further underscore this male preeminence by deleting any female reference.[4] The story of the ascent of the family unrolls against the historical backdrop of the wars that marked the birth of the Italian nation. In every generation the future paterfamilias of the family fights in one of those wars: the Gran Mastèn's son, Pidrèn,[5] fights in the army of Napoleon; Luìs, Pidrèn's son, participates in the revolutionary uprisings of 1848; and Pietro Giuseppe, Luìs's son, is hurt in the naval combat of Lissa in 1866. Thus connected, family and nation appear as twin ventures; both are conceived as male enterprises, built by a series of masculine acts and founded on the acquisition of land, the accumulation of capital, and the need for male progeny.[6] The official history of the family, like the history of the nation, is patrilineal and all-encompassing.

In line with this historiographic tradition, the founder of the house, the Gran Mastèn, is depicted like every mythic pioneer and conqueror as quintessentially male. Larger than life, triumphant over nature, he builds his fortune out of nothing by ceaseless work and indomitable will. He doubles his possessions, marries, and has children because he needs more hands to work his land, which he straddles like a giant. Of his wife little is said, a fate ultimately shared by most women who appear just as names on genealogical trees. At the end, Antonia, Luìs's wife, also disappears from the pages and presumably from history. Since the inside pages of the novel teem with women, their absence at the beginning and the end of the novel is even more noticeable.[7] This strategy directs us to go beyond the readerly text, to crack open and penetrate its encasing structure. The obvious parallel between Camurà, the successful merchant, and the Gran Mastèn should refocus our reading. From an off-center perspective, the Gran Mastèn, divested of his mythical attire, is a speculator who enriches himself by taking advantage of the incessant wars, hoarding and selling grain and wine as Camurà does with fabrics two generations later.[8] By foregrounding men's actions and relegating women's stories to the submerged text, *Le strade di polvere* mimics patriarchal history while subtly subverting it. It enacts the stifling and stultifying effect of official discourse on the stories of women whose lives, like their stories, are circumscribed and defined by the lives and stories of their husbands, sons, brothers and lovers. But we can reconstruct the labyrinth of their lives if we follow Ariadne's thread backward, rolling it up into a ball again, retracing the twists and turns of life with our imagination. Women's history has been colored over by that of men but it can coalesce anew.

If our lives are *strade di polvere*, [dust roads] trajectories in time and space that inevitably end in dust and can only live on in memories, women's lives are, if possible, more radically dust than men's; having been deleted from history, erased from its texts, they are denied the power of memory. Woman, writes Hélène Cixous, "has always functioned 'within' the discourse of man, a signifier that has always referred back to the opposite signifier which annihilates its specific energy and diminishes or stifles its very different sounds" (1981, 257). Thus "muffled throughout history, [women] have lived in dreams, in bodies (though muted), in silences, in aphonic revolts" (256). Dispossessed, woman had no voice, no place, no history, thus *voler*, flying/stealing, "is woman's gesture. . . . we've been able to possess anything only by flying. . . . stealing away, finding, when desired, narrow passageways, hidden crossovers" (258). In *Le strade di polvere* Maria, Pidrèn's wife, exemplifies the entrapment while her unmarried sister Matelda appears to have found the passageway by belonging not to a flesh and blood man but to a dead lover, Giai:

> After Gavriel and Luìs it will be the turn of Bastianina, of Manin. . . . and finally of Gioacchino. . . . But Maria doesn't know any of this yet. . . . Her thoughts go to the eggs to be gathered in the hen coop, the wool to be carded. To Luìs's first dress. *In that life that Sacarlott wants to enclose like an arena she has found a shadowy corner, she has drawn a circle even smaller,* and from there at times, with no more suffering, she watches her sister become leaf, wind, knowing no circle, great or small, but only the vast spaces of the birds. (35)[9]

Maria's life, like Antonia's and Sofia's after her, is confined and delimited by her husband, children, and domestic chores. In the confined space of the patriarchal home, in a circle contained by another circle, the women must fight to maintain their own space and identity.

In Loy's text the insidious nature of the house is progressively revealed. The house, a multivalent symbol usually associated with motherhood, shelter, and the cradle, is here the space of estrangement, entrapment, and mental alienation. It visibly represents the englobing and metabolizing power of patriarchal discourse. The house is like a carnivorous plant: innocuous and enticing outside but deadly inside. Almost by magic, the simple yellow building, with its long sequence of rooms one after the other, permutes into a disturbing place where mysterious presences are felt. For Gaston Bachelard, the house represents a "psychic state" that discloses the inner world of a character (1969, 79). For Maria it becomes a labyrinth with painted ceiling from which a fearful man with a pointed beard seems to give her some order and where she gropes in the dark.[10] Slowly the house metamorphoses. It changes into a living entity. As a labyrinth it may have contained a monster at its center, but Antonia discovers that, in actuality, the monster is the house itself. Women have from mythical times guided men through the labyrinth of life and death, giving them the thread that would save their lives, only to be deceived by them. Loy's text uncovers another dimension of Ariadne's myth. As in a series of receding planes a different picture emerges. The myth implodes: woman herself is the thread of life and the labyrinth does not contain but *is* the devouring beast who is man himself. Thus man metaphorically comes to represent death for woman.

Pidrèn, like the Gran Masten, lives life as a battle, a duel to be fought and endured without showing any weaknesses: "he has learned that life must be enclosed in a circle, like those arenas he saw in Spain" (34) [ha imparato che la vita bisogna chiuderla in un cerchio come quelle arene che ha visto in Spagna (29)]. Man is a matador or alternatively the trapped bull. It is a lesson he learned as a soldier, a vision of life that inevitably poisons man's relationship to woman. In the novel, except for Gavriel, men are adept at separating present from past and reason from emotion and at repressing memories because of their painful associations. Pidrèn erases the traumatic memories of the Russian campaign till his final moments. His decision to forget, to deny the reality of pain inevitably limits his capacity for empathy and narrows claustrophobically the confines of his life. He

> has learned to direct his gaze at a distance closer all the time, not to look around, not to ask himself questions, never allow his desires, his future, to go beyond the fields and the house, the dusty road that rises towards Lu. (54)[11]

Memories are for Pidrèn the sure way to hell; his is the "unswerving conviction that the only way to save your soul is to forget what has happened, good or bad" (54) [incrollabile convinzione che l'unico modo di salvarsi l'anima sia dimenticare quello che é stato, nel bene come nel male (49)]. Emotionally he grows a hard shell. When after the first child Maria refuses to have more children, he sweeps away her feelings as fanciful or childish. He likes making love to her and considers children important "for the land and for the house. . . . he decided to pay no attention to what she had said" (31) [per la terra e la casa. . . . decise di non tenere in nessun conto quello che aveva detto (26)]. Maria must concede defeat. Her everyday life is channeled again, its flow checked and controlled by domestic cares:

> she hadn't calculated Pidrèn's strength, the strength of someone who has convinced himself and others that what is good for him is good for all. . . . forced, dominated by his will, her thoughts once again were guided, like letters on the lines of a copybook, along the path of family life. (31)[12]

Her only escape is within, into her small circle—a shady refuge that Pidrèn's masculine power cannot easily obliterate as he symbolically does by cutting down the top of the walnut tree (1990, 31; 1987, 26).

Luìs's second wife, Antonia, suffers the same fate as Maria. The busyness of their domestic duties represses and keeps their feelings in check, but with the passing of time their yearning for their maternal home and childhood increases. At the window of the yellow house they peer through darkness, space, and time. Their memory forms a different picture. Trapped in the house, Antonia contemplates the bell tower, which reminds her of Braida, her maternal home. When she lets her guard down, her body talks.[13] Her desire to escape is betrayed by her neurotic compulsive behavior. Her secret pain is expressed by the spilling of her blood:

> She should have been happy, perhaps at times she was. But at other moments, when fatigue created a sudden emptiness in her, she would make a mechanical gesture that gave her away. With the nail of her forefinger she would scratch whatever object was within her reach, even the most delicate. Irresistibly, she scraped away the paint, arrived at the wood, the plaster, until her finger bled. . . . Often she would stare, spellbound, out of the little window . . . at the spire. . . . She seemed to be waiting for the hours to strike, the only thing that could tear her away from the closed circle of her suffering as her nail scratched away the dry putty that held the pane in place, and the sill was stained with little drops of blood. (159)[14]

The house is a prison, a stone coffin; her life is a circle that asphyxiates. She scratches to get out, to find air, freedom; perhaps she bleeds to feel alive. Scratching also reflects a need to expose something hidden, to see its true nature. She feels like a foreign body in her house: "the house slowly rejects her, expels her like an alien body, the rooms no longer recognize her as theirs" (216) [la casa lentamente la respinge, la espelle come un corpo estraneo, le stanze non la riconoscono piú dei loro (207)]. The house has acquired a personality of its own. It is an organism that only tolerated her in its own body; its hostile nature was hidden while she was busy producing children for the house. Then, her duty done, it lets her see its true nature and rejects her for being different, for desiring more.

The word "house," *casa* or *casato*, refers not only to a building housing a family but also to the family line associated with it. In our society a family line is inherently patrilineal and relies on sons for its continuity. Maria reacts to the birth of her first son with fear and repulsion because she instinctively fears annihilation. By that act of "reproducing," she had been transformed into common farm stock, "flesh that reproduced more flesh" (30) [carne che riproduce altra carne (26)], whose function is to increase the capital of the family. By exercising his ontological power of naming, Pidrèn immediately appropriates the son. "He'll be called Gavriel" (23) [As ciamerá Gavriel (27)], he says and, having claimed him as his own, goes back to his work. With his father's staff, symbol of power and patriarchal continuity, "where the job hadn't been done perfectly, he simply undid it with the stick that had been the Great Masten's" (28) [dove il lavoro non era perfetto, si limitó a disfarlo con il bastone del Gran Masten (23)].

Rather than threatening his annihilation, the first son assuages Pidrèn's need for affirmation and confirms his identity. Gavriel is his projection in time, another way to assimilate and possess the land even after death. Pidrèn wants his son to be like him. He is proud of his step behind him "as if son and land comprised one thing, something squared off in time. A geometric progression where each would be transformed, but not lost" (42) [quasi il figlio e la terra formassero una cosa sola, un quadrato nel tempo. Una progressione geometrica dove ognuno si sarebbe trasformato senza perdersi. (37)]. Once again we find the concept of transformation, although in this instance it really means sameness because the son is conceived as the father's replica. Pidrèn is confident that his permanence, his eternity, resides in the body of his firstborn son who is thus burdened by the obligation of being like his father. To be different would be a betrayal. The Gran Masten's staff will later be used by Luìs the second son, visibly expressing the otherness of Gavriel. Gavriel will incur Pidrèn's wrath for being a dreamer, for being different, as will Pietro Giuseppe incur the wrath of Luìs, who likewise refuses to accept or even contemplate any identity other than one that mirrors his own. Antonia realizes that could easily be her fate: "it would take very little . . . to make her, too, slip away, out of his (Luìs') life for ever" (210) [anche lei sarebbe potuta scivolare via, fuori per sempre dalla sua vita (201)]. Except for their obligations, the status of women is not unlike that of children. There seems to be no escape for them: if they transgress, they are erased from family and society; if they conform, they are inscribed in the symbolic order and thus also disappear.

Erased by official history, if woman tries to find her story in prehistory, in myth, fairy tales, and folklore, she must again contend with the phagocytising power of hegemonic discourse. Archetypal and mythological studies of the past have focused on male experiences, male visions, and male interpretations, as we have seen with Ariadne's myth. In fact Estella Lauter contends that in Western mythology we see

> the emphasis on the masculine in our images of God; the confinement of the mother to the realm of intimate relationships; the emphasis on the seductress in every woman; the definition of creativity in terms of a heroic (masculine) quest; the identification of woman with nature to the detriment of both; the assumption that the woman is the guardian of love; the hierarchical arrangement of the species, as if the ladder were the most "natural" principle of relationship; and the dichotomizing tendencies of our language and thought, as if it were really true that "without contraries there is no progression," or as if "progression" were the only viable option in our lives. (1984, 204)

In *Le strade di polvere*, Rosetta Loy matches official history with her history by using the language of a storyteller, exploiting common fairy tales motifs to reveal the damaging effects of masculine myths of dominance and love. The informal language and conventions of oral storytelling tradition invest reality with a fabulous sheen. It is another way to break the symbolic order. At times her use of similes that permute humans or human parts into animals or inorganic matter and vice versa confers on her prose a disturbing, oneiric quality.[15] The logical, hierarchical, rational order changes color, *trascolora*.

Le strade di polvere does not try to mirror reality, but to decipher it.[16] It is clearly symbolic[17] and overtly constructed. It is based on a loop structure, somehow ending with its beginning, and there is a strong cyclical sense in the repetition of dramas from generation to generation. Contrastive and symmetrical portraits abound, as in fairy tales and myths. This magical dimension is established at the outset with the blurring of boundaries between people and nature, this world and the other world. Gioacchino and the revenant Giai still walk among the living. People become inanimate matter, while matter acquires human connotations from this mingling. Matelda is coupled to the Monferrato land by the color of her hair; they share the same tonality. It is the color of the land, the mud, the fog, a mimetic color common to its inhabitants (1987, 4; 1990, 8). Her secretive eyes are mollusks beneath her lids (1987, 24; 1990, 29) and when she cries, after Maria tells her of Giai's visit, the tears appear to flow not from her eyes but from all her face as if her skin were permeable layers of the earth. As in many fairy tales, two brothers, Pidrèn and Giai, vie for the same woman. Pidrèn is the powerful man of action; Giai is a blond artistic dreamer. This pattern of complementary opposition is repeated in the next generation with Gavriel and Luìs, one lunar and the other solar, while in the third generation Pietro Giuseppe, named after the first two, symbolically unifies what was split before. Pidrèn has five children, of whom two die; Luìs also has five children with Antonia, and two die. Maria marries twice, first to the blond Giai, then to the dark Pidrèn; in the next generation it is Luìs who marries twice, first to Teresina, the childish blond beauty, and then to Antonia, the dark waif. Pidrèn's daughter Bastianina is an unusual strong-willed child as will be Luìs's daughter Piulott. Also the two sisters Maria and Matelda are a study in contrast: one beautiful the other plain; one solar and the other lunar. And seventeen seems to be the liminal age to enter adulthood. Maria is seventeen when she meets and marries Giai; Gavriel is seventeen when he falls in love with Elizabetta; Teresina is seventeen when she marries Luìs; and Piulott is also seventeen when she falls in love with her half brother Pietro Giuseppe who is double her age and who was also seventeen when he left his family after his own first love delusion. The numbers

seven and three so common in fairy tales keep cropping up in
the narrative. Giai lies sick three years. Pidrèn comes back
seven years after his death and sleeps three days and three
nights. Errors are repeated: Gavriel leaves home after a fight
with his father, like Pietro Giuseppe who left after a fight with
Gavriel. Luìs dislikes Evasio's liberality, as Pidrèn disliked
Gavriel's. Piulott's attraction for her half brother recalls Gavriel's sin with Signora Bocca. Pietro Giuseppe saves Limasa
from the flooding of 1859, as Gavriel saves Rosetta del Fracin
from the flooding of 1939. History and people keep repeating
themselves with slight variations.

Lauter wonders if women, freed from many past constraints,
can now overcome the restrictions built into our symbolic code
and create their own myths and weave new patterns. What
unites the women artists whom Lauter examines is a reluc-
tance to dichotomize (i.e., Margaret Atwood's "there is no
other" and Susan Griffin's "the light is in us") and the embracing of the concept of transitionality. Transitionality, according
to Gloria Bonder, is

> a permanent process in life . . . and it is a process more characteris-
> tic of women than men. [It is] that type of subject-object relation-
> ship which is neither total fusion (confusion of boundaries) nor
> total separation, but a relationship that is paradoxical, intermedi-
> ate and dynamic. In ideological discourse the certainty of this dis-
> tinction is challenged: Thus one need not, indeed cannot,
> differentiate subjectivity and objectivity so sharply. All objects are
> subjectively experienced as part of the subject, yet not *as* the sub-
> ject; that is, object and subject are not coterminous but *are* and
> *are not*, simultaneously. (Lauter 1984, 212; Lauter's emphasis)

This translates into a landscape populated by interwoven
forms of life. These permeable boundaries manifest themselves
in shape-shifting images, in metamorphoses in animal, vege-
table, mineral, and spiritual forms.[18] Thus Gioacchino's death
(1990, 61; 1987, 56) echoes in cosmic oneness the death of the
eels he had just seen slaughtered (1990, 59; 1987, 54). The eels
"slither" with "glints of mother-of-pearl." The men slam them
on the stones, and their sticky blood "spatters" their hands.
They die with a "final shudder." After his eerily silent fall,
Gioacchino's boneless body lies on the ground in a tragic parody. He "shudders" in a last spasm; a line of blood trickles
from his ear. The dish he was carrying breaks and "spatters"
fragments all around him. Gioacchino's death with its cosmic

reverberations affects Maria and Pidrèn as cataclysms affect continents: "an upheaval, like an earthquake, the searing eruption of a volcano. Or perhaps rather like the beginning of an ice age that imprisoned them in its emptiness" (58) [fu uno stravolgimento pari a un terremoto, all'eruzione rovente di un vulcano. O forse invece l'inizio di un'era glaciale che li imprigionava nel suo vuoto (53)]. Only death can crack the frozen crust, as we see when Pidrèn's wild death cry breaks the ice on the window sill. But the secretive, witchy Matelda by her familiarity with nature is able to cross corporeal boundaries. She can see through space and time. She can experience Giai's pain and mirrors it in her body. At the moment in which "something incomprehensible, like a pin jabbed into the works of a clock, subverts the silent order of his body" (12) [qualcosa di indecifrabile, come uno spillo conficcato nell'ingranaggio di un orologio, sovverte l'ordine silenzioso del suo corpo (7)], Matelda pricks herself with her needle—a reworking of the folk motif Sleeping Beauty. She sees inside him, she "senses the crazed beating of the heart. She sees the maze of the veins, the wrench of the viscera" (12) [ne avverte il battito impazzito del cuore. Vede il labirinto delle vene, lo spasimo delle viscere (8)]. Like him she faints, and the drop of blood on Giai's head is mirrored by the blood on her finger. Giai's body is compared to a clock, a traditional symbol of the inexorable passing of time, which reduces the human body to a mechanical machine. But the images of the beating of his heart, the meandering of his blood, the contractions of his bowels are powerful organic images of time that by contrast reflect the pulsating rhythm of the universe.

For Loy official history is coming and going, *andare e venire,* a frenetic senseless activity similar to the movement of ants. It is only from narrowing the focus that the swarming acquires individuality and meaning. For this reason *Le strade di polvere* alternates between macronarrative and micronarrative, between long shots and close-ups. The author uses a zoom technique that foregrounds the domestic events and keeps the historical ones in the background. She also imitates the accelerating and decelerating speed of a movie camera. From a flash pan of historical events, the focus of narration returns, always in lingering close-ups, to the domestic occurrences of the family, magnifying them and dwarfing in importance the historical events. While the battlefields of war fade, the house comes into focus.

Because of their off-center or ex-centric perspectives, Loy's close-ups of people produce at times the surrealistic effects that characterize the literature of magic realism.[19] The same fantastic effect is achieved by viewing the events of the war from afar, as if with long, high angle shots that shrink and pin the participants to the ground. We see the battlefield from the height of a tower or on a map, where it is a miniscule flag. This optical perspective confers on the war an illusory dimension; it reduces it to a chess game or a play of mirrors. Rivers and valleys can be crossed with the movement of a finger if not with the step of a magical boot as in fairy tales. If space is compressed, so is time. Historical events pass like a whirlwind. Borrowing once again from the cinema, in a series of wipes, the temporal sequence is lost and the events appear as though happening simultaneously. The tempo accelerates vertiginously without "then and after" [poi, dopo] by substituting "but already, meanwhile, once again" [ma giá, intanto, ancora]. The rapid speed of sequences recalls the effect obtained by rapidly flipping the pages of a picture book. Like dominoes, one image falls to be covered by another and another:

> Pidrèn meanwhile is in Lombardy, the Veneto, Mantua. He even reaches Egypt and sees there the Pyramids and the Mamelukes. He's at Marengo. . . . (11) Pidrèn is already well away, on his horse with the checked blanket and the worn saddle. (13)[20]

The sequence also recalls the children rigmarole *Volta la carta* [turn the page], while Pidrèn's peregrinations turn into a parody of the common folk motif of the girl who must wear out seven pairs of iron shoes to save her brothers. This accelerated sequence is repeated several times (1990, 132, 136, 178; 1987, 125, 129, 169). At times the narrator not only compresses the action by the use of the present tense but runs ahead and tells us the future. In the novel, time is not an abstract concept but a tangible, physical process that imprints every being and object.

For Loy, history is essentially memory, that is, a sequence of events that must be interpreted and therefore reconstructed because time's obliterating force does not spare bodies, objects, or memories. To recover the story of a life we must recompose a puzzle from a few remaining fragments; we must see and smell what that person saw and breathed, contemplate what she or he loved. We must stop, pause, and look back. Pidrèn is not willing to do it. He prefers to forget:

> Giai left behind such faint traces, fragments which it is hard to put in any order, and reassembling them would demand infinite patience. As if Giai had been a light breath of air, a gust in the great storm of life. . . . Pidrèn. . . doesn't like to lose himself in the labyrinths of the past, or linger now to contemplate one place; he doesn't even have the time. (33)[21]

To recapture Giai's presence Pidrèn needs to imitate a hunter, look for traces and interpret them.[22] Maria does the same when she lifts the curtain she had imposed on her imagination and reconstructs the love story of her sister and Giai. So does the narrator of *Le strade di polvere* who does not hide the fact that she is reconstructing, imagining, fleshing out the event.[23] When Gioacchino dies, all that is certain is that he fell. The why is not known; only conjectures are possible.

> Maybe it was the fault of those two eggs . . . but what really happened nobody would ever know. If it was because of the ladder. . . . It was known for sure that Gioacchino climbed up from the stable. . . . Maybe he tried to reach his friend. . . . Or else he had only meant to escape. (60–61)[24]

This narrative segment is, like many others in the book, replete with such phrases as: no one knows, who knows why, maybe, perhaps. Fabulation is inevitable. After all, as Robert Scholes observes, "fabulation is not simply something that happens after the events, distorting the truth of the historical record. Fabulation is there before, making and shaping not merely the record but also the events themselves" (1979, 208). The myth of history's scientific objectivity has long since been debunked. The shared characteristics of history and fiction—both "cultural sign systems, ideological constructions whose ideology includes their appearance of being autonomous and self-contained" (Hutcheon 1988, 61)—are increasingly exposed.

In *Le strade di polvere* objects—the violin, the shoes, the snuffbox, the house—are icons of memory. They also *trascolorano*, reveal traces of the past, suggest a story. In fact Loy summarizes her novel as

> A moment of time, seen through a house, in other words the only thing which is real, true, concrete, tangible. Everything else arises

out of this house. That's also why I mixed in the element of fantasy, because the house seemed to me almost magical.[25]

And it is the aging chapel that provokes Bastianina's meditation on the fleetness of life:

> That chapel emanated an irrepressible sadness, the frescoes made unrecognizable by mildew, the altar crumbling with some sickness of the stone. The thought of death dominated that stratification of events, making unrecognizable all that has been vital and shining. (154)[26]

Inanimate objects exhibit the inexorable signs of time; like bodies they suffer the insult of time. Likewise, bodies, especially female bodies, lose their humanity during their aging process. Old Maria and Matelda are compared to two totems (1990, 163; 1987, 155). People slowly metamorphose, lose vitality, stonify, ossify, fossilize, swell or shrink, close themselves the way mollusks or turtles do into their shells. Human bodies seem to invert the evolutionary process and gradually reveal their different shapes and multilayered structures to finally return to the primordial dust. Life appears to be a progressive draining of vital fluids and desires until, as Matelda proclaims, what was left on this earth was nothing, "less even than those empty larvae that you crush in the grass in springtime when the insects have flown away" (18) [meno ancora di quelle larve vuote che si schiacciano nell'erba a primavera quando gli insetti sono volati via (14)].

In her last days Luison regresses to infancy. Like a child with a doll, she pets and cares for the copper wig the family bought her. Before dying she asks that they give her food to the princess, the wig. She has reverted to her native dialect; her eyes have become empty pools, "glaucous and watery" (98) [glauco acquoso (93)]; and she is deaf. She of the splendid tresses dies a bold puppet, the glory and beauty of her hair gone in a cholera epidemic that shrinks her head to the size of an orange, and further insults her by giving her the appearence of an obscene newborn: "she has gone completely bald and on her head she wears a bonnet that Bastianina wore in her cradle, the old woman's head has become that small" (67) [è diventata tutta calva e in testa porta la cuffietta che era della Bastianina tanto la testa le è diventata piccola (62)].

Matelda too, with her few wispy hairs, reverts to infancy and calls for her mother, her sister:

> It was a sound that carried the vibrations of earliest childhood, when the green of the trees and the wandering of the clouds are still like liquids dissolving one into the other, and words and things, not separated by the perception of the senses, assume forms in constant metamorphosis. And from afar, from its source, that chant dragged with it, like the magic piper, the formless characters of dreams. Things similar to the first years of life, or perhaps the same things. (218)[27]

Matelda is a baby again, about to disappear into the primordial time. Death is the last metamorphosis, the final *trascolorare*. Maria dies with her hair still dark and dense, but her face has shrunk so much that her head looks like a scalp. Under the pillow she keeps the snuffbox now full of dust, maybe what is left of Gioacchino's flute. Antonia's mother is in the end a whale, "slumped on the dormeuse . . . [with] the sharp odour . . . of a great whale cast up adrift on the last beach" (154) [afflosciata sulla dormeuse [con] il suo sentore acre di cetaceo abbandonato alla deriva sull'ultima spiaggia (146)]. She is already dissolving; her face is a "melting cake" (163) [torta sfatta (155)].

Beauty and love are missing from these images of death. Little, if anything, is left of dreams, desires, and love. Aging is seen as a progressive isolation, a steady fossilization of the flesh and spirit, the atrophy of the power of imagination. Memories become obsessions; Matelda's thoughts turn into frenzied bees and Gavriel's into the maddening creaking of a chain: "he has given up imagining, and his thoughts, like the chain of a well, have always the same creak" (178) [ha finito di immaginare e i suoi pensieri come la catena di un pozzo dànno sempre il medesimo cigolio (170)].

In *Le strade di polvere* life is a labyrinth full of deceiving mirrors: power, beauty, love, and the lover in whom one thinks to reflect oneself, in search for completion. In his blurb on the jacket of the book, Cesare Garboli states that Loy finds her most authentic voice [*si esalta*] when narrating about love, war, children, and death. But the catalytic force in the novel is the illusionary nature of love. Besides entrapping Antonia and Maria, love or the refusal of what it entails influences the life of the artists and virgins: Matelda, Luison, and Bastianina. Imperious and headstrong, Bastianina suffers the limitations imposed by her gender and refuses to fall into the trap: "she will not fall into the trap, she will not end up like her mother, like Luison; she will not end up like Fantina" (89) [Lei non cadrá nel tranello della madre, della Luison, non fará la fine della Fantina (84)]. It is not just marriage she rejects—Luison and Fantina never married—it is the giving of one's heart, the caring, the sacrificing for love. She chooses to follow the road to power. As a mother superior, a *badessa*, she will be able to command and be obeyed like the Gran Masten, Pidrèn, and Luìs. But her repressed passions are betrayed by the round, sensual, opulent fruits she paints. The "witch" Matelda becomes Hecate and embroiders her "blasphemous" refusal to let Giai go. He becomes the Angel of the Annunciation depicted on the priest's garments. The "amazon" Luison, described as a lady of the beasts and a Genoveffa di Brabante, only wants her two nieces, her kneading trough painted with flowers and birds, and her "tombolo" for making laces. Like a wild fairy, with unbound hair she dances when she is with her people from the wooded land of ferns and running water, but she refuses to marry because ironically she "did not feel 'nature'" (19) [non sentiva la natura (15)]. Our androcentric culture has so perverted the meaning of "nature"—and love—that it has come to signify submission to man. Thus paradoxically Luison is too wild "to feel 'nature.'"

When Maria and Matelda are young and curious about love, Luison's answers are like those of a sibyl:

> They (the answers) could mean one thing and also its opposite, as if the difference between man and woman, the realm and the adventures of love were things belonging to a future so remote that, like dreams, they were part of a life unpredictable in its eccentricity. (99)[28]

The last image of the book is the image of the house like a ship ready to sink, without women, full of silence and sterility. The house is a fossil like the bodies it contains, like the burned dead wood in the fireplace. But all was alive before. The fossil is a text waiting to be read, to be made flesh again. Like Luison's sibylline answers, this last picture is a text to be interpreted, an image ready to dissolve, *trascolorare*.

Notes

Portions of this paper were delivered at the Seventeenth Annual Conference of the American Association for Italian Studies, Winston Salem, NC, 21 February 1997.

1. This cinematic technique is evident in the sequence where Luìs reads aloud Monette's letter while Antonia remembers Monette's betrayal. She stares at the window, misty from the condensation, past the fog outside, and sees the events of the past summer fade in the distance. The closing frame shows the backs of Rosetta and Monette leaving (1990, 167; 1987, 159). Similarly, Limasa visualizes Pietro Giuseppe's imminent departure as a train fading into the country, carrying away images of her youth and Pietro Giuseppe (1990, 197; 1987, 189).

2. Ma adesso non pensiamo a quello che sarà, il destino chi lo conosce, chi sa come e dove gli eventi si sovraporranno alle immagini prefigurate; la vita *trascolora* e lascia apparire quello che era nascosto (Italics mine, 126).

Henceforth, unless otherwise stated, italics in the text are mine.

3. Loy's treatment of time has been analyzed by Brizio (1992) and Wood (1993), while Figliola (1994) has investigated the role of space in *Le strade di polvere*.

4. The chapters are: "Pidrèn," "The Cossacks," "Gavriel and Luìs," "Rust Apples," "Braida," "The Dragon Junot," "Giai's Violin" [Il Pidrèn, I cosacchi, Gavriel e Luìs, Le mele rusnent, Braida, Il dragone Junot, Il violino del Giai].

5. Pidrèn is also called Sacarlott and his real name is Pietro. Giai is Giuseppe. Matelda is also called Fantina; Sebastiana is called Bastianina. Later she will be Magna Munja which means the nun aunt.

6. See Rodríguez 1994.

7. As in real life, women outnumber men in the novel, which not only tells the story of the wives of the family—Maria, Teresina, and Antonia—and of the daughters—Bastianina, Sofia, and Piulott—but also of Matelda, Maria's sister; of Luison, their aunt; and the Cavaliera, Antonia's mother. It also lingers on Rosetta, Gavriel's lover, and the female servants, Gonda, Limasa, and Marlatteira.

8. The English translation hides the analogy between the Gran Masten's actions and the war's. It is the vocabulary pertaining to wine that connects them. While the Gran Masten pours wine from one vessel to another, selling it to people of all nationalities, the wars pour people into different nations, thus changing the colors of the map of Central Europe (1990, 7; 1987, 3). The mercenary source of the Gran Masten's fortune associates him with Camurà whose ascent lacks any mythical disguise: he profits from the increased need for fabric to dress the army (1990, 130; 1987, 123).

9. Dopo Gavriel e Luìs sarà la volta della Bastianina, della Manin . . . e infine del Gioacchino . . . Ma questo lei ancora non lo sa . . . I suoi pensieri vanno alle uova da raccogliere nel pollaio, alla lana da far cardare. Alla prima veste di Luìs. In quella vita che il Sacarlott vuole chiudere come in un'arena lei ha trovato un angolo d'ombra, ha segnato un cerchio ancora piú piccolo e da lí a volte, senza piú sofferenza, guarda la sorella farsi foglia, vento, non conoscere nessun cerchio né grande né piccolo ma solo i vasti spazi degli uccelli (31).

10. "She . . . anxiously waited to cross the threshold of the house with the painted ceiling; and instead she entered a maze with a candle in her hand" (53) [aveva aspettato con ansia di varcare la soglia della casa con la volta dipinta; e invece era entrata in un labirinto con una candela in mano (48)].

11. Ha imparato a posare lo sguardo a una distanza sempre piú ravvicinata, a non girarsi intorno, a non farsi domande, a non lasciare mai che i desideri, il suo futuro, vadano oltri i campi e la casa, la strada di polvere che sale verso Lu (49).

12. Non aveva valutato la forza del Pidrèn, la forza di chi ha convinto sé e gli altri che quello che va bene per lui va bene per tutti. . . . costretta, dominata dalla sua volontà, i suoi pensieri tornarono ad incanalarsi come lettere nelle righe di un quaderno lungo il sentiero della vita familiare (27).

13. Hélène Cixous observes that "more so than men . . . women are body. . . . For a long time it has been in body that women have responded to persecution, to the familial-conjugal enterprise of domestication, to the repeated attempts at castrating her" (257).

14. Avrebbe dovuto essere felice, forse in alcuni momenti lo fu. Ma in altri, quando la stanchezza le creava un vuoto improvviso, usava fare un gesto meccanico che la tradiva. Con l'unghia dell'indice scalfiva qualsiasi oggetto le fosse a portata di mano, anche il piú delicato. Irresistibile ne grattava via la vernice, arrivava al legno, al gesso, fino a sanguinare. . . . Spesso si incantava a guardare dalla piccola finestra in fondo al corridoio il campanile. . . . Sembrava che aspettasse il battere delle ore che solo avrebbe potuto strapparla dal cerchio chiuso della sua pena mentre l'unghia grattava via il mastice secco che teneva fermo il vetro e il davanzale si macchiava di goccioline di sangue (151).

15. Luìs comes back from the war with a body so lean he appears to have been kept under salt (1990, 137; 1987, 130)]. Fantina's thoughts are compared to bees, or better worms, under her fat brow (1990, 127; 1987, 121). Her face is like the skin of a featherless chicken and her eyes those of a snake. Lice climb up and down Mandrognin's hair like crickets along heads of wheat (1990, 1987, 133).

16. See Cannon 1989, which underlines the fabulist quality of Italian postmodernist fiction.

17. The house, the well, the moon, the raven, the circle, and the labyrinth are just a few recurring symbols.

18. For example, Piulott is compared to a bird, a mouse, a puppy, a small vulture; her fingers are described as "kneaded from earth, ready to crumble" (191) [impastate di terra pronte a sbriciolarsi (182)].

19. Linda Hutcheon considers magical realism "less a rejection of the realist conventions than a contamination of them with fantasy and with the conventions of an oral storytelling tradition" (1988, 208). In fact, the feeling of unreality and mystery is produced by the strange juxtaposition of otherwise ordinary elements that brings them into sharp focus.

20. Intanto il Pidrèn è in Lombardia, nel Veneto, a Mantova. Arriva fino in Egitto e là vede le Piramidi e i Mamelucchi. È a Marengo . . . (6–7). Il Pidrèn è già lontano con il suo cavallo dalla coperta a scacchi e la sella consumata (9).

21. Il Giai ha lasciato dietro di sé tracce cosí labili, frammenti cui è difficile dare un ordine e il ricomporli richiederebbe infinita pazienza. Come se il Giai fosse stato un'aria leggera, uno spiffero nella grande burrasca della vita. . . . Pidrèn . . . non ama seguire i labirinti a ritroso, fermarsi nella contemplazione di un luogo, non ne ha neanche il tempo (29).

22. Carlo Ginzburg writes: "Perhaps the actual idea of narration . . . may have originated in a hunting society, relating the experience of deciphering tracks. . . . [T]he rhetorical figures on which the language of venatic deduction still rests today—the part in relation to the whole, the effect in relation to the cause—are traceable to the narrative axis of metonymy, with the rigorous exclusion of metaphor" (1989, 103).

23. Retracing in her memory past events, Bastianina understands many years later what happened between Gavriel and Pidrén. Thinking back she has an illumination.

24. Forse era stato proprio per colpa di quelle due uova ... ma come erano andate veramente le cose nessuno lo avrebbe mai saputo. Se era stato per la scala.... Di certo si sapeva che Gioacchino era salito attraverso la stalla.... Forse aveva cercato di raggiungere l'amico.... O invece aveva solo cercato di scappare (55–56).

25. Un momento del tempo, visto attraverso una casa, ossia l'unica cosa reale, vera, concreta, tangibile. Il resto nasce da questa casa. Anche per quello ho mescolato quell'elemento fantastico, perché la casa sembrava quasi magica (quoted in Wood 1993, 135).

26. Una tristezza irrefrenabile trasudava da quella cappella dagli affreschi resi irriconoscibili dall'umido, dall'altare roso dal mal della pietra. Il pensiero della morte dominava quella stratificazione degli eventi che rende irriconoscibile quanto è stato vivo e splendente (147–48).

27. Era una nenia che divideva le ombre.... Era un suono che riportava le vibrazioni della primissima infanzia, quando il verde degli alberi e il vagare delle nuvole sono ancora simili a liquidi che si riversano gli uni negli altri e le parole e le cose, non divise dalle percezioni dei sensi, assumono forme in continue metamorfosi. E da lontano, da dove quella cantilena arrivava, si trascinava appresso come il pifferaio magico i personaggi informi dei sogni. Cosí simili, o forse gli stessi dei primi anni di vita (208–9).

28. Potevano significare una cosa o anche il suo opposto, quasi la differenza fra uomo e donna, il regno e le avventure dell'amore, fossero cose di un di là talmente lontano da appartenere, come i sogni, a una vita imprevedibile nella sua stravaganza (93–94).

References

Bachelard, Gaston. 1969. *The poetics of space.* Translated by Maria Jolas. Boston: Beacon.

Brizio, Flavia. 1992. Tempo e strategie narrative ne *Le strade di polvere* di Rosetta Loy. *Quaderni di Italianistica* 13, no. 1: 71–83

Cannon, JoAnn. 1989. *Postmodern Italian fiction.* Rutherford, NJ: Fairleigh Dickinson University Press.

Cixous, Hélène. 1981. The laugh of the Medusa. In *New French feminisms,* edited by E. Marks and I. de Courtivron, 245–64. New York: Shocken Books, Inc.

Figliola, Arthur. 1994. Space and its role as a medium for human interaction in Rosetta Loy's *strade di polvere. Romance Languages Annual* 6: 248–52.

Ginzburg, Carlo. 1989. *Clues, myths, and the historical method.* Baltimore: Johns Hopkins University Press.

Gollin, Richard M. 1992. *A viewer's guide to film.* New York: McGraw-Hill, Inc.

Hutcheon, Linda. 1988. *The Canadian Postmodernism: A Study of Contemporary English-Canadian Fiction.* Toronto: Oxford University Press

Lauter, Estella. 1984. *Women as mythmakers.* Bloomington: Indiana University Press.

Loy, Rosetta. 1987. *Le strade di polvere*. Turin: Einaudi.

————. 1990. *The dust roads of Monferrato*. Translated by William Weaver. New York: Knopf.

Nedderman, Stefania. 1997. Fossilization and stratification of memory in Rosetta Loy's *Le strade di polvere*. Paper read at the Seventeenth Annual Conference of the America Association for Italian Studies, Winston Salem, NC, 21 February.

Ostriker, Alicia. 1982. The thieves of language. *Signs* 8, no. 1 (autumn): 68–90.

Rich, Adrienne. 1979. When we dead awaken. In *On lies, secrets, and silence*, 33–49. New York: Norton.

Rodríguez, Ileana. 1994. *House, garden, nation*. Translated by Robert Carr and Ileana Rodríguez. Durham, NC: Duke University Press.

Scholes, Robert. 1979. *Fabulation and metafiction*. Urbana: University of Illinois Press.

Wood, Sharon. 1993. Rosetta Loy: The paradox of the past. In *The new Italian novel*, edited by Zygmunt G. Barański and Lino Pertile, 121–38. Edinburgh: Edinburgh University Press.

List of Contributors

Maurizia Boscagli is associate professor of English at the University of California, Santa Barbara. She is the author of *Eye on the Flesh: Fashions and Masculinity in the Early Twentieth Century* (1966) and of numerous articles and presentations on comparative literature, film, politics, and women's studies.

Rodica Diaconescu Blumenfeld is assistant professor at Vassar College. She has published articles on narratological strategies in Ariosto, on gender and representation in Carlo Emilio Gadda, and on feminist historiography in Dacia Maraini. She is working on a collection of essays on gender and the politics of cultural repression in classic and contemporary Italian cinema.

Gabriella Brooke is associate professor of Italian and director of the Italian Studies program at Gonzaga University. She is the author of a historical novel, *The Words of Bernfrieda* (Eastern Washington University Press, forthcoming 1999), articles and presentations on women writers and coeditor of the present collection. She is working on a series of short stories.

Paola Carù earned her Ph.D. from Columbia University with a thesis on Anna Banti. She is a lecturer at the University of Bergen, Norway, where she teaches courses in Italian literature and cinema. She has published essays on authors of the Italian Renaissance and on twentieth-century women writers. She is currently working on a study of Jewish Italian women writers.

Lauretta De Renzo is completing a Ph.D. in comparative literature at the University of Oregon. She is interested in twentieth-century Italian and Russian literature with a focus on crime and detective fiction.

Davida Gavioli is assistant professor of Italian and comparative Literature at Oberlin College. Her work focuses on the writings of contemporary women in a comparative perspective. She has published essays on Francesca Sanvitale, Carla Cerati, Alba de Cespedes, and Joyce Carol Oates. She is currently working on the emergence of the maternal voice within the mother-daughter relationship in works by Italian, ethnic American, and Francophone women writers.

Carol Lazzaro-Weis is professor and chair of the Department of Foreign Languages at Southern University, Baton Rouge. She is the author of two books, *Confused Epiphanies: L'abbé Prevost and the Romance Tradition* (1991) and *From Margins to Mainstream: Feminism and Fictional Modes in Italian Women's Writings 1968–1990* (1993). She is also the author of numerous articles on Italian and French literature. Dr. Lazzaro-Weis is currently working on a comparative study of the dynamics of autobiography, history, and fiction in the works of selected Italian, Caribbean, and African-American women writers.

Bernadette Luciano earned her Ph.D. from Columbia University. She is a tenured faculty in the Italian department at the University of Auckland, New Zealand. She has published in the field of dialect poetry, Dante studies, and Italian women writers. She is currently working on a book that explores how female narratives of the Italian Resistance revisit and reinvision history.

Maria Ornella Marotti is an independent scholar in North American and Italian studies and in women's studies. She has been on the faculty at the University of Rome, La Sapienza, the University of California at Santa Barbara, and the University of California at Santa Cruz. She is the author of *The Duplicating Imagination: Twain and the Twain Papers* (1990) and the editor of *Identita' e scrittura: Saggi sull'autobiografia Nord Americana* (1988) and *Italian Women Writers from the Renaissance to the Present: Revising the Canon* (1996), as well as coeditor of the present volume of essays.

Giovanna Miceli Jeffries is an independent scholar in Italian literature and culture and an honorary research fellow in the Women's Studies Research Center at the University of Wisconsin, Madison. She is the author of a book on Italo Svevo, *Lo scrittore, il lavoro e la letteratura: la rappresentazione del lavoro nella narrativa di Italo Svevo* (Piovan, 1989) and the editor of *Feminine Feminists: Cultural Practices in Italy* (1994). She is the director and coordinator of an Italian language and culture program in Madison, Wisconsin.

Stefania E. Nedderman is assistant professor of Italian at Gonzaga University where she teaches Italian and Spanish literature. A Renaissance specialist, she is the author of presentations and articles on Cervantes, Góngora, and Castiglione. Dr. Nedderman is working on a book exploring early modern women conduct books.

Gerda Reeb was born in Timisoara, Romania, and grew up under the regime of Ceausescu as part of a German Hungarian ethnic minority group. She has lived in Austria, Italy, Germany, and the U.S. She has presented papers and is currently finishing a Ph.D. in comparative literature with a dissertation on testimonial writings from political prisoners in Italy, Germany, and Eastern Europe.

Monica Rossi is a Ph.D. candidate at New York University. She is the author of presentations, interviews, and articles on Italian cinema, the historical novel, and Italian feminist writers. She is currently teaching at Vassar College.

Index

Diaconescu-Blumenfeld, Rodica, 24, 178–89
Diamond, Irene, 187 n
diary, 20, 64, 72, 73, 211, 213
Dilthey, Wilhelm, 31–32
Diotima, 93; Banti: symbolic female order, 93; entrustment, 26, 93. *See also* Muraro

Eco, Umberto, 129, 137; *The Name of the Rose*, 129
Elshtain, Jean Bethke, 153; violence as life preserving, 153; *Women and War*, 153
Enlightenment, 194. *See also* historical novel
epistolaries (letters), 20, 54, 107–8, 114

fairy tale, 36, 130, 131, 184; as motif in *Le strade di polvere*, 230–32; Sleeping Beauty, 130–31, 184, 233
Farina, Rachele, 152
Fascism, 152, 153, 165; anti-fascist movement, 62; knowledge, 170; women under, 152
female: agency, 104; body, 214; bonding, 22, 92; desire, 62; empowerment, 22, 51, 92; genealogy, 65–66; oppression, 170; order: symbolic, 93, 96, 191; perspective, 89; presence: invisible, 99; qualities, 155
feminism, 17, 31, 49; as treatment of resistance, 192; Banti and *Diotima*, 93; cultural revolution, 112; entrustment, 22, 93; feminization, 139; herstory, 18; historicism, 21, 205, 215; history: reappropriation by women, 16, 24, 214–15; historiography, 18, 24; Italian feminist movement, 63, 205, 215; symbolic use of myth, 191; theory, 82, 93; thought, 17, 49
fiction, 35, 49, 72, 87, 88; fabulation, 235; fictional memory, 38; fictionalized narratives, 71; invention 212; metanarrative, 142; narrator's alter ego, 41; non-fiction, 87
food, 139–42; and eroticism, 142; as metabolization of the past, 145

Foucault, Michel, 73, 83 n, 164, 176 n, 187; knowledge-power, 73
Frederick II, 123, 124, 125

Garboli, Cesare, 237
Gargani, Aldo, 63
Garro, Elena, 39
Gavioli, Davida, 22, 111–20
gender, 17, 26 n, 31, 54, 62, 167, 169; and power, 57; as tool of historical analysis, 74, 186 n; awareness of, 20; biased interpretations, 72; categories of, 20; consciousness of, 77; destabilization of, 20; knowledge and agency, 74; microtechnologies of, 71, 75; perspective, 56, 99; relations, 53; subversion of roles, 23; theory, 73
genealogy: female (women) 21, 65–66, 80
Gentileschi, Artemisia, 40, 41, 45 n, 57, 91, 99 n; as maestra, 91, 92, 93; as virile woman, 57; Holofernes' decapitation, 96
Gilbert, Sandra and Susan Gubar, 95
Gilligan, Carol, 83 n
Gilmore, Leigh, 33, 44 n; *Autobiographies*, 33
Ginzburg, Carlo, 20, 50
Giuffrè, Maria Teresa, 118 n
Gonzaga, Camilla Faà, 35, 36, 40; *Historia*, 35
Gonzaga, Ferdinando, 35
Greenblatt, Stephen, 83 n
Griffin, Susan, 232
Groppi, Angela, 50
groups, non-historical, 49, 63, 66

Heilbrun, Carolyn, 34, 36; *Writing a Woman's Life*, 34
Heller, Deborah, 45 n
Higonnet, Margaret, 155
Hildegarde of Bingen, Martyr, 34
historical background, 22; knowledge, 19, 114, 133, 164; materialism, 24, 164–66, 175; narrative, 19, 23, 24; orthodox materialism, 175; referents, 133; research, 19, 22, 25, 49, 53, 76; subjective interpretation, 115
historical novel, 81, 89, 102, 111, 117, 157, 202; antihistorical novel, 18;